T0203287

Also by Polly Toynbee:

Leftovers: a novel

A Working Life

Hospital

The Way We Live Now

Lost Children

Hard Work: Life in Low-Pay Britain

The Verdict: Did Labour Change Britain?
(with David Walker)

*Unjust Rewards: Ending the Greed That is
Bankrupting Britain* (with David Walker)

The Lost Decade: 2010–2020 (with David Walker)

*

Polly Toynbee is a journalist, author and broadcaster. A *Guardian* columnist and broadcaster, she was formerly the BBC's social affairs editor. She has written for the *Observer*, the *Independent* and *Radio Times* and been an editor at the *Washington Monthly*. She has won numerous awards including a National Press Award and the Orwell Prize for Journalism.

An Uneasy Inheritance

My Family and Other Radicals

Polly Toynbee

Atlantic Books
London

First published in hardback in Great Britain in 2023 by Atlantic Books, an imprint of Atlantic Books Ltd.

This paperback edition first published in Great Britain in 2024 by Atlantic Books, an imprint of Atlantic Books Ltd.

10 9 8 7 6 5 4 3 2 1

A CIP catalogue record for this book is available from the British Library.

Paperback ISBN: 978 1 83895 837 4
E-book ISBN: 978 1 83895 836 7

Printed and bound by CPI (UK) Ltd, Croydon CR0 4YY

Atlantic Books
An imprint of Atlantic Books Ltd
Ormond House
26–27 Boswell Street
London WC1N 3JZ

MIX
Paper | Supporting responsible forestry
FSC
www.fsc.org   FSC® C171272

To my family, past, present and future

Contents

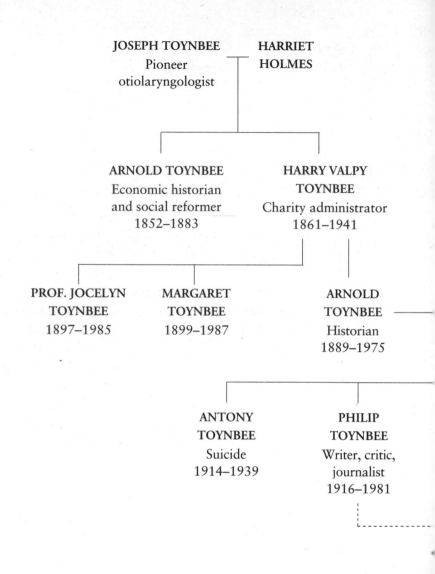

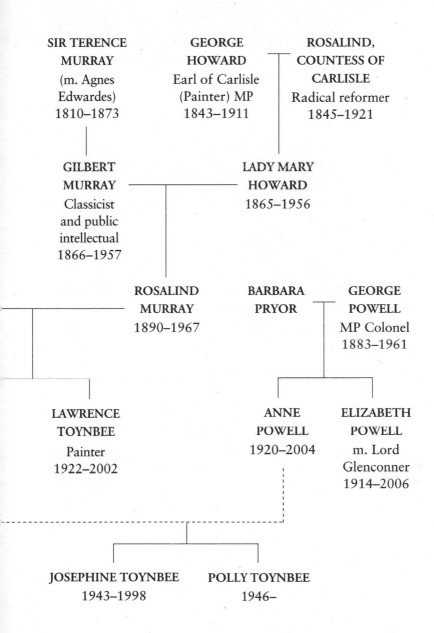

An Uneasy Inheritance

Josephine and Polly

Introduction

My Class

'When Adam delved and Eve span, who was then the gentleman?' That was my father's riddle as he delved and dug every afternoon in the garden or in the next-door allotment at Cob Cottage. 'Tell us, tell us!' Josephine and I pleaded, jumping up and down in irritation, trying every answer we could think of. Was it like 'Constantinople is a very long word: spell it'? Was it like 'I saw Esau sitting on a see-saw, how many S's in that?' What sort of a riddle was it? My father would smile cryptically as he drove his spade into the heavy Suffolk soil and say that one day we would work it out for ourselves, and when we did, we would understand many things. That made the words magic, a spell to reveal the tree of knowledge.

Those Peasants' Revolt words are wrapped up in my memory with two ceremonial swords with gilded hilts, the pommels wound round in faded golden threads. My father had plunged them deep into the earth, their tarnished silver blades only just poking above the ground. I have no idea how he came by them, certainly not from his own wartime military career. You can have one each, he said. When you are strong enough to pull them out, then you'll be old enough to have them. We tugged and pulled but couldn't loosen them.

Not long afterwards Josephine told me she had the answer to the riddle, but she wasn't telling me, ever. I was too young and stupid to understand and I probably never would. I begged and offered her anything I could think of, including my pocket money, but she just smirked like a ginger cat. I kicked her and she let fly her fists. I cried as I always did and she sneered 'Cry-baby!' as she always did. That same afternoon we wiggled and yanked and pulled and tugged the Arthurian swords out of the ground. Still quarrelling over her refusal to tell me, we lifted those heavy weapons with both hands and clashed them over and again until somehow, suddenly, blood gushed from her ankle, her Achilles heel: I was the one that screamed, not her. She dropped her sword and ran, leaving a trail of bloody drops while I ran after her shouting out that I'd killed her. But she didn't run for help; that was not her way. She plunged under a huge upturned wooden vat my father used for stamping out his pungent experimental wines, pulling it down on top of her in the middle of the grass. I thumped on the tub, implored her to come out, said I'd never ever annoy her in any way again if she would come out and not die, but she groaned louder and louder. 'Go away! I'm going to bleed and suffocate and it's your fault! Let me die in peace!' she said, and I rushed for help.

The cut wasn't mortal, not even worth a stitch, and a simple sticking plaster stopped the bleeding, but she always had that small white scar on her ankle just above her heel, my scar, another harm I'd done her. She never told me the answer to the riddle, though I did find out a while later. I asked my philosopher stepfather first, but he never gave a straight answer to any question. 'It all depends what you mean by...' When my mother finally explained that it was about social class, about a time long ago when people were equal with no aristocrats, I felt cheated. It wasn't a proper riddle at all, not one you could tell in the playground. It was a shaggy dog riddle. Neither Adam nor Eve? No one? What kind of an answer was that?

The question of who delved and why was embedded deep in my family's thoughts, for as many generations as I know about. Liberal ancestors agonized over the excruciating moral embarrassments of social class. My father would wag his finger and say people will look back on us with horror, just as we look back on feudal serfdom and slavery. He was unwavering in his trust in the inevitability of social progress, though so often outraged at its frequent backsliding. People in the future (if there is one, if we are not annihilated by the bomb or environmental catastrophe) will be shocked at how we live now while half the world starves, he said, as he set out to turn his family home into a (would-be) self-sufficient agricultural commune, with (would-be) sharing of wealth and income among all communards. People in the future won't be able to imagine our moral state of mind, he said. They won't comprehend the hypocrisy of people like us.

Everyone is class-conscious in their own way, but the liberal and left-wing middle classes writhe in the particular contortions of their own moral inadequacy. Though it is, I suppose, no different to the double-think of generations of comfortably-off occupiers of the front pews in church who were warned that they could no more reach heaven than a camel can squeeze through the eye of a needle. If they genuinely believed only the meek and the poor at the back of the church would inherit the kingdom of God, wouldn't they have lived differently? There are many ways of accommodating contrary beliefs and the cognitive dissonance of failing to live up to the beliefs we profess.

To the left-wing middle classes, how the charge of hypocrisy cuts to the quick. With great glee, enemies on the right spit at 'champagne socialists' – David Cameron hurled that one at Ed Miliband across the floor of the House of Commons. How easy for the right who can bathe in champagne without qualms because life on their moral low ground is easy on the conscience. The hard truth is that those of any politics or faith who claim concern for others are faced with the shaming incompatibility between life and belief, unless they take the Mahatma Gandhi way of loin cloth and self-denial. No political movement can be built on the expectation of a society of saints, but the moral contortions spring from searching for some liveable ground somewhere between Gandhi and hypocrisy.

I started writing this book after making a series for Radio 4 in 2011 called *The Class Ceiling*, when the producer asked me to include something about my own experience of social class. I clammed up. Of course I would have leapt at self-exposure with pride if I'd had some satisfying pulled-up-by-my-own-bootstraps-from-tough-council-estate story to tell. Lock-jawed, I couldn't think where to begin. Must I? It was a fair enough question. I set out to make these programmes on social class keen to ask as many people as possible how they felt. Facts, figures and statistics about Britain's rigid social immobility are revealing, but more powerful still is how people feel about their background and how social divides affect their own lives and attitudes. Richard Sennett and Jonathan Cobb's fine book written in 1970s America, *The Hidden Injuries of Class*, says it all: class hurts, deeply and emotionally, not merely economically. So while making the programmes I started a habit of asking everyone I met for stories about their experiences of class: I asked the experts, the academics, pollsters, politicians and sociologists, alongside friends, people in the street and anyone I came across. Could they remember an event when they had bumped up against class barriers, either feeling not classy enough or too embarrassingly posh, put upon, put down or mocked on account of their origins, occupation or status? Everyone, it turned out, has strong stories to tell of themselves or their family. If they rose in the world from humble roots, they are full of guilt about family, neighbourhoods and school friends socially left behind. Those, like myself, born into the middle classes, have their own shame and anxiety too. Social mobility, which every politician advocates, means many people rising up and falling down, which is rarely without emotional cost. But a world more equal would be a world less painful too. Literature is rich with social class agony, none more poignant than in *Great Expectations* when the newly enriched Pip treats gentle Joe Gargery shamefully on the blacksmith's visit to his elegant London chambers, leaving the fine old son of toil awkwardly uncertain what to do with his hat. Most writers are absorbed by the pain of social class, its gin traps and its barbed wire boundaries.

The Clapham omnibus was too difficult for radio interviews, so I went instead to Clapham Common, my home for forty years, where I talked to a group of elderly working class men, drinking tea from thermoses by the boating pond. Yes, they had tales to tell of being snubbed, quite often. In the old days it was 'Use the tradesmen's entrance', that kind of insult. These days it was only a little more subtle, people identifying them by class with just a first glance. Or worse, they talked of school opportunities missed and regretted because staying on was not an option, intelligence wasted in jobs that didn't require their brain. When I asked the chic young mothers drinking lattes at the café by the Clapham Common bandstand they had other mortifications to tell, toe-curling moments of sudden shame at culture clashes over their children across the class divide. At other people's houses what should they say if their children were exposed to the wrong television programmes, wrong video games, wrong food, and how could you say to a mother of a different/lower social class, I don't want my child to watch, eat or play with the same things as your children? These women were not suffering any social injuries, just blush-making awkwardnesses.

Outside Asda in the Isle of Dogs, looking up at the great glass palaces of the new world of Canary Wharf finance, so near and yet a planet away from the unrewarded East End where we stood, I interviewed a welder who talked indignantly of sitting with his children in his work clothes in a first class train carriage, when an upper class-sounding man summoned the guard to check his absolutely correct first class tickets. His son later did well and went to Oxford University, he boasted.

Professor John Goldthorpe of Oxford, the distinguished expert on class and social mobility, who keeps his Yorkshire accent despite a lifetime in upper academe, told of the letter he had received from an Oxford college after passing the exam to get in: 'It said, "We need you to come to interview to check you are appropriate in dress and manners." I sent a rude reply,' he recalls. He went elsewhere and keeps the framed letter in his bathroom. Maybe it helped propel him on his life's research. Deborah Mattinson, a pollster and social researcher into class, recalled arriving at university from a working class background and being stumped by what to do with an avocado. Andy Burnham, Labour politician, Manchester's first elected mayor, man of impeccable working class origin, talks of the awfulness of arriving for a date with a posh girl at Oxford for 'dinner' at lunchtime instead of in the evening.

Writing in 1941 in his great essay on patriotism, 'The Lion and the Unicorn', George Orwell thought the war effort was being imperilled by England's shameful state as 'the most class-ridden country under the sun'. Five Etonian prime ministers later – Eden, Macmillan, Douglas-Home, Cameron and Johnson – England keeps a firm grip on that undesirable top ranking.

So, said the producer, wasn't it only reasonable that I should say something or other about my own class background? But what? I have travelled nowhere, not made my own way in the world, staying socially more or less where I was born. As far as I can tell, stretching far back into the past, my father's family and his father's and grandfather's family, and those before them remained remarkably socially static, writers, teachers, professors, civil servants. Certainly, I can find not one drop of working class blood – though the history of wives is usually ignored and lost.

Nor do these people come from any particular place, this peripatetic rootless class of professionals who were roundly abused by Theresa May as 'people from nowhere'. Yes, that's who we are. In the olden days this was the clerk class, indeterminate, dressed in black, holding a quill, doing quite well in a quiet way, not landed but educated, footloose to follow professions. The peculiar name Toynbee is found in Danelaw lands, invaders and settlers up the Lincolnshire coast, where Norse names end in -by and -bee. 'Over with Canute, don'cha know?' my father would mock, trumping the upper class pretensions of those who claimed they came over with William the Conqueror. Nonsense of course, but that was exactly his point. Few of us truly come from anywhere. I talk about the male line, my father and his father and his father's father – but that's only half the picture. My great-grandfather, the Australian-born classical scholar Gilbert Murray, unexpectedly married into a branch of the aristocracy, so when I firmly describe us with the portmanteau expression 'middle class', sometimes that ought to include the borderlands of 'upper middle class' and 'aristocracy'. But once we plunge into those quicksands of disputed class gradations, we risk losing the main thread.

Idiosyncrasies and oddities invade every family tree, defeating every attempt to shoehorn ancestry into a coherent pattern. My mother's father George, as we shall see, was a perplexing mystery, origins and birth unknown, propelled into the upper class by some benefactor, but once arrived there, left penniless to sink or marry money. Once you look at the gigantic size of anyone's family tree within a couple of generations, you can see how absurdly people have to pick a dainty path through thickets of forebears to claim any one particular origin: any selected bloodline of ancestors dilutes in a generation or two to less than a thimbleful, less than a little toe.

I hunted hard for any redeeming twig of a working class branch of my family tree, without success. Not a shadow of a distant root emerges from good working class earth. That's a ridiculous middle class habit, trying to justify itself by proving working class origins. I enjoy a 2021 piece of research from the London School of Economics (LSE) that shows how many of the indisputably middle class these days lay spurious claim to being working class. An astonishing 47 per cent of all those in professional and managerial jobs actually call themselves working class. Even a full quarter of those who have middle class parents still claim working class authenticity by reaching back to grandparents and even to great-grandparents. I understand the urge, but it's ludicrous. (My wise daughter interjects here: am I being unfair? If we had working class grandparents, wouldn't our lives and attitudes and self-confidence be subtly different? She may be right.) The search for these origin stories springs, the LSE researchers suggest, from the need to prove their own merit, to assert that we do really live in a meritocracy, against all the evidence. To show they made it to their present status by their own effort and talent alone, they need to believe they earned it. US political philosopher Michael Sandel's book *The Tyranny of Merit* explodes these self-delusions. Most of us acorns don't fall far from the trees we come from. If I can't find a shred of working class credibility to boast about, I have to assume, from the way I stayed exactly within my own social class, that had I been born into a family with no advantages, I would probably have stayed there too, equally static.

But I digress, avoiding the question. How do I feel about social class? That's what this book is about. I can make myself blush all over at embarrassing scenes remembered. All my family, my father, my mother, my sister, my brothers, my stepfather, my late husband, my present partner and my children too, tussle with questions of class. Those who claim to be resolutely immune are either crassly insensitive to their own privilege or from their own niche, high or lowly, they live in some insulated social zone where they rarely glimpse beyond their own kind, except on television.

The fashionable – and politically convenient – view is that 'we're all middle class now', apart perhaps from the feral underclass of *Daily Mail* nightmares. Class is old hat. The useful political myth declares class is dead. *Downton Abbey* deference is no more and look how often vocal differences among the young meld into universal estuary and mockney accents. Classlessness may be modern and hip – yet that affectation is no more than an unsuccessful disguise of the extent to which birth determines destiny more, not less, than it did fifty years ago. Never mind irrelevant Hyacinth Bucket and Nancy Mitford wars over the niceties of napkins versus serviettes; in everything that matters class holds sway more, not less than it did and that needs saying loudly and often. Things are going backwards. That's why it matters.

The dangerous tendency now is to replace class with other identities – ethnicity in all its variations, gender, transgender, sexual orientation or religion. I realize that, in describing previous eras, this is a very white book about white people. Other identities have other stories, but class still stands out as the overarching determinant of most lives, an identity everyone is born with, and too few escape. Platitudinous politicians talk only of upward mobility: the truth the middle class knows and fears is that for some to rise up the ladder, others must slip down it. But not our children.

Look, I have skated away again from the personal. Pondering the difficulty of describing my liberal family's intense convolutions about class, I agreed with my producer to give a modest nod to acknowledge my middle class background – not that Radio 4 listeners could have missed the unmistakable inflections of my voice. So I said, 'I come from a family of writers and academics, we had every advantage – and it was dinned into us how lucky we were compared with some children I played with. But what if I hadn't grown up surrounded by books and parents who talked to me about everything, how do I know if I'd ever have made it into journalism?' I don't – and never will. Secretly, I think how admirable and enviable are those who have risen from hardship, without privileges, through sheer talent and determination into a job like mine. But how rare too. The *Guardian* also writhes with discomfort at figures showing how private school and Oxbridge educated its staff have been – like so much of broadcasting, the press and the most desirable jobs. It has taken conscious effort to hire a more diverse younger generation.

In the office at the *Guardian* I discover that the mother of the leader writer I sit next to went to school with me, both at Kensington High School, a private primary school, and together again in the sixth form of Holland Park comprehensive. Where you come from matters a lot less than what you stand for, I hear some say, with some justification. It's not which side of the tracks you were born on, but whose side you fight for that counts: I hold onto that thought but I also partly doubt it. Collectively, it still looks bad for newspapers, the broadcasters and all the other commanding heights of privileged jobs that are effortlessly occupied by we silver-spooners. When I started writing this book, Alan Milburn's final report for the Social Mobility Commission reported that the private school educated make up 54 per cent of leading journalists and medics, 55 per cent of partners in top law firms, 68 per cent of barristers and 70 per cent of judges, with a far higher proportion than that drawn from Oxbridge. In the legal profession, the numbers of privately educated are actually on the increase again, a warning that in these tough times, as competition gets harsher for fewer good jobs, the proportion of the sharpest elbowed, the most intensely tutored, crammed and bred for success may well rise, not fall. Progress has gone into reverse in my lifetime.

The story of social class since the Second World War has followed the story of British politics. A reasonably steady progressive consensus secured upward mobility and an expanding white collar middle class. I was taught social history in the 1960s as we lived and perceived it in the post-war decades: it was taught as an ineluctable onward march from factory acts and trade union rights to the universal franchise, the welfare state and universal free education, including expanding universities. From the start of the twentieth century, incomes became more equal while income tax and inheritance tax chipped away at Victorian levels of inequality. In the mid-1970s Britain reached its most equal era with its highest levels of social mobility. Why wouldn't that social democratic improvement continue forever onward under the flag of Fabian gradualism? But then came the 1980s, when everything went into reverse, when incomes shot off in opposite directions. Accelerating poverty and soaring wealth have stayed relatively unchecked ever since. My father died in 1981 at the age of sixty-five, steaming with anger both at Margaret Thatcher and at me for joining the Social Democratic Party that year, splitting from Labour and, in his view, making her continued victory the more certain. (That historic argument has never been resolved.)

Britain's social story since the 1980s can be told in numbers and statistics, slice it any way you like. The top 10 per cent gained greatly, the top 1 per cent insanely, while, especially since the turn of the millennium, the middle stagnated and the bottom half fell back. That means the habit of measuring national wealth by GDP as if it were per capita is meaningless for the majority of people who saw very little increase in their own living standards, while hearing that the country was apparently motoring ahead. Almost all of that growth of the last fifteen years was gobbled up by the top tenth, so an 'average' figure for growth is useless in a country as unequal as ours. Statisticians may be satisfied with national numbers that express GDP growth as if the spoils were fairly shared, but in such an unequal country, never accept an average. Average out the living standards or the GDP of Good King Wenceslas and the poor man underneath the mountain, and by statistical magic the poor man is doing just fine. The turmoil of the last decade that delivered the great Brexit cultural division and the Red Wall of 'left behind' northern towns turning blue in Boris Johnson's 2019 landslide general election springs in part from the simmering disruptions of Thatcher's heedless de-industrializations and forty years of those consequences.

In one way or another I have spent most of my working life chronicling social change or, in recent years, social stagnation, reporting and writing about it in newspapers, broadcasting and books. I inherit my parents' indignation at the wrongness of things, personal guilt over privilege and an obligation never to forget it. But it is not as easy to be good as it is to imagine what a good society might look like. This raw awareness of undeserved good fortune was in my parents' marrow, though mercifully they didn't express it with solemn Quakerish puritanism but with a measure of rueful self-mockery at the impossible difference between how we live and how we think society should be. Delight in life's pleasures was blended with an awkward guilt, a hallmark of my father's writing. My older sister was more tortured and struggled harder than I to correct the distortions and convolutions of our lives. I was indignant but, if I'm honest, not truly tormented, not tormented enough or I would have lived differently. But I do feel lucky and so do my children, the luck every human has from haphazard randomness of birth. 'Aren't we lucky' is what we keep saying when enjoying life, and I have so enjoyed myself.

* * *

No family story is simple. No family history can be boiled down to class, though class is at the heart of the way everyone describes the history of their antecedents and their origins. But stirred in with social context, in my family as in every other on earth, there is a rich mix of the nuts and raisins of odd characters and illogical passions. Anyone looking at mine through a Freudian lens would ask what might my father have been like had he not had a fiendish mother? Might he have been a happier man, and less wracked by cycles of sin and guilt? He was a romantic by nature who believed that romantic agony is the price to be paid by artists, writers and truth-seekers. If he had not suffered the deep wound inflicted by his mother, a believer in the idea of romantic agony might wonder if he would have had the spur to make him the clever, comic, self-knowing writer and good companion he was. At the end, in the grip of severe clinical depression, the agony overwhelmed everything else. So, inevitably this is a story of inherited anguish and of alcoholism passed through the generations, as well as a tale about the angst of the middle class left.

Spare us from the fate of being remembered only through the eyes of our children. Children are grasping creatures, by nature programmed to require just one thing of their parents – that they devote themselves unstintingly to the wellbeing of their offspring, and nothing much else. Parents' independent state of being is beside the point to children. It has been the fate of too many interesting people of every kind to be remembered only by their grumbling offspring. Did Edmund Gosse's recollections of his abominable father begin the child-as-victim autobiography? Or did the fashion start with the misery memoirs by the daughters of Joan Crawford and Bette Davis about their alcoholic mothers? There followed a succession of family revenge sagas, no doubt justified by aggrieved children of the famous with neglectful or abusive childhoods. But being an unsatisfactory parent or a bad spouse is only one aspect of a human life, not enough to blot out every other talent or attribute. I don't know if, say, Louis Pasteur or Marie Curie were good parents, but it would be the less important or interesting facet of their lives. Sex has overwhelmed the biographies of many, remembered more for their bedrooms than the workrooms that were the reason why we should care about them at all. Ill treatment of their wives is no reason to stop reading Tolstoy or Dickens. Sometimes children's recorded resentments of their parents overshadow everything else: Philip Larkin gave everyone permission. I bear no grudge against my parents or my upbringing, complicated and disrupted though it was: on the contrary, I always felt fortunate.

My father, however, was entirely justified in his sense of the damage his poisonous mother Rosalind had done him. To a lesser extent he blamed his father Arnold's inadequacy, for the harm they both did him. But blame is never that simple. Rosalind's own upbringing may have harmed her, with a domineering and chilly mother in Mary Murray. But was that altogether Mary's fault? Her mother, the Countess of Carlisle, was far worse, a famously radical but terrifying tyrant, ending up at war with all her eleven children. So where did it all begin? Deuteronomy says the sins of the fathers – and in my father's family the sins of the mothers – are visited on the children and the grandchildren even unto the third and fourth generation.

My family have a long generational habit of writing, so plentiful evidence abounds. They all leave trails of book after book, and what I write here is in part a book about their books.

This is a back-to-front way to tell my family's story. Everyone has two stories: a personal, psychological, emotional family tale to tell, but also a social setting, tracing histories that travel up and down the social scale. Beyond the personal, this book is a particular history of a liberal heritage, generations of lives lived on the left, mostly struggling to be good but inevitably never being good enough. For as far as I can reach back to uncover, on all sides of the family, of Toynbees and Murrays and Howards, here is an assembly of the old liberal world of social reformers, concerned philanthropists, good internationalists, communists, socialists, liberals and social democrats. In each generation they are always in the minority and forever locked in combat with the perpetual old enemy, the forces of conservatism. To live on the left side is to live with inevitable hypocrisy and painful self-awareness, with good intentions forever destined to fall short of ideals, social concern never enough. And there are, of course, those admirable few who genuinely do live their ideals, and put the rest of us to shame.

Liberal/left idealism doesn't, it seems, make for contentment. In a conversation with economist and psychologist Daniel Kahneman, he told me research shows how much less happy are those on the left: in the US, Republicans have always far outscored Democrats on the happiness scale. You can see why there is not an abundance of happiness to be had from all that seething outrage at social injustice, anger at governments that protect the interests of the rich and confused despair at the incomprehensible inertia of the masses who inexplicably fail to rise up against their oppressors, despite our indefatigable urgings. Life on the left is a destiny of indignation, illusion and disillusion. As I hunt back through my family's life and times, from liberal grandees to earnest academics, from passionate communists to my own duller social democratic endeavours, looking back at the liberal/left life of the last 150 years my family has faced a long chain of inherited disappointments. To be sure there has been progress, but the steady two steps forward, one step back has often felt like two steps back. For most of the time covered in these stories, certainly for most of my lifetime, the right has been complacently triumphant, a Conservative Cheshire Cat beaming down on us from the high branches of power. Oh for the contentment of conservatism! The uncomplicated class confidence of the Conservative life, unwracked by who you are, unashamed by birth privilege, certain that merit has propelled them to the top and just as certain their children will merit their inheritances. Life untouched by social guilt must be easeful, while the contradictions of the lives of the middle class left are, of course, excruciating – and often inherently comic.

1

What Children Know

CHILDREN KNOW. THEY breathe it in early, for there's no unknowing the difference between nannies, cleaners, below stairs people and the family upstairs. Children are the go-betweens, one foot in each world, and yet they know very well from the earliest age where they belong, where their destiny lies or, to put it crudely, who pays whom. From a young age their loyalties are torn, betrayal of both inevitable, colluding in complaints with gossip passing each way, upstairs and down. Every autobiography, every story about middle class childhood is riddled with guilt, complicity and awareness. Love that nanny, au pair, housekeeper or any paid employee – but never forever. Never equally. Tiny hands are steeped young in the essence of class and caste.

In their first view from the pushchair, they know as ineffably as they know about male and female how others compare, who fits, who's the same, who's different. No one need speak a word. Good liberal parents will strain every nerve to deny it's there, to blank it out and protect their offspring from the awkward truth of their lucky lives, but the harder they pretend, the more a child sees and knows. In nursery school, in reception they see the Harry

Potter sorting hat at work. They know. And all through school those fine gradations grow clearer, more precise, more consciously knowing, more shaming, more frightening. Good liberal parents teach their children to check their privilege – useful modern phrase – but it swells up like a bubo on the nose. There's no hiding it.

Maureen

I can summon up the childhood shame at class embarrassments. Aged seven like me, Maureen, with her hair pinned sideways in a pink slide, lived in a pebble-dashed council house in the Lindsey Tye, the small row by the water tower. They lived at the other end of Lindsey, more hamlet than village, half a mile down the road from my father's pink thatched cottage set in the flat prairie lands of Suffolk. I envied Maureen for what looked to me like a cheerful large family tumbling noisily in and out of their ever-open front door. They never asked me in, so I would hang about the door waiting for Maureen to come out and play.

I thought they were the Family from One End Street, the Ruggleses from Eve Garnett's children's book. In that classic 1930s story, Mr Ruggles was a dustman, Mrs Ruggles was a washerwoman, and Lily Rose their eldest looked out for their other six children, including the twins and baby William. It was a groundbreaking book at the time, seen as radical, these stories of everyday working class life, though it was read, I imagine, mostly by children like me envying the daily scrapes and the scraping up of pennies for an annual family treat.

Polly, aged seven

Maureen (whose name wasn't Ruggles) and I played fairies in the corn fields, crept about scaring each other in St Peter's churchyard next door, water-divined in the ditches with hazel switches, drew hopscotch squares on the road and threw five-stone pebbles on and off our knuckles. One day we had a cart, an old orange box set on pram wheels. Was it her brother's? Where did we find it? I don't think we made it ourselves. We took it in turns pulling along the rope harness and riding in the box, up and down the flat road outside her house, shouting Giddy-up and Goa-on, waving a stick as a mock whip. It was my turn, I was in the box and Maureen was yoked in as my horse, she heaving me along making neighing and whinnying noises while I whooped and thrashed the air with my stick. Suddenly, there came a loud yell, a bark of command. 'Maureen!

Get right back in the house, now! Right now!' Her mother was standing in the doorway with the baby in her arms. 'You, who do you think you are, your ladyship, getting my girl to pull you around! What makes you think she should pull you, eh? Off you go home and don't you ever, never come back round here again!' Maureen dropped the rope and scuttled back home. I thought she'd explain we were taking turns, but she was scared of her mother. I jumped out of the cart and ran all the way back to my father's house in tears of indignation. Not fair, unfair! But something else in me knew very well that there was another unfairness that wasn't about taking turns, that couldn't be explained away. Somewhere deep inside, I knew it meant Maureen would never have the turns I had. And Maureen's family knew it well enough. They were plainly nothing like the Ruggleses in the book, who were always cheerful, not overly bothered by their lowly place and not resentful of the better off. Nor were Maureen's family like another book I loved, about Ameliaranne Stiggins and her five siblings. Of similar disposition to the Ruggleses, the Stigginses were ever grateful to the squire and his tea party for poor children.

Jackie

I was always looking for friends in the lonely weekends and holidays at Cob Cottage, where my sister and I, children of divorce, had our time parcelled out precisely between South Kensington and Suffolk, staying with my father and stepmother. Josephine was rarely companionable: when we were sent out to 'play' she always asked me which way I was going, and then walked off in the other direction. When she grew too tall for it, her knees knocking the handlebars, I was passed on her old purple Raleigh bike and I pedalled it all the way to Kersey, the chocolate box village with a steep hill that races down to a ford running across the road at its foot, a zoom and a splash well worth the bike ride.

Beside the ford was the Bell Inn and one day I met Jackie riding her bike in and out of the water too, slow pedalling around the minnows and the pebbles. I went back to play with her often and I looked up at her village school just up the hill with longing as she talked about their playground games there. But most of all I envied Jackie her home above the pub, where her father was landlord. Up the winding back stairs, into a small snug, she had things I wasn't allowed – a big tin of Quality Street ever open to dip into, bottles of Vimto whenever we wanted and a knee-high pile of comics – *Dandy*, *Beano*, *Girls' Crystal*, *Bunty*, *School Friend*, all the best.

'Ask her here,' my father and stepmother kept saying, 'ask her to lunch,' so I did, with fearful trepidation. But when I pedalled back to Kersey, she was surrounded by village friends. 'Here she comes, Miss La-di-da!' one shouted out at me. 'Oh I say, I'm just going to check my Rolls-Royce is in the garage!' mocked another. 'Oy, poshpants! Bet you think you're better than us!' a boy called out, with more of the same. I thought Jackie would stand up for me, but I was the outsider. And every time I opened my mouth, the noise that jumped out like a box of frogs only drew more mimicry.

When they had gone, I asked Jackie if she'd come to my house for lunch, and she said yes, but with a sort of shrugged diffidence. I was gripped by anxiety: she wouldn't like our food, it wouldn't be as good as hers. Nothing I had was as much fun, no sweets, no comics. Did she play board games? She'd be bored. I played country games, camping in the old hay wagon beside the allotment, but she wouldn't reckon much to that. I lit fires and cooked up soups made of nettles and herbs, playing witches, but she'd think that was disgusting.

Here's the damned subtlety of class: she had more stuff that children want, but I was posh. My father's cottage didn't even have electricity until a few years later, only paraffin lamps with mantels, pumped up and lit at dusk. Her clothes were smart, I only wore baggy jeans too short up the calf and a home-knitted jersey. My plaits were old-fashioned, she had a cool bob like Bunty. What of our cooking would she eat? I begged for sausages and mash, the only thing that seemed safe. And please no cabbage. The next day I stood by the window and waited and waited and waited, but she didn't come. I cried. My father was perplexed. When I rode back to Kersey the following day I waited and waited by the ford until eventually when I saw her she was with the same group of friends, and she just said, 'You're not my type,' and rode off with them. And that was that. I knew it was true, but not fair. Jackie Bull of the Bell and Maureen of Lindsey Tye, where are you now?

Joe the Milkman

If I couldn't find friends in the half of my life and the long holidays I spent at Cob Cottage, I did find work, or an early fascination with it. Three mornings a week at exactly 5.45 a.m. Joe came by Cob Cottage on his milk truck and I, aged about nine, would be waiting for him at the gate, alarm set not to miss him. He was a whistler, but not much of a talker. 'Jump up,' he'd say and off I'd go with him for the morning, counting out the right bottles for each house in one village after another. I read out the notes tucked into the empties, sometimes orders for cream in glass bottles too, eggs, white sliced loaves, and money in a twist of paper to be noted down in his cash book, tucked into his aged leather pouch slung round his overalls on a strap.

This was the job I wanted when I grew up, real work, useful, practical, pounding up and down pathways, clinking bottles, wary of barking dogs. 'You're a useful lass,' he'd say when the round was done and I glowed with more pride than if a teacher had given me a star and a red tick – which they never did. In my family no one did proper jobs. My father (journalist, poet and critic) and my stepfather (philosophy professor), my grandfather (history professor), my great-grandfather (classics professor) disappeared into their studies dark with books and wrote, wrote, wrote, boring, incomprehensible, inexplicable and not useful. Now that's all I can do, write, write, write. It took the pandemic of 2020 to remind this labour-despising hyper-civilization that the people we really depend on don't work from home in their book-lined studies, but they bring in the food from earth to shelf. Or they care for people, or they keep the electricity and the water flowing, they fix things, make things, transport things. That has always transfixed me, real work of tangible value. In the Covid crisis praise and clapping came for the deliverers – but afterwards there followed no reversal of values to say the workers by hand deserve money and respect to match those of us working in thin air producing books or newspapers, our clean hands well rewarded in cash, esteem and status.

The Morley Brothers

The Morleys farmed the great wide fields that stretched in every direction as far as the eye could see all round my father's cottage. It was desolate country, wide acres with grubbed-up hedges short of coveys, copses or clumps to interrupt the getting of grain in summer or sugar beet in winter. I never knew why my father had chosen this bleak prairie land to bring his new wife from America and plant her here. It's not as if she came in on a tornado from Dorothy's Kansas, which this part of East Anglia imitates in its small way. Sally came from Shaker Heights, a well-heeled Cleveland, Ohio suburb when he met her in Tel Aviv where she worked in the secretarial pool of the American embassy. Many days of the week – four at least – he was in London at the *Observer*'s offices, or off reporting or interviewing, doing journalism or roistering with friends, leaving her, just as he used to leave my mother in the Isle of Wight. Sally was parked there in the middle of nowhere with a thatched roof but not one mod con, not even electric light.

Out there in the fields was the rich and fecund Suffolk earth. I don't know how I persuaded them, taciturn and silent by nature, but the Morleys let me jump up on their tractors in the ploughing season, perched in the biting cold on those giant mudguards watching clods of earth turn over in the scything silver churn of the ploughshares. Those gigantic ridged tyres threw up divots, followed by birds swooping down for worms. These great wide fields that reached up to the flat horizon came into their own at harvest time, swaying with wheat brushed by the wind into rivers of swirls and streams. The Massey Ferguson combine harvester was a wonder of a machine, its front reapers devouring the corn, its innards flaying the stalks, a monster munching its way across the fields, a Kraken only half-tamed. Cutters, threshers, augurs, belts, screws, reels and rams churned away inside. The chaff blew out of a chimney on top, the straw emerged in bales ready tied with string, dumped down in rows as we trawled up and down those seas of corn. The bounty from these yellow oceans was the unbroken stream of wheat that poured like liquid gold down chutes into sacks. My job was to stand on the platform at the back and fix the new sacks onto the hooks, as each full sack was heaved aside, making sure no corn was lost from sack to sack. I can feel the wheat pouring through my fingers, even as the dust and flecks of straw choked the throat, sneezed the nose, sorely rubbed into the eyes. The roar of the engine was deafening. The sight of rabbits, hares, nesting birds and mice dashing away from the jaws of this beast was heart-stopping: some didn't make it, mashed up by the great red field-eater.

What pride I felt, as if it was I who was tending this animal, obeying its commands and needs, the glow a child feels at a rare chance to be useful, though no doubt only in a very small way. No child now would be allowed anywhere near such agricultural machinery: it was frightening – easy to imagine falling under those crushing tyres, slipping down in front of the ploughshares or the harrows behind, minced to pieces. But I have always loved machines and admired the engineers who coax and ease them into life, oil their cogs, fix their glitches. Later as I was writing about the drudgery and hardship of life on factory production lines, describing workers as slaves to the greedy unforgiving speed of the conveyor belt, I always found in the machines themselves a captivating fascination. Their hammer-blow precision wrapped and packed, filled and sorted, stamped, mixed and fixed. But nothing matched the magnificence of the mighty combine harvester and the people who worked it.

Only a middle class child would sentimentalize the glory of hard manual work. You soon grow up to understand the penalties of labouring by hand, and the rewards of thin-air product-less work by brain. All other things being equal – the status and the pay – keeping a machine running with spanner and oily rag might have suited me better than tussling with newspaper column-writing. But all other things never are equal, so no one knows how many labouring hands would have been better suited to wordsmithing on a laptop or how many word-warriors would have been happier fixing things. When, interminably and dishonestly, every politician of every hue pledges each child will 'fulfil their potential', who ever knows what a child's natural skills might be when most of our lives are more or less predestined by background, accident and luck – good or bad? In my working lifetime social immobility has grown more rigid, not less.

Servants

For a child, class bites hardest with the people you love. In the other half of my divorced childhood, in my London life, Aurelia arrived with her two sisters in London in

1953 in a wave of Italian immigration, from Fano on the Adriatic coast. Bianca and Maria went to work for neighbours, while Aurelia came to live with us in our tall South Kensington house. Fiery, tempestuous, emotional, superstitious, uproariously funny and frequently obscene, with wild black hair, a hooked nose and coal black eyes, she called herself a 'strega', but she was our witch, living in our basement front room, next door to the kitchen. Josephine, myself and my twin younger half-brothers came to speak her blended pidgin Ital-Anglais, but she taught me much more than Italian. She sang Italian songs of every kind with a fine voice, not just 'Nel blu, dipinto di blu' but streams of others, some Neapolitan folk tunes too. The twins were toddlers when she came and they too loved her gusts of laughter and storms of fury. She told me rude gossip she got from her sisters about the neighbours, eye-popping tales of the unlikeliest ladies of the house screwing a tradesman on the kitchen table. I never repeated these upstairs.

Hers was a hard life, up early lighting the kitchen boiler: there was no central heating. This grand stuccoed house in Pelham Crescent put on a fine show outside but inside only two rooms kept up appearances, the ice-cold rarely used dining room and the drawing room, with its Pither stove devouring anthracite beans. It was cold everywhere else, especially the shared bathroom with rationed hot water, and the chill attic rooms for children. The house, like many smart London addresses, was all fur coat and no knickers, rented not owned. For years there was no fridge, just an outside pantry with a stone shelf for keeping milk and butter cool. No washing machine, but a copper boiler and a mangle for sheets, nappies and towels we took

Pelham Crescent

turns to wring. 'Dodici camicie!' Aurelia protested to us at my stepfather's hyper-fastidious elegance of dress – he wore at least three silk shirts a day for her to wash and iron: he was phobic about many things, including dirt. She complained a lot and I sympathized, sitting at the kitchen table, but it was me and mine she was complaining about.

I listened to her stories from Fano, tales about her lovers and other people's. She told of her London nights out with GIs. Her friend Pina often brought her GI boyfriend Vito home to us, bringing chewing gum and strange American grape-flavoured sweets. We have a photo of my little brother wearing Vito's GI uniform. I heard in graphic detail what the Italian girls and their Italian-American GIs got up to in the Chenil Gallery dance hall in the King's Road and the Hammersmith Palais. 'Is that a stick you got in your trousers?' another of Aurelia's friends, Yolanda, told me she'd asked her GI. I didn't know what she meant but it was definitely rude. From the earliest age I knew that I inhabited these two lives, two sets of worlds apart, never to be mixed.

Rita

Aurelia's Fano family was large and dirt poor. She and her sisters had worked at a fruit-packing factory since leaving school at the age of twelve. But there was something no one knew and she never told until she had been with us a few years. One summer she was taking my twin half-brothers back home with her to Fano for a holiday, and so the secret couldn't be kept any longer. She had a daughter, Rita, born when she was only fourteen, who she'd left behind all these years with an aunt, and not happily. Aurelia had been sending money back for Rita's upkeep and no one knew. She told me how she'd kept her pregnancy quiet, wearing tight bindings round her stomach, hoping it would just go away. No one knew until she gave birth alone one night in the local graveyard, the same graveyard where she'd been raped frequently on the way back from the factory by someone she feared who used to lie in wait for her. My mother was horrified that she had never known about Rita for all these years: she said she must come at once to live with us too.

Rita was exactly my age, just eleven when she arrived. I waited for her full of excited expectation. She would be the sister I wanted, my own twin to play with me, an ally on my side as my actual sister never was. I thought she would be all mine, like a new doll. I could model her into exactly what I wanted her to be, as if she was newly made of clay.

Of course that wasn't it at all. By accident I got off to a bad start. Rita unpacked her small suitcase and stood in front of the mirror brushing her long black hair. I thought she was beautiful. Her skin was a deep olive, darker than her mother's, smooth and glowing, her eyes luminous, her features faultless, I thought. She was wearing big gold hoop earrings I yearned for: no eleven year old was ever going to be allowed pierced ears and gold hoops in my family. 'You're so beautiful! Che bella!' I said. She made a face at herself in the mirror. 'You look like a gypsy girl, come una zingara!' She turned on me with double the fury of her mother in a tempest and screamed, 'Zingara! Putana!' Hurling her hairbrush at me, she stormed out of the room yelling for her mother, 'Mi ha chiamato zingara!' Aurelia was angry with us both. I had no idea that zingara was the rudest thing I could have said, but in Fano there was no lower anyone could sink.

Things didn't get much better. She'd lived an unloved life and there was no recovering her relationship with her mother. They fought and shouted, and Aurelia just couldn't love her, nor could Rita love her mother, unforgiving of the miserable years abandoned to a brutal aunt. I couldn't love Rita and she certainly couldn't and wouldn't be moulded into my imaginary twin.

Besides, I was sent off to boarding school soon after she came, and she went to Holland Park, the brand new comprehensive that had just opened. By the time I escaped boarding school and insisted on going to Holland Park too, she was leaving, though she passed on to me some warnings and all the lowdown on gropers, bullies and teachers who she said were trouble. In London she had settled in fast, made friends, took to mod clothes, pleated miniskirts and Peter Pan collars. Even with a helmet of Cilla hair and her skin plastered with bright white panstick to hide her olive tones, she still looked beautiful. When we talked, she was Moody Blues and The Beatles, I was more Stones, The Who and The Kinks. But otherwise our lives diverged almost immediately. She was always out, escaping her mother, in trouble for being late. Beyond friendly hellos as we passed on the stairs, in our lives we just passed each other by.

Her life didn't turn out happily later. When I thought of her of course I felt guilty, nothing specific I had done or not done, just that same old class guilt, living under the same roof, same age, but each with a destiny more or less etched out at birth, hers in a graveyard.

Aurelia left soon after my stepfather walked out on my mother. To me, her going was the greater shock. To my mother it felt like a double betrayal. How could she? She'd gone off with Denis the decorator who had been painting the outside of our house. She upped and went, never came back, but took a job as a caretaker that came with a basement flat in a mansion block behind Harrods. Well, why not? Wouldn't anyone, given the chance? It hurt. But this is no misery memoir. Add up all these pains, slights and embarrassments, and frankly, the price of privilege is pretty low. We of the middle classes seem to live comfortably enough within our skin most of the time, despite these social disquiets.

The Glenconners

But we were only middle class – middle middle or upper middle, I'm not sure. But definitely not upper class, because I knew that difference from a very young age. My mother's only sibling, her elder sister Elizabeth, married into the real upper class, into aristocracy. She married Lord Glenconner, and became Lady Glenconner, with a vast London house looking onto Regent's Park. And she was chatelaine of Glen, a great baronial castle in Peeblesshire where we spent most Christmases and many Easter and summer holidays. In its turreted splendour, with its long drive leading through a stone archway emblazoned with 'Salve' on the entrance, and 'Vale' on the other side, its rolling lawns, peach- and flower-filled hot-houses, its stables and gun rooms, it was a world apart. So was its maze-like life below stairs with a gigantic kitchen, and quarters for cook, butler and housekeeper. All this was a romantic Scottish paradise, set among the bracken- and heather-covered hills that we strode along singing Jacobite songs, 'Charlie Is My Darling', 'My Bonnie Lies Over the Ocean' and the like. There were two lochs with boat houses filled with fishing tackle; returning fishermen would throw their fat trout trophies into a wide Chinese platter in the entrance hall, the hall that in December held a Christmas tree reaching to the high ceiling, lit in the evening with real candles. Shooting parties in plus fours and tweeds had the whole village out beating the pheasants and the woodcock from the covers; my sister and I would join the village beaters driving the plump-fed birds into the

guns, a bit embarrassed by the village children's deference to us from the big house and a bit cheesed off at not
getting the pay the villagers received at the end of the
hard-walking, up-hill-and-down-dale day.

The youngest of my three cousins, Catherine, was my
age, and I shared her room, fond friends all our childhood, but losing touch as adults. From an early age she
was bewitched by old books of magic spells and astrology:
later she wrote horoscopes under the name Wanda Star
for the *Telegraph*. Under her own name she had a website
with a fleet of clients following her astrological advice. At
Glen she had a magnificent four-poster I yearned for, while
I slept in a camp bed by her side. That was the nature of
things. You get the picture.

With Catherine at Glen

The Glenconners were, by Scottish aristo standards, a bit nouveau. The family fortune came from manufacturing bleach and other chemicals in Glasgow, the foundation stone of ICI, the peerage only bestowed on Edward Tennant, the first baron, in 1911. They were a Liberal family, elevated by the Liberal government: the first baron's daughter Margot married the Liberal prime minister Herbert Asquith. The first Lord Glenconner's eldest son was killed in the First World War, and so the younger brother, my uncle Christopher, unexpectedly inherited the title and estate. My aunt Elizabeth was his second wife, so the title and estate went afterwards not to her three children, but to his son by his first wife, the notorious Colin Tennant.

Colin was the lavish, extravagant, exotic wastrel beloved of the gossip columns for nearly marrying Princess Margaret, to whom he granted a house on his fantasy Caribbean island Mustique. His outrageous behaviour is brilliantly described in his wife Anne's surprise 2020 bestseller, *Lady in Waiting: My Extraordinary Life in the Shadow of the Crown*. She was a maid of honour at the coronation and lady in waiting for life to Princess Margaret. We met her now and then but we didn't know her. Because of her loyalty to royalty we had always assumed she was monumentally dull, until reading her startling book. She was regarded as a great catch for Colin, he the son of a mere baron capturing the daughter of the Earl of Leicester: 'I married somewhat down,' she tells interviewers. Worse than that, she married a bullying lunatic. All this I only perceived dimly from afar: my mother was the un-wealthy, un-grand left-wing sister of Lord Glenconner's second wife so we had very little to do with the louche world of Colin, her sister's stepson. But we would read in magazines about his legendary Mustique parties, such as the Golden Ball which was photographed by Robert Mapplethorpe when Bianca Jagger was carried in by a troupe of boys painted entirely in gold, wearing almost nothing else. We read how they travelled several times to India to choose the right costumes for one fancy dress party – but not until reading Anne Glenconner's book had I any idea of his psychotic cruelty, his uncontrollable rages over minutiae, fury so ferocious that he would lie down in the middle of a London pavement in a yelling tantrum.

Colin Tennant

I met him only when I was a child, when I looked up with devoted fascination at his dashing elegance, wit and charm when in company, but he rarely came to Glen, as it was his stepmother's domain. He blew most of the immense family fortune, millions and millions and millions of it, and then left the remnants to a bartender in St Lucia where he ended his days: the family went to court to get it back, but lost. In her book his wife asks him why he screamed at people so often and he replied: 'I like making them squirm.'

We grew up with a sense that the Glenconner family was cursed: do I detect a little lemon-sucking middle class glee at our own respectability and seriousness compared with all that wild extravagance? But as one tragedy piled upon another, we looked on appalled. Colin publicly disinherited their first son when he became a drug addict and later died of hepatitis. Their second son abandoned his wife when he came out as gay, and later died of Aids. Their third son suffered a severe brain injury in a motorcycle crash. In Anne Glenconner's book she keeps using a phrase that I remember hearing often around the Glenconners: 'Don't dwell'. Goodness knows, the tragedy of her three sons and her deranged, sadistic husband required fortitude to survive – and survive she plainly has. There is something admirable about the spirit of 'Don't dwell', keeping on come what may. Looking back, I do sometimes find 'Don't dwell' useful, but there is something deathly chilling about it too, a denial of pain, a refusal to face suffering.

Glen belongs now to Colin's grandson, but without the money. I went back there one last time in 2013 for my aunt Elizabeth's funeral in nearby Traquair. The estate was hanging on, just, trying to make a go of it as a conference centre, but, freezing cold and down at heel, this castle in the middle of nowhere looked an unlikely commercial venue, though rentals from the old tied cottages do well. It was snowing in January and my brother and I wandered around the frozen sunlit grounds, out to the loch, past a sad memorial to the two dead heirs at the end of an avenue of trees. This was a melancholy *Cherry Orchard* scene as we sat down with a few family members round the vast table in the dining room, eating a Chinese takeaway from Innerleithen out of cardboard cartons and remembering very different banquets here. The silver covers over an array of breakfast dishes, perfect pats of butter from the farm's own dairy for toast cut magically without crusts, the long whole honeycomb stretched out on a platter, and the shooting party lunches served with gigantic steak and kidney puddings by butler and footmen, all gone now.

Late in the evening after much wine, I talked to the young heir in his early twenties, who had trained as an electrician, but seemed dangerously eager to hold onto Glen against the odds. Why, I asked? Don't chain yourself to the upkeep of an impossible building, I warned. Live your life. But I feared he felt his identity was tied to this place, these hills, as if the last shreds of his aristocracy resided here. My family have all been footloose, peripatetic people from nowhere, so perhaps I would never understand this castle-bound family my aunt married into.

That day my brother and I walked through the village that belongs to the house, its stone cottages once inhabited by estate workers now let out as holiday homes.

Tramping through the thick snow, we came to one of the small Edwardian sandstone cottages that I had forgotten all about. The Alveses lived there, where as young children Catherine and I would go often for tea, or just to play. Mr Alves was a gamekeeper, Mrs Alves helped in the kitchen at the great house. I don't know why this was our special place, these our special friends, or how we came to be so close to them. We loved them for their warmth, homeliness and kindness, a little haven of our own, a cosy nook away from the grandeur of Glen. She would bring out old-fashioned board games and a toy tin chicken that laid tin golden eggs, along with her homemade bannock bread, thick with dried fruit.

But one day as Catherine and I walked along the high road towards their house, we saw my uncle, Lord Glenconner, standing outside their door and shouting at them at the top of his voice, red-faced with anger. Mr and Mrs Alves just stood there saying nothing while he berated them. We shrank back and retreated, appalled by the scene, hoping we hadn't been spotted. Until then I had always considered my uncle to be the most indulgent and benevolent old man, a munificent spoiler of his children and me. He would give his children anything they wanted, any time, often to my astonishment. I remember once Catherine calling for him from her four-poster after we had been put to bed and the house party were about to go in for dinner. 'I want some eggy bread, I'm hungry and I need it now,' Catherine demanded. I hid under the bedclothes to make it clear this outrageous request was nothing to do with me. Of course the answer would be no? But he said, 'Yes, darling. I'll get Mrs Mackay to make it right away.' And two plates of eggy bread arrived on a silver tray, despite my aunt's protest, with the kitchen trying to heave a large dinner up the lazy Susan lift from the kitchen into the dining room pantry. Until then, that's the only way I had ever seen Uncle Christopher, kindly, generous to a fault, a Father Christmas who indulged his children's every whim. He would take us at Easter to ask the farm chickens to lay us coloured eggs. He would take us to climb the haystack in the barn to hunt for duck eggs. As a benefactor of London Zoo, he would take us inside the enclosure to throw cabbages into the yawning mouths of hippopotamuses. He would row us across the loch to picnic on the island with a wicker hamper and fishing rods. So what was this magisterial explosion of rage at our dearly loved Mr and Mrs Alves?

Later that afternoon I found my mother in her room shaking with indignation. I overheard her talking to my stepfather, so I made her tell me. This is what we had crashed in on: we had seen the Alveses being evicted, immediately, with barely time to pack their life's possessions. Why? Some dispute about the game or the organizing of the stands for the shooting party or some technical gamekeeping detail my mother didn't understand. But the upshot was that we never saw the couple again, or knew where they went or how they lived once they were turned out of their tied cottage in the village where everyone was dependent on the Glenconner command, living there only on his sufferance.

Memories can be wrong: after reading my account in the first edition of this book, the Tennant family say that what my mother thought she knew was not accurate. They checked letters in the Glen archives and say: 'Jimmy Alves was not sacked or evicted. He resigned when he was asked to join the farm staff, because Christopher could no longer afford to run a separate shooting department. This meant giving up his house, which went with the keeper's job. Had he accepted the job on the farm, he could have stayed there until he retired. In the circumstances, he stayed in his house, The Kennels, until he found alternative accommodation and Christopher gave him a pension for life.'

Due to the finer points of class difference, Catherine's life and mine always diverged. While I was sent to a sensible middle class boarding school where we were expected to earn our livings, Catherine was sent to Cranbourne Chase, a more upper class school where most girls were not expected to do anything. She left at sixteen, and had an immensely grand coming-out ball, the only debutante event I ever encountered. She and her much older sister, the exuberant and sharp-witted writer Emma Tennant, seemed not to be expected to earn their livings – though as it turned out, they needed to. But later in life Catherine, who was cleverer than her school, took herself off to University College London and got a good degree, and Emma worked for *Queen* and *Vogue*, founded a good literary magazine, *Bananas*, wrote novels and clever books about everything that happened to her, including an affair with Ted Hughes. But although both were given a hefty slab of money, earning enough – or marrying richly enough – to suit the life they had been brought up to expect eluded them, and both ended up relatively penniless with nothing much to hand on to their children. Seeing all that splendour falling away from the castle walls of my childhood was unexpected: that grandeur had felt so solid and permanent. Does some smug, weaselly middle class part of me and my family look on with a knowing nod at the perils of a spoilt upper class upbringing without the fortune to sustain it? I hope not, because I loved as well as feared them. I remember once as a child in the drawing room, tall glamorous Emma waved her cigarette holder at us and asked what wildest dream trip we would choose. Catherine rolled out some great South Sea island fantasy, but when I said I wanted to go to the Edinburgh Festival everyone howled with laughter. I was just so, well, boringly bourgeois.

Catherine and I went our separate ways, though on rare occasions when we met we picked up at once on our childhood closeness: she was funny, dashing, eccentric and curiously unworldly with an elliptical take on life. In her presence I felt my plodding pursuit of a career with a pension seemed materialistic: through earnings and buying a London house that, like everywhere, had exploded in value over the decades, I found it strange that I ended up with more money than her.

Public school

The older children grow, the more refined their social antennae become. You might think that at a middle-ranking girls' boarding school, Badminton School in the dull Bristol suburb of Westbury-on-Trym (nothing to do with the stately home of Badminton horse trials), every one of us belonged to the same social class. In the crude weighing scales of sociologists, that would be so, all AB children with parents or grandparents able to stump up the middle-ranking fees. But from all of English literature, from your own life, you will know the importance of subtle gradations of social difference. This was not a school for the aristocracy but everyone knew the significance of money, eyeing the cars and clothes each other's parents arrived in. But the devilry of English class is that money is not the whole story. More important than wealth was parental occupation, status and education, with that great gulf between profession and trade. From high to low, there can barely be a schoolroom in England where children can't rank one another's families fairly accurately. I have often reported on the misery of desperately poor children first arriving in school, branded from day one for the wrong uniform, cheap trainers, no lunch box, no lunch money, no PE kit, nothing to write in an essay on 'My Summer Holidays' or 'My Christmas'.

The rule isn't absolute: clever, talented, funny, interesting or just plain lucky children break free of low social origins. Dim and dull richer ones do sometimes slide down in their peers' esteem. But class at my school was subtle and always unspoken: too flash parental Jaguars and fur coats were despised as vulgar. Nonetheless, the big picture of social class destiny was played out in microcosm even in my apparently homogeneous middle class schoolroom. Aged twelve we were divided into A streamers and B streamers; let's call them sheep and goats. Sure enough, the daughters of doctors, academics, scientists, teachers, lawyers, diplomats, a Nigerian daughter of the governor of Kaduna, an Indian politician's daughter, one bishop's daughter and any similar children of highly educated professionals glided effortlessly up to the A stream. But the daughters of trade were more likely to be relegated to the B stream, often day-girl daughters of local Bristol businessmen or farmers from around the West Country. This was unconscious bias on the school's part: they simply went by children's results, or their perceived intelligence or intellectual interests. In this subtle grading, parents' education predestined most of us either to the Latin set or to the domestic science stream. The Latins were headed, it was presumed, to university, the cooks to secretarial college. Since we were usually hungry, the Latins hung around outside the cookery room yearning for the pies and cakes the others carried out in silver tins – and yet we Latins knew perfectly well that we were glad to be designated A streamers. Since I hated Latin and failed it at O level, I'd have had a better time with the domestic science stream, but of course I'd have been appalled at relegation to the B stream: social status trumps cakes.

One school memory of class still makes me blush. For a little while Jane was a best friend, but she was a Group B, a cook not a Latin. She tagged along, copied what I said and did, remembered the right books and PE kit to stop me getting into needless trouble, and I doubt I treated her well. Think Jane Austen's Emma and Harriet Smith.

One half term she invited me to stay at her home, a bungalow in a suburb of Torquay, where her parents treated me as if I were a prize. Inviting friends round for a coffee morning to meet me, her mother read out to them a pretentious poem of mine in the school magazine.

When I was finally escaping the school after (virtually no) O levels, heading for a comprehensive, Jane immediately decided to do the same, but her parents wouldn't let her go to a state school when they had saved for her private education. So I persuaded her that the next best would be Dartington Hall, the notorious Devon free-thinking, free-living, artistic progressive school I'd always longed to move to. I never stopped to think for a minute how unsuited quiet and conventional Jane would be to this bohemian enclave. Soon I was off and away, preoccupied with my own London comprehensive life, and of course I forgot all about her. Only years later, bumping into someone from Badminton, asking what had become of various girls we knew, she told me Jane had been miserable at Dartington. Teased for her ordinariness, she had turned into 'a rather bitter and unhappy person', she said. 'Badly done, Emma, badly done,' reprimanded Mr Knightley.

I have plenty more to say about rebellious years at that school, the running away, the getting caught and sent back by the police, ferocious matrons and PE teachers who condoned the bullying by sporty girls. About Miss Griffin, the junior school matron who reigned with unfettered absolute power, clicking down the dorm corridor in her crisp Wrens uniform, tormenting her unfavourites. I could write about punishments, forced lumpy porridge-eating and being in endless trouble. Why was I there? The imposing and intelligent stateliness of the headmistress persuaded my mother this was a liberal institution; it was a member of something called the Conference of Internationally Minded Schools (CIS), founded in 1951

School photo, Badminton

imbued with United Nations fervour, with many foreign exchanges. (Wikipedia tells me that CIS was wound up in 1969.) Sunday evening talks were lantern slides of Pestalozzi children's villages, Oxfam and third world needs. The ethos was that we should go out and do good around the world – and many did. There was an honour system where you signed yourself up for a black mark on the noticeboard if you caught yourself breaking rules, such as talking in the silent corridors: a friend and I resisted the honour rules by signing ourselves up to hundreds of these confessions, to general outrage as it lost our house the cup for good behaviour.

Just before I finally managed to leave, I started a Bristol schools branch of YCND – Youth Campaign for Nuclear Disarmament – and wrote to every head boy and girl in every Bristol school inviting them to a public meeting in the school hall with a CND speaker down from London. Hundreds turned up, mainly, I think, to get a look inside the forbidden bastion of this private girls' school. There was trouble. The *Bristol Evening News* reported it and interviewed me (I didn't know how to pronounce 'annihilation' which I'd written in our leaflets, and the reporter laughed at me). Some Bristol parent governors were incandescent at the school's good name being dragged into this communistic cause, but I was off and away soon after. Julia Clarke, my co-YCND leader, was the real heroine. She ended up sitting on the art room roof hurling down tiles before she was expelled: now she's a splendid radical doctor.

As for privilege, I left with four bad O levels, no maths, no science, no Latin, so the value for money was poor. Those marks were not, directly, the school's fault: much of the teaching was conventionally good but I was too rebellious to work, too angry to obey, too impatient to get out of there. Observing the many schools my four children have attended, the few schools that succeed concentrate first on happiness: learning is drudgery without it. And schools are undoubtedly happier places for my grandchildren than they were when my children experienced them, let alone back in the late 1950s when I was sent away. Why did my mother do that? Her friend who had a daughter there persuaded her, and I thought it would be Malory Towers. I was excited by the extraordinary uniform and equipment assembled in my school trunk, from ten pairs of knickers and five woollen vests, to a shoe-cleaning kit, a letter-writing set, a lacrosse stick, divided-skirt PE shorts in gun-metal flannel, a tweed winter coat, a round brown hat like a cowpat and two long-sleeved afternoon frocks called 'mufti', non-uniform for Sundays, all bought from Daniel Neal, the private school outfitters in Kensington High Street. 'Mufti' was just part of the colonial and military language that was deep-dyed into those schools.

Why private? She would have sent me to a London grammar school, but my sister and I both failed the 11-plus, for the same reason. We both hated Kensington High School, the Girls' Public Day School Trust junior school of nightmare detentions, rules, bullying and cramming. The more we were crammed for that cursed life-determining 11-plus exam, the more we baulked at it. Neither of us could spell and my sister was still writing 'Josephine' with the J backwards, though later she took off to academic brilliance.

Comprehensive

My social class guaranteed I would never be sent to a secondary modern, so boarding school was my punishment. But at sixteen I took myself out of that detested school and into the sixth form of Holland Park, the gleaming new first comprehensive in Notting Hill that Rita had attended, and one of my twin half-brothers followed on after me. There for the first time I found pleasure in education. As for the missing O levels, I took them again my first term at Holland Park where I was steered through retakes with kindly persuasion, under the mentorship of Mr Stedman Jones, the scholarly head of the English department, devotee of Dr Johnson. This fine teacher, against all family expectation, guided me into winning an Oxford open scholarship too,

by passing on to me his deep fascination for and knowledge of Jacobean drama, studying far beyond the ordinary
curriculum, engrossing me in his literary obsessions. Luck
in finding that teacher played its part, for by then my
parents had lost any hope for my academic success: as I
left my boarding school, the stately headmistress told my
mother there was little chance I would ever apply myself
sufficiently to get into a university.

But now when I think about it again, probably that extra
help from a great comprehensive teacher wasn't pure luck.
What if I'd been a working class O level failure, who would
have bothered to see if I was worth a second chance? Mr
Stedman Jones may have picked on me for special coaching because he knew of my family's literary and academic
background and just assumed I must have an inherited
talent hidden away somewhere, though I had nothing
much to show for it. I was once told by an academic of
an appealing education experiment conducted some years
ago that alas I haven't been able to trace: a group of teachers were picked and told they had been especially selected
as the most highly skilled to teach some particularly brilliant children, children who were also told that secret tests
had revealed they were exceptionally gifted. Both teachers
and pupils did extraordinarily well, though all had been
chosen at random. Expectation is everything.

* * *

Since the hardback edition of this book was published,
several people have written to me to say this important
piece of research is well known, called 'Pygmalion in the

Classroom', published in 1968 by Robert Rosenthal and Lenore Jacobson in *The Urban Review*.

Since writing about Mr Stedman Jones I was glad to receive messages from a few others at Holland Park, who were from working class backgrounds and had benefited from his extra coaching. Here's Susan, a few years younger than me. 'My cousins closest in age had gone to a Secondary Modern. I think an A level was not something I even thought about. We lived on a council estate in Fulham. For two years during lunch break and free periods we took lessons with Mr Stedman Jones.' That propelled her up to university.

The truth is, the Oxford scholarship exam of those days was designed to reward people of exactly my background and journalistic state of mind. Its general paper was one of the most enjoyable and encouraging exams ever devised, with scores of essay questions to choose from on every conceivable subject, open-ended, imaginative and even fantastical in their scope. Choose any question on any subject and show off to us! Intrigue us with a parade of ideas! It searched for what you could do best, while most exams aim to catch you out on what you know least. That should be the guiding spirit in all exams, I thought. But that's because it best suits dilettantes already exposed to wide reading, precisely as encouraged by my background. It favours those who know a little about a lot, we who had been brought up to skate across the cultural landscape, conversant with the canon of everything important from Tintoretto to Nietzsche to Wagner. But only lightly acquainted, sliding across a thin veneer, enough not to be wrong-footed in that world punctured by T.S. Eliot in

'The Love Song of J. Alfred Prufrock': 'In the room the women come and go / Talking of Michelangelo'. I could do that. The Oxford scholarship paper encouraged those superficial traits. It gave an undeserved chance to shine to someone who had regularly done badly in exams through idle failure to learn theorems or foreign grammar by heart, ignoring what I found boring, studying only what I enjoyed. This heavily class-biased exam would disadvantage very clever applicants who had worked exceedingly hard at every subject at school but lacked the family or an Alan Bennett *History Boys* teacher or my Mr Stedman Jones to open their wings at this early stage in their life. This was the perfect exam to select future newspaper columnists.

2

Arnold

OVERNIGHT MY FAMILY'S view of me was transformed by winning that scholarship, no longer the disappointingly unserious academic failure. From the moment that telegram from St Anne's College was opened, it was 'We always knew it all along, of course we did.' My grandfather Arnold gave me a complete leather-bound set of the works of Ibsen: typically tight-fisted, a note showing these were review copies fluttered out. My father Philip gave me his old set of Dickens, which still sits on my top shelf. My philosopher stepfather, a Balliol man with a tendency to look up what degree people got in a sinister little red book, looked on me in a new light. I had neither expected nor intended to go to Oxford, not until Mr Stedman Jones pushed and pulled me there: to my mind, Oxford was uncomfortably overfreighted with a family history of phenomenal academic prowess and scholarly fame or else by my father's dashing literary and political triumphs. From my childhood stays with my two great-aunts in their Oxford house in Park Town, those spires didn't dream but loomed, daunting and dusty, smelling of old libraries and musty dons, the dark corridors filled with ancients in long gowns bending down to say, 'Ah, you're Philip's daughter? Arnold's granddaughter? Gilbert's great-granddaughter? Ah!'

There were two quite distinct family brands of Oxford nostalgia: first there was that winning-every-essay-and-classics-prize heritage and then there was my father's glorious past as a great debater, elected as the first ever communist President of the Union in 1934, accompanied by feats of drunkenness to outdo Sebastian Flyte of *Brideshead Revisited*. My father's tuft-hunting success in recruiting great names to the Communist Party included the likes of Stephen Spender and Denis Healey. From all sides the shades of Oxford cast their shadows over me – and all of these relatives in their opposite ways plied me with unwelcome advice and sentimental memories of their salad days.

Within a week of opening that telegram, the three old Toynbee siblings swept me out to lunch with them to the ladies' annex of the Athenaeum, the ancient gentlemen's club in Pall Mall. Here they are: first, and always foremost, is my grandfather, Arnold Toynbee, world-famous historian, author of an epic twelve volumes of *A Study of History*, whose 'challenge and response' theory of the rise and fall of all civilizations caught the American imagination and became a global bestseller. In the year of my birth his face was on the cover of *Time* magazine and all my childhood he travelled the world giving lectures and receiving honours. Since the name is odd, wherever I go as a child, adults and teachers ask awe-struck if I am related to him, as if some of that world-embracing civilization might have rubbed off on me: these days it's only elderly Americans, Japanese and Turks who tend to ask, agog, if I am indeed descended from him: memento mori, fame and intellectual fashions move on.

Great-Aunt Jocelyn and Great-Aunt Margaret

His two distinguished sisters are my maiden great-aunts, Jocelyn Toynbee, Cambridge Professor of Archaeology, and her younger sister Margaret, who, as a mere history don at St Hugh's College, Oxford, was a little condescended to by the other two. Bearing down on me, this is a rare London visit by the great-aunts from their spinster fastness in Park Town, where they have an airing cupboard with seven shelves for seven cats, the top one reserved for fleecy white Minerva who sits on Great-Aunt Jocelyn's shoulder and they purr together in unison, the whiskers of the cat entwined with the thick crop of whiskers on her own chin: she is the only human I've ever known who could purr perfectly. But her aura was austere.

To give some idea of how heavily their seriousness weighed down on me that day, here's a thumbnail of their work: Jocelyn's doctoral thesis was on Hadrianic sculpture, and she became the leading British authority in Roman artistic studies. However, she is now probably best remembered within the Vatican, not for her most scholarly work but for her more dubious commission from the Catholic Church, for which copious Catholic references remain. As a trustworthy convert to Rome, she was summoned by Pope Pius XII as the right kind of distinguished archaeologist with the right kind of beliefs to dig up and investigate without sacrilege the tomb of

Jocelyn Toynbee, painted by Catriona Jane Cursham

St Peter under his basilica. As a result of her digging, in 1950 the Pope proclaimed in his Christmas message that the bones were indeed St Peter's, a claim blazoned across the front covers of *Time* and *Newsweek*. Great-Aunt Jocelyn was not quite so unequivocal in her verdict on the holy bones, but nor did she refute the Pope's more or less infallible assertion. As a historian, it must surely have occurred to her as odd that among all the detailed Acts of the Apostles listed in the New Testament as they roamed among the Galatians, Corinthians and Ephesians, no one remembered to record so important a matter as Peter tipping up in Rome, leading the Church as first pope and being crucified upside down by Nero right there at the heart of the empire. The Acts contain no such record. But Jocelyn's less than strictly pure academic judgement on St Peter's tomb will be her own epitaph for as long as the Catholic Church requires a Cambridge professor's archaeological validation.

As for Great-Aunt Margaret, she was much the cosiest and warmest of the three siblings, affectionate, a bit giggly and spontaneous. But that made her despised as a bit dim by the other two, a mere Dr and St Hugh's don, lacking a professorship. In the sisters' household, she was the housekeeper, compelled into the domestic role of Martha to Jocelyn's haughtier Mary. Besides, her specialism was not classical, but a vulgar admiration for Charles I and a taste for Cavalier tales of derring-do which I confess guiltily I loved as a child before I knew any better, as she told me the stories of the King up the oak tree and brave Flora MacDonald rowing over the sea to Skye. Her liking for the Cavaliers didn't suit the

Roundhead flavour of their upbringing. (I find Margaret's book on Charles I is for sale second-hand on Amazon at the alarming price of £0.01.) What a tough and competitive childhood these three must have had, where all that mattered was coming top in exams to get the scholarships they needed: in any other family Margaret would have shone, but her brother and sister consigned her to the second rank. So if I was daunted, who wouldn't be?

Arnold greets us at the Athenaeum door, leading us down the outside steps to the dark basement, to avoid even the passing breath of women contaminating the club's all-male portals. As ever, the three chuckle coyly at the inscription in ancient Greek over the doorway of the ladies' annex, which they can read and I can't: 'Come in dear ladies and lie down'. I am wearing a micro miniskirt that shows my knickers if I bend even slightly and white PVC boots that smell terrible when taken off – but to wear anything else in 1966 is unthinkable.

Over the brown Windsor soup, the dark brown slices of dry beef and gravy followed by apple pie and solidified custard, I am grilled about my precise academic interests, as they inform me in minute detail of the history curriculum, the best tutors at St Anne's, the many important lectures to attend: Gibbon and Macaulay, mediaeval French, mediaeval Latin, Old English, the Venerable Bede's *Ecclesiastical History, Beowulf*. They know all my tutors well and will regularly confer with them as to my progress. Of course, they say, swelling with familial pride, 'a scholar' such as myself is expected by the college to get a good first. Whatever air-punching moment of euphoria I felt on opening that telegram was deflated here.

Yet, to be honest, winning this most unexpected academic honour changed not just how others saw me, but how I saw myself. No longer the hopeless case in a hyper-academic family but overnight the most serious scholar among my siblings, half-siblings and cousins. Taking on the mood of their Anglo-Saxon theme, I had always relished the story of Caedmon, Bede's illiterate cowherd of Whitby, who, he records, was one night miraculously struck lyrical with the gift of poetic song. Everyone secretly hopes they may suddenly be 'discovered' for some previously unseen talent. But these new family expectations filled me with foreboding: this was a fluke, a cheat and not for nothing was it named the Gamble Scholarship. It should have been plain: I didn't have the right A levels to qualify ordinarily, but the rules in those days decreed that the magic of a scholarship swept away all mundane matriculation requirements. In my case, impostor syndrome wasn't a syndrome: I was an impostor.

To the self-centred young fretting over their own uncertain future, older people's pasts seem unimaginably distant, dull and alien. But now I look back at that Athenaeum lunch and a hundred other missed opportunities to ask these three about themselves, their childhood, their determination to succeed against the odds – or maybe even their lost loves. I knew nothing of their childhood or of their tiger mother who propelled them forwards. She was by all accounts an early fearsome hot-houser. I knew nothing of the hardship of their childhood, perilously perched as poor relations. What of their father who vanished from all conversation, never spoken of? Why did I never ask any of them of the horror hidden behind that silence about their father? I was shamefully incurious, but in the course of writing this book, I have uncovered their sad secret now.

As a young child I was fond of all three as their literary enthusiasms illuminated the tales they told me from classical mythology, stories of ancient Greece, Rome and Valhalla. I liked the aunts taking me into secret vaults beneath the Ashmolean Museum to view serried ranks of Greek and Roman emperors, recounting their foibles.

I savoured trips with Arnold to the Tower of London, up to the whispering gallery of St Paul's Cathedral, round the tombs of Westminster Abbey, through the British Museum's array of lost civilizations or climbing up the Monument to the Fire of London: he too was good at telling a child stories, conjuring up history with great verve and imagination, as he sailed away on cloudy evocations of the past. He would tell excellent world traveller's tales too, surprisingly well adapted for children. There are faraway places in the world I still associate first with his stories. The Andes? A land of spitters, where someone once spat inside his sock. Until my sister and I became sulky teenagers when both he and we became embarrassed by all our combined awkwardnesses, he was a good companion for children with his treasury of legends and myths.

But as teenagers do, by the time of that Athenaeum lunch I found these three elderly ancestors depressing and alarmingly demanding. They could intuit as little of my modern life as I could envisage their distant youth, though I now know that apparent clash of generational civilizations is a needless mutual incomprehension: human life changes so much less than each generation imagines.

A narrow escape

But these three ancients certainly knew nothing of how narrowly I had escaped teen motherhood and an end to any educational expectations. I was bowled over in love with a clever and cerebral boy, son of a high Catholic convert mother but humanist father, sent to Ampleforth, though by then he had thoroughly shaken off all that. His breadth of cultural and intellectual interest was beyond anything I had come across among friends of my age. I was awe-struck not just by him, his avid reading, zeal for jazz, poetry and left-wing politics, but also by his cool and detached air of grace. His father was a wise and humorous international human rights lawyer, who reminded me of Mr Bennet in *Pride and Prejudice*. As for his older sister, who became a good painter, I looked up to her with a kind of hero-worship for her wild and funny exuberance.

But as he was about to go to Oxford, I was appalled to find I was pregnant and even more appalled at his anti-abortion mother pressing us to marry. She suggested we would live in an Oxford flat, where I would bring up the baby while he studied: the end of my own future worried her not at all. We paid a visit to his newly married sister, who was living in Oxford's Summertown, up the road from my great-aunts. I was pleased to see her, this lively, funny and magnetic character. But she was living, as far as I could see, the life their mother expected me to live, married and cooped up in an Oxford flat with a baby. Though she was herself a student, wifedom and life with a baby looked to me like a brutal curtailment of studenthood, locked in at home. There was her baby, Alexander, a few months old, lying naked on a bath mat, kicking his feet in the air, round, pink and fat with a remarkable shock of electrically bright blond hair. As I gazed at him, I didn't find that baby at all appealing, too pink and too noisy. I shuddered at the prospect of this motherly existence, threatening an end to my life before it had even begun.

Afterwards, as we both contemplated this scene, looking at his sister and at the vision of our future stretching out ahead of us, he broke off with me. His mother was plainly glad, but she called me many times to insist that I have the baby and give it away to a Catholic adoption agency. I was aghast that anyone could suggest anything so cruel. This was still before abortion was finally legalized in 1967. But I was lucky, again. My family's local GP was a disreputable and amenable practitioner, who we always thought made extra money on the side by dispensing more or less anything anyone wanted, and so he prescribed what were then illegal abortion-inducing pills: after two days of great pain, to my immense relief, that was the end of the pregnancy. But I didn't know if my boyfriend's mother might investigate and report me and I feared she might. The end of that relationship left me heartbroken and bereft, taking revenge by writing him into my (not very good) first novel. That baby on the bath mat, who so decisively put me off the idea of teen motherhood, grew up to be the most disgraced prime minister under his ludicrously changed name of Boris: he looks much the same.

As for my former lover, he is a serious writer and thinker and a remote friend: odd how impossible it is to recapture old passions. I simply recall the fact of the agony of unrequited love, but look at him now as an interesting but distant person, all passion spent. As for Boris Johnson, I look back with a morbid incredulity at what that baby grew up to be. It's a not particularly good joke to surprise people with the fact that I am one of the many women to have seen him naked.

All this was, of course, entirely unknown to my grandfather and his sisters that lunchtime as they busily filled me with advice on how to shine as they had shone at Oxford. And I, of course, asked them nothing of their young lives either, only wishing this Athenaeum ordeal of expectations to be over and to escape back to the modern world.

Arnold and his sisters' family

Now, far too late to ask, I start to dig into their history. Arnold and his two sisters had an upbringing of genteel poverty after both parents suffered a plunge downwards from the comfortable worlds of their own childhoods.

Their father Harry was the youngest child of a successful otologist, Joseph Toynbee, ear specialist to Queen Victoria. I find there is a blue plaque to him at 49 Parkside, Wimbledon where they lived: he saved Wimbledon Common from the avaricious Earl Spencer's attempt to enclose and build over all that common ground. He founded a Wimbledon Village Club to provide reading rooms and lectures for local agricultural and manual labourers. On his death a public drinking fountain, known as the Toynbee Fountain, was erected in his memory and there it stays, recently restored, inscribed, 'Originated by the working men of Wimbledon and erected with funds contributed by them and his friends and others interested in the public good. AD 1868.' A strong liberal, yes, striving for 'the public good', he was what *Spectator* types would call a 'do-gooder'. He campaigned for working rights, inheriting that spirit from his antecedents, a gene, an impulse, a moral cast of mind he passed on just as strongly to his own nine children. But he passed them no money. He died young conducting a typically selfless but lethally dangerous experiment on himself, seeking a cure for tinnitus: he bequeathed his family his fine values, but meagre means.

That meant Harry, the youngest, was denied a university education and went to work unhappily for a tea company. But he became repelled by commerce, so he gave up his quite lowly job in the tea industry to take an even lower salary as general secretary to the main poverty charity of the day, the Charity Organisation Society, of which more later. His wife, Edith Marshall, came from a reasonably affluent Birmingham industrial family, but her father went bankrupt, losing his rail rolling stock factory and everything else in bank debts. By then Edith was as well educated as a girl could be of her generation when women were not admitted to universities: she had enrolled into what later became Newnham College, Cambridge, where she could study and take the same exams as men, but without receiving a degree. She was awarded one of only two firsts in modern history that year – but was never formally granted a degree. She was earning her living as a teacher when she married Harry.

The young couple had too little to set up house on their own, so they moved in with Harry's uncle, an irascible retired sea captain also called Harry, living in a shabby-genteel Paddington terrace that, like them, was hanging on by its fingernails to middle class respectability. Edith was to act as this difficult widower's housekeeper, as her husband's family couldn't or didn't help. His rich and idle brother Paget had married well, lived the life of a country squire and collected Dante manuscripts, but he offered not a penny of support. His clever sister Grace was a distinguished biologist at Birmingham University, but not earning enough to help.

So Harry and Edith's children, Arnold, Jocelyn and Margaret, were all born there in Westbourne Terrace, off Praed Street by Paddington station, one of those in-between, doubtful districts that always surround city railway stations. The children grew up tiptoeing around a house that wasn't theirs, penny-pinching on their father's pitifully low charity salary. Of his sad life and fate, I discover more later, but he suffers a nervous breakdown and vanishes from this family scene.

Left on her own, Edith was the powerful, dominating figure in her children's lives, pouring all her own frustrated education into driving them on to academic success. From the youngest age the three children knew they could afford no education unless they won scholarships and prizes all the way, and so they did. Edith did earn a little as archivist of Florence Nightingale's papers and she earned £20 for writing a child's history of Scotland (I find Edith Marshall was not, alas, H.E. Marshall, the bestselling author of *Our Island Story* and *Scotland's Story*).

Arnold's biographer, William H. McNeill, describes Edith thus: 'She was a strong-minded woman, utterly firm in her Anglican faith, her English patriotism, her sense of duty and her attachment to her son.' The moral code of the household was liberal in politics, imbued with concern for the unfortunate and strongly anti-Tory.

Edith and Arnold

Though humiliated as a penurious poor relation, Edith kept 'an appropriate façade of gentility, culture and independence by dint of the utmost economy of daily expenditure'. Into her son she distilled all her own hopes – and she was not disappointed. All three children grew up to be parsimonious to the point of family parody: though Arnold would have made considerable sums from his bestselling books and lucrative globe-trotting lecturing, we ridiculed his miserly thrift and his tight-fisted anxiety about money. All his life he lived in fear of 'ending up in the workhouse' as I heard him say often. But we, in our comfort, who mocked him, knew next to nothing of the scars left by the hardship of a childhood keeping up appearances. Later, as a Balliol Fellow, he was rightly shocked at the extravagant gluttony and luxury of high table life. He wrote to a friend, 'Why need they fare so sumptuously? I shall get myself made junior bursar and feed them all on bread and water. I want to smash and melt the college silver.'

Edith coached and pushed, so the two girls won scholarships to board at Winchester High School for Girls, and then scholarships to Newnham, followed by firsts. Arnold won the top scholarship to Winchester College where his youth was spent entirely in relentless study, winning every available school prize for essays in Latin and German, and Latin and Greek verse, awash with the study of ancient civilizations, an education unthinkable these days. He was unsociable with few friends, detesting team sports yet not an aesthete either. He was plainly lonely but he ferociously devoured all the learning on offer every minute of every day, as trained by his mother. When he writes to her in capital letters 'I HAVE WON THE GODDARD: is that not splendid?', she annotates the cherished letter at the bottom with maternal pride, 'What a boy it is!' In those days Winchester prize-winners were gazetted in *The Times*.

He arrived as a scholar at Balliol College, Oxford in 1907 gauche and socially clumsy but with an inner conviction of his own secret brilliance. It was a college that combined high aristocracy with top brains, an awkward mix since the two were rarely compatible. His biographer notes that nineteen out of fifty-two entrants to the college that year were Etonians, nearly all were aristocrats and only ten were students whose brain alone was their main reason for admission. Poor Arnold had an abiding interest in aristocracy, wistfully respectful of notions of blue blood with an instinctive weakening of the knee at the thought of pedigree, perhaps because his own experience of school and university had made his lack of blue blood painful. He once wrote an odd letter to me about seeing in me my 'Stanley blood' which he said made me impetuous and passionate. I had no idea what he was talking about, but it turns out there was a distant Stanley connection: my great-great-grandmother, the Countess of Carlisle, was a Stanley, daughter of Lord Stanley, a Whig politician. Jessica Mitford (known to us as Decca, as I shall call her from now on), who later in life designated herself as my official non-godmother, discovered that if she went back a similar number of great-greats, she and I were related and did indeed share half a fingerfull of Stanley blood. How odd and how sad for Arnold, as a serious historian, to take such pernicious nonsense seriously, but living despised among yahoo Oxford blue bloods may have done that to him.

At Balliol, Arnold became an atheist and briefly a Fabian socialist. He wrote, 'Economic laws are wholly man-made', so that 'trades union "co-ops" may succeed in mastering economics and bridling it and riding it along whatever road we choose'. He remained distantly sympathetic to socialist causes, but a quintessential liberal. As for his social life, he knew no women and was exceedingly shy when he met any. He wrote to a friend at the time of finding himself sitting in a train compartment with a suffragette. 'When she got out I gallantly lifted my cap and wished her success in her cause. I have been amazed at my temerity ever since.' I can see his flustered, staccato

Arnold at Balliol

gestures even now, as to the end of his days, and despite worldwide success, he was a man who fumbled most encounters. As a child on expeditions with him, his shyness and awkwardness made the simple business of buying a bus ticket, paying a waiter or asking the way hideously uncomfortable.

Arnold's awful mistake

Unaccustomed as he was to women, it's no surprise that he made the worst decision of his life in proposing to my grandmother, Rosalind Murray. He had no notion of her character, no understanding of the full monstrosity of her nature, holding onto a dreamlike impression of her, even after she divorced him. The light only finally broke in on him with the full shocking revelation of her profound hypocrisy long after her death.

Fatefully, the shy young Arnold spied her across the room at her parents' Boars Hill home, outside Oxford, where her father, the Regius Professor of Greek, Gilbert Murray, and his wife Mary held Sunday evening gatherings for classics scholars. Arnold fell instantly in love, stricken as if touched by a Puck-like piece of mischief. Of that epic error, more later.

But first I set off to explore what had happened to Arnold's father, the disappeared Harry, who neither he nor his sisters, Great-Aunt Jocelyn or Great-Aunt Margaret, ever mentioned to me. Why did I never ask? Now that I know my great-grandfather Harry's story, I find it's a tragedy that began with striving too hard to be good, a would-be-good broken by reaching beyond his mental or physical strength, a social reformer overwhelmed by the task.

Father — April — 1890

3

Harry: A Social Reformer's Tragedy

TOYNBEE HALL IS not quite an ancestral home. This strangely out-of-place edifice is tucked away in the heart of London's East End. In search of Harry's story, I pause in Toynbee Hall's familiar courtyard to look up at its mullioned windows where it stands proud in Commercial Street, a pastiche of an Oxford college. Inside, its wood-panelled lecture hall is curiously decorated round its cornice with shields bearing all the coats of arms of Oxford colleges: I am tempted to claim it as an ancestral home, in its unlikely magnificence.

But its true stateliness is in its wellspring of idealism. For a century and a half it has been the home of social reformers, the progenitor of ideas and policies about poverty, inequality and the welfare state. Here Clement Attlee worked as a young man, later writing that he learned his left-wing politics living there, as he joined the East End's Independent Labour Party. Here at the same time a young William Beveridge lived as sub-warden for a few years, studying 'social problems in a scientific way'. He claimed the origin of his 1942 welfare state plan was born in Toynbee Hall, after seeing the damage done by the

Toynbee Hall circa 1900

Poor Laws. Here too my great-grandfather Harry Toynbee spent time in his work on the Poor Laws, as the settlement movement urged on local authorities to build libraries, playgrounds and washhouses in this poverty-stricken district where few of the middle classes ever ventured.

Toynbee Hall was named after Harry's eldest brother, another Arnold, under whose powerful influence Harry fell after their father, Joseph the otologist, died of his own experiment when Harry was still very young. This older Arnold was a charismatic leader of the Oxford settlement movement of social reformers and a radical historian who earned his reputation young when he coined the phrase 'the industrial revolution'. He was a promoter of working rights, of trade unions and co-operatives, an ardent reformer and a stern puritan who drew a following of young people to work with him in the East End. But he died young of something described as a 'brain fever', caught, it was said, in Whitechapel where he was working with the poor. His close friends and colleagues, the Reverend Samuel Barnett and his wife Henrietta, founded Toynbee Hall in Spitalfields a year after his death in 1884 in honour of his work. The purpose of this university settlement movement was to bring well-heeled undergraduates to live and work in Whitechapel, so they could learn about the lives of the poor in exchange for offering them free classes.

If there is something embarrassing now about the notion of transporting privileged students to do good to East Enders, the institution's history as a pioneer of political radicalism has more than overcome those patronizing strains. The fine Whitechapel Art Gallery nearby, also founded by the Barnetts, now home of cutting edge ultra-modernism, tends not to mention its de-haut-en-bas founding mission to ensure that 'even the lowest people of London could appreciate higher art'.

Toynbee Hall has stood as protector and support to a host of often unpopular new migrants arriving in waves to the East End, at first Jews, Russians and Poles, eager to attend English classes and lectures. Nowadays the area is mostly Bangladeshi. I have attended Toynbee Hall's English classes with their outings for women, listening to Bangladeshi women's tales of being trapped indoors, some never daring to travel by bus or underground until taken on expeditions, but keen to learn from students who still get cheap accommodation here in exchange for giving free support and lessons. The first ever Jewish scout troop was here and the first pacifist National Peace Scouts. R.H. Tawney set up a first Workers' Educational Association here and a Poor Man's Lawyer service continues to this day (renamed). Lenin spoke here in 1902. In the General Strike Toynbee Hall provided money and concerts to strikers' families. In the war it received refugee children from the Kindertransport and set up the first Citizens Advice Bureau. Here was founded the Children's Country Holiday Fund, taking urban children to the countryside, where my mother worked for many years. Here too, famously, John Profumo, Secretary of State for War, served out the rest of his days as a volunteer as if in penance at a moral reformatory, after resigning in disgrace for lying to parliament about his affair with Christine Keeler in 1963.

The East End has long been treated as a place of duty for the upper classes to expiate their guilts and privileges, a place to boldly dip a toe in class experiments. My father writes of his Rugby School days when the boys were sent reluctantly to do good at an East End boys' club by treating them to games of football – revoltingly sneering at the local boys as 'blogs'. There is a long tradition of all this: I particularly enjoy Decca Mitford's description in her book *Hons and Rebels*. Her nanny signed up the Mitford children to join the Sunbeams. 'The idea was that a rich child would be given the address of a poor child, they would correspond, and the rich child would send old clothes or toys from time to time. Nancy [the oldest Mitford daughter] had once belonged when she was little, but she had lost the address of her Sunbeam and had addressed her letter "Tommy Jones, The Slums, London", much to the fury of Nanny.' Decca signed up. 'I imagined that my letters, which consisted of a highly romanticized account of life at Swinbrook [their Oxfordshire stately home] must bring great rays of joy into her otherwise drab existence.' Her Sunbeam, Rose Dickson, sent back descriptions 'in heart-rending detail' of the 'miserable, overcrowded conditions in which they lived – all six of them in two beds in one tiny room'. Decca begged her mother to let Rose come and stay, but her mother said firmly, 'Think how dreadfully *uncomfortable* she'd feel.' Eventually Lady Redesdale suggested they hire Rose as a tweeny – a between-maid. Rose arrived – but the two were instantly struck dumb, tongue-tied, with nothing to say to one another. Rose was whisked up the back stairs, and Decca only saw her now and then, heaving heavy slop pails on the upper landings. Not long afterwards, weeping floods of tears of homesickness, Rose asked to go home and was put back on the train to London. Decca, shame-faced, far too late looked up the role of a tweeny in Mrs Beeton's *Household Management* and was appalled to find this: 'The Between Maid is, perhaps, the only one of her class deserving of commiseration: her life is a solitary one, and in some places her work is never done.' The good intentions of mixing the social classes, is, as I often found as a child, frequently fraught with shame.

* * *

Toynbee Hall these days has thrown off these upper class do-gooding connotations. In my own time, I was at Toynbee Hall on the morning of Tony Blair's extraordinary visit, when he addressed the packed lecture hall to make the seminal social policy speech of his prime ministership, on 18 March 1999. To listen to his remarkable Beveridge lecture, he had summoned a hall full of poverty experts, economists and academics, along with social affairs journalists such as myself, to astound us with an unexpected commitment to abolish all child poverty by 2020. Abolish it! Jaws dropped, everyone in the room was amazed and partly disbelieving: did he understand what that would take, the enormous heavy lifting in redistribution and the colossal long term social programmes? He did, as did Gordon Brown, and they have never had enough credit for how far they reached their goal before being ousted. By Labour's departure in 2010 they had reached a third of that

Tony Blair with John Profumo at Toynbee Hall

target, not only taking a million children out of poverty, with many more lifted up closer to the poverty line, but they had also set up a network of 3,500 Sure Start children's centres, and a host of good anti-poverty programmes drawn up by eighteen different social exclusion task forces defining every cause and remedy. But all that they achieved was swept away within a month with David Cameron and George Osborne's first austerity budget in 2010. Had Labour stayed in power, that 2020 pledge might, just, have been realized. There could have been no better memorial to Toynbee Hall's history or to my great-great-uncle Arnold, after whose social reforming endeavour Toynbee Hall was founded.

Broken by good intentions

Harry, my great-grandfather, named his son, my grandfather Arnold, after that charismatic elder brother whose pioneering work set Toynbee Hall in train. Harry himself had conducted some of his research here for Beatrice Webb. But here the good news ends. As I go in search of him, Harry's tragic story turns out to be a striking case of liberal inner conflicts, a wrench between his need to earn a living to support his family, and his shift towards working with Beatrice Webb and the nascent Labour Party. That rift may have cost him his sanity.

I knew he had suffered a serious nervous breakdown when his children were young. I knew he had been taken away to an asylum but I always thought Harry must have died young in a psychiatric hospital. Not at all. I am shocked to find he was locked away for nearly forty years, only dying just before I was born, but never again set free. Arnold never spoke of him and nor did my father or anyone else mention my shut-away great-grandfather. What was his madness? Reading between the few lines available it sounds as if he began by falling into an acute depression that turned into a nervous breakdown of total collapse. But why did he never recover enough to emerge, not even for short stays outside? I wondered if institutionalization in a series of grim psychiatric hospitals had broken his spirit, incapacitating him: at first he was moved to ever-cheaper asylums as family finances tightened. As I looked into it, I began to suspect Edith, his powerhouse of a wife, fiercely protective of her children, didn't want him back as she was struggling hard to bring up her children respectably on very slender means. As she hothoused her three offspring into precocious academic success, I suspected she was not eager to have her husband return to a household where they were precariously only residing as poor relations. They were lodgers, she as a housekeeper, scraping by on a pittance. Would Harry's return have been a burden too far and a social embarrassment beyond enduring? I suspected this when I discovered that he didn't die young, but lived to be tragically old.

Harry's sad story turns out to be a tale of trying to do good that broke him in the end. As a young man, after his elder brother Arnold died and Toynbee Hall had been founded, Harry gave up his relatively humble job in the tea business to follow in his brother's footsteps into social reforming work, joining the staff of the most influential charity of its day, the Charity Organisation Society. It had an old-fashioned liberal philanthropic ethos, describing its mission as to 'heal the breach' between the poor and the middle classes and to help the poor help themselves. The foundation survives to this day unrecognizable in function or ideals as Family Action, recently renamed from the Family Welfare Association. In those days funds came from well-to-do private donors with well-heeled but amateur volunteers who were sent out to do case work among the poor.

This charity job meant taking a drop in salary to only £400 a year, below what he needed to sustain his family and well below what it took to keep up a London middle class life. That was in sharp contrast to his brother Paget who married into the ease of life as a country gentleman, who, despite his fortune, offered no help beyond patronizing advice to his hard-up brother. Nor did he lift a finger to help the impoverished family after Harry's removal to the asylum 'for the mentally deranged'. The crisis that tipped Harry over the edge and into the asylum was political and moral, as well as financial.

The Charity Organisation Society for whom he was general secretary had seemed benevolent, liberal and kindly a generation ago in Victorian eyes, set up to draw together a host of small private charities. But by now it was becoming increasingly out of step with changing times. Arnold's biographer, McNeill, writes that 'The condescension implicit in asking well-to-do persons to volunteer to help the poor by giving advice, approving small payments when their morals, on inspection, proved deserving, and, more generally, trying to establish commonality between rich and poor by the exercise of noblesse oblige' was something Harry found increasingly distasteful. As a paid – and underpaid – staff member, he was in an awkward social position with his rich and leisured volunteers. He was the professional, yet he had to defer to the volunteers' superior social status and their command of the financial whip. 'Harry's chosen life of service to the poor compelled him to fawn on the rich to elicit a condescending benevolence,' writes McNeill. That sounds all too familiar and there is nothing, alas, Victorian about it. Ask most people running charities today and it's the same old story: fawning on financiers while being subjected to intense and ignorant quizzing on how deserving their clients are and whether the right prescriptions are being applied to the undeserving. I have often listened to the sheer arrogance of the rich insisting that their philanthropy should buy control over the charities they support in whatever whimsical way the benefactor thinks fit, however clueless they may be about the lives of others they could never comprehend.

But that was only part of the problem with the Charity Organisation Society. Socialist ideas were starting to undermine the old liberal and moral foundations of charities such as this. What had been called 'the social question', where good was done to the poor, was beginning to be subverted by assertive socialist demands from the ungrateful working classes themselves. Harry's work was starting to crumble beneath his feet as the value of the Society's philanthropy was increasingly questioned.

The Royal Commission and Beatrice Webb

In 1905 a leader of the organization, Helen Bosanquet, was appointed to sit on the Royal Commission on the Poor Laws and Relief of Distress. She took Harry with her as a professional staff member to service and research for the

Commission, where he found himself working alongside another staffer, a young William Beveridge, then at Toynbee Hall. Together they travelled the country collecting evidence of social conditions for reports to the Commission.

The Commission turned into a pivotal political and ideological battleground between the old liberal world and the new emerging ideas of the Labour Party. On the one hand there were Commissioners like Helen Bosanquet and Octavia Hill who thought the poor must be helped and goaded to stand on their own two feet. They thought moral dereliction was responsible for poverty and family cycles of deprivation could be broken only by individual effort. They regarded the handing out of state benefits as creating a great risk of dependency: charities not the state should be the conduit of voluntary help. Bosanquet wrote: 'I have always held that poverty and pain, disease and health are evils of greatly less importance than they appear except in so far as they lead to weakness of life and character; and that true philanthropy aims at increasing strength more than at the correct and immediate relief of poverty...' Plus ça change, not much changes, as still these days the right warns of the 'moral hazard' of state benefits. These are the very arguments dredged up by David Cameron and Iain Duncan Smith on coming to power in 2010, introducing a meaner benefits system in universal credit under cover of what they called The Big Society, where voluntarism would fill any gaps.

On the left side on the Commission were Beatrice Webb and George Lansbury who saw poverty and unemployment as a systemic failure of society and the economy, insisting it was the state's responsibility to alleviate and insure against these economic and social dysfunctions.

The Commission's task was to reform the increasingly confused Poor Laws, which organized workhouses and in theory, if not in practice, banned local authority Boards of Guardians from handing out any kind of 'outdoor relief', benefits paid outside the workhouse. Workhouses were supposed to ensure a standard of living below that of the lowest paid workers, to prevent the moral hazard of anyone choosing to enter one except in the direst need. They were designed to be punitive, separating women from men and both from their children into different houses, forcing them to wear uniforms so only the utterly desperate would voluntarily enter these humiliating portals. But the system had never worked. Workhouses were inordinately expensive to build and run. The original idea was that work would finance them but there was little profitable work for the inmates to do, and most of them were too old and sick to be capable of any labour. It was impossible to keep the food rations below the standards of the poorest workers without starving people. I once examined the account books of a workhouse in Leeds and the food was of a considerably better standard than most of the lowest paid working families could have afforded. This was because scandals in Huddersfield and Andover workhouses had exposed *Oliver Twist*-like gross starvation that was not acceptable for those in public care. Increasingly, local authorities were choosing the cheaper option of making small payments to the old, the sick and the unemployed outside workhouses. In the years of taking evidence and servicing the Commission as a member of its staff, Harry travelled the country examining workhouses, especially in the north of England, and reporting back on the anomalies in the outdated Poor Laws.

Royal Commissions, often created to shunt difficult issues out of the immediate political scene, famously 'take minutes and last years', assembling great volumes of evidence that no one reads, consulting a public whose opinions are largely ignored. So when the Commission finally reported four years later in 1909, the Lloyd George government duly ignored its findings altogether. That was easier to do since the Commission emerged at daggers drawn, split between two warring reports. But nonetheless, one of the Commission's reports became a landmark manifesto for social reform.

The dramatic clash at the ending of the Commission seems to have tipped Harry over the edge into nervous collapse. As it finished its work, it split between the Beatrice Webb and the Helen Bosanquet factions, with a majority and a minority report. That split ran right through Harry himself as he was an employee of Bosanquet's, summoned by her to work on the Commission, but inevitably he supported the Webb minority report. Here was the deep ideological divide that remains all too familiar still in today's political debates on welfare policy – and as polling keeps showing, it still divides public attitudes on benefits. The result was that his job came to an abrupt end with no other work immediately in prospect when he broke with his old employers: his family finances were painfully tight.

Bosanquet's majority report said the origins of poverty were essentially moral, the Poor Laws and workhouses should remain, local Boards of Guardians were providing too much relief outside workhouses and the able-bodied poor were not being sufficiently deterred from seeking assistance. In the opposite corner, Webb's minority report called for the abolition of the Poor Laws and a new state insurance for all 'to secure a national minimum of civilised life... open to all alike, of both sexes and all classes, by which we mean sufficient nourishment and training when young, a living wage when able-bodied, treatment when sick, and modest but secure livelihood when disabled or aged'. The majority report fell into the dustbin of history but Beatrice Webb's famous minority report sold 25,000 copies and became the battle-flag for a Labour campaign against the Poor Laws. Oddly, it occurs to me that my two great-grandfathers in their very different social spheres could have met long before they could imagine their children were to marry, since Gilbert Murray took up Beatrice Webb's cause with the minority report while Harry Toynbee was working on it.

It took many years, but eventually the minority report became the basis for the welfare state founded by William Beveridge's 1942 report and finally enacted by the Labour government in 1948. My poor great-grandfather Harry was never to be part of that final success. Instead he was broken by it and was locked away at the age of forty-six until he died just before he turned eighty. Had he lived just a few years later, he would have died in a National Health Service prefigured by that minority report he worked on.

Madness

Was he unjustly incarcerated, abandoned and neglected into old age in an asylum? Was he locked away as a source of shame, a bit odd, perhaps? A hundred years ago people were institutionalized quite easily and could be all but forgotten. No, I am glad to find I have accused his wife and family unjustly. Edith visited him regularly and wrote about their father's progress, or lack of it, in letters to her children. Was it a family secret? Not quite. It was known but not known, not talked about. I never remember my father talking about his grandfather or delving into his story, which is curious, since he himself suffered much mental illness in later life. Arnold certainly never mentioned it to us, although his father's illness and the family's impoverishment cast a long shadow over his life. How could it not?

I wondered what Harry Toynbee had suffered from and where he was kept. Recently quite by chance, researchers investigating other families came across information about him and told me about it. Suddenly his story emerged into the light – and it is worse, far worse than I imagined.

His medical records tell a story of decades of extraordinary suffering. This turns out not to be a tale of cruelty or ill treatment but a revelation of the sheer raw agony of mental illness in the days before there were any effective drugs or treatments. His wife was not neglectful: there was just nothing else to be done but shut him away. Those who doubt the value of modern psychiatry, and, in particular, of modern psychiatric drugs, should look back and see what mental illness was like without them.

In 1909 – that significant year when the Commission reported and Harry took the Beatrice Webb side against his employer – when he was put away, his wife Edith is listed as the 'petitioner' who had him restrained, or 'sectioned' as it would be now. By 1912 he was moved to

St Andrew's Hospital in Northampton to a locked ward where he stayed until he died. The hospital is not only still there, but it grows and beds in its locked wards are in high demand, with an ever-expanding long waiting list. What a relief to find not some run-down workhouse of a place, but a fine building with its own elegant chapel set in parkland of apparent tranquillity.

In the dusty leather-bound archives at St Andrew's, all the records remain for every patient who was ever treated there. By chance, the archives are now stored in the very rooms that were the locked wards where Harry Toynbee was kept. Here the archivist pulls out for me the record of his first admission, sent on from another poorer institution in Hillingdon: 'Age: 51. Religion: Protestant. Whether suicidal: Yes. Whether dangerous: Possibly. Whether any near relative insane: No. Supposed cause: Overwork.'

His first medical assessment reads: 'Believes and says he is utterly worthless. He says life is not worth living. He is very violent requiring physical control.' The second doctor adds: 'General incoherence. Sleeplessness, suspicion of conspiracy to detain him. Morbid dread of impending suicide. Sister in charge reports violence to attendant, threat of suicide.'

His physical description is 'Average height, brown hair, grey eyes, beard and moustache. Pupils equal.' This last, I discover, is an important check, a sign that he did not have GPI, general paralysis of the insane due to syphilis, a common cause of insanity in those pre-penicillin days.

A further early report on his condition states: 'Patient is suffering from chronic melancholia. He has a dejected aspect. He keeps repeating the same sentences – for instance he says – "Simply a patient, sir" dozens of times, also "Silly fool, sir." He is restive and will not let anyone treat him without struggling. He cannot converse rationally and is weak-minded. Takes no notice of what is said to him.' And the horror is that this goes on and on and on, hardly changing from year to year. He is still repeating 'Silly fool' over and over, year in year out. 'Delusions of unworthiness, silent, solitary, unoccupied and worried,' the notes keep reporting. Physically he is losing weight, eating too little, so at times he is force-fed. 'Very silly, very silly, silly fool, silly fool!' he is still repeating years later.

Incidents are noted: he is hit in the face and bruised by another patient. Then he takes to standing in one position, catatonic, for hours on end. 'He is dirty in his habits, slovenly in his dress. Apt to strike anyone near him.'

In 1919 he catches Spanish flu in the great global pandemic that swept away more lives than the Great War. What an irony that this poor soul who might have been better off dead survived to suffer decades more of mental torture. But this was a good hospital, state of the art then, and still now provides secure mental health services for the most severe cases. They cared for him well. Where other hospitals tied people up and kept them in straitjackets, St Andrew's was ahead of its time, a charity set up in 1838 by local wealthy families, whose descendants still sit on its board. It remains a private charity hospital, with mostly NHS patients admitted at high cost. Who paid for him to be there? His family certainly had no money for fees. According to the history of the place, he was almost certainly a charity case – and then as now, his care here would have been exceptionally expensive. The notes show

how much personal attention he had: his survival to such an old age shows how well he was cared for physically. There was nothing to be done about the agony of his mind.

He recovered from Spanish flu to live on, if you can call it a life. 'He is restive and requires careful management. He requires considerable supervision. Occasionally answers questions and says he wishes he were dead.' He gets worse. 'Suffers auditory hallucinations.' In 1928 he is on the way to the dining hall when 'a patient in front of him turned round and knocked him over'. His hip is broken – sometimes an event that hastens death. But not for Harry. He is put in a splint and recovers from that too, though 'the alignments of the fragments will not be good' as he is 'extremely restive'. 'He is receiving special attention from a special attendant.' A few months later 'the utility of the limb is nil'. He is 'noisy, restive and difficult to nurse, occasionally impulsive'. All kinds of physical illnesses assail him in the next years – but none shorten his miserable life. 'He is suffering arterial sclerosis but he resists any attention and his only reply when spoken to is "Go away sir!"'

1932: 'He is impossible to examine. He is completely unoccupied and disinterested in his surroundings. Any attempt to examine him is met with resistance and cries of "Leave me alone!" He will pant like a frightened animal when assessed. If he is handled he will struggle fiercely muttering "Shameful, shameful!"'

By now, it emerges, he has been bedridden for some years, never recovering from the broken hip. 'He is almost completely inaccessible, heedless when addressed. When examined he says, "It's all futile" or "I will kill you!"

Looking at his notes for 1939, I note with horror that he weighs just four stone nine pounds.

Finally, in 1941, he weakens. His pulse is faint, he has a fever, he stops eating altogether and at last pneumonia, that dilatory old man's friend, takes him away at the age of almost eighty, too late, far too late.

I take these notes to Professor Sir Simon Wessely, President of the Royal College of Psychiatrists, and he tells me all this 'melancholia' displays the classic symptoms of severe depression. But he says no living doctor now would ever have seen a case such as this, because drugs would stop anyone reaching this desperate state.

No wonder Arnold had worried all his life that his father's madness might be hereditary. No wonder, approaching marriage, he felt he should find out if it was genetic. But unfortunately he seems to have spent more time worrying about that distant threat than in learning about the character of the woman he had chosen to marry, of which he knew next to nothing.

4

Rosalind

WE PICK AND choose who we think we are descended from, devising our own origin myths. I choose not to inherit anything from my obnoxious grandmother Rosalind, who I never met. I wish I could add any shred of a reminiscence of my own, but it was her choice not mine to keep me well away from her. Apparently she did once examine and prod me as an infant but viewed any progeny of my father Philip with such physical disgust, spawn of her sinner son, that she never saw me or my sister again. Now, of course, I wish I had steeled myself to insist on meeting the old monster, to roll up at her door and demand to see her for myself. But there is evidence enough in all that I discover. And evidence enough in my father's suffering at her hands.

Approaching the marriage made in hell, foolish Arnold, Puck-struck in love with her, poured out his lover's agonies in letters to his best friend over the next two years, without daring to speak a word to her. Poor unknowing sap that he was, he saw Rosalind Murray as a 'faery princess, no merely human creature', as he yearned for her across the room at Gilbert Murray's Sunday night dinners for Oxford classicists. There was a magic spell cast over him by this

Murray household, with the charismatic Regius Professor and his entourage that included not just the great thinkers and writers of the time, but leading lights of the London theatre for whom he wrote his Greek plays. If the atmosphere in those Sunday evenings in Boars Hill was heady for a naïve young classicist, it was certainly not due to the drink, as the Murrays were strict teetotallers as well as vegetarians.

'It is a weird thing not to know really what she is like and yet to be in love like this,' Arnold confided. Yes, weird indeed. 'I am certainly just one of a casual crowd she comes across.' He calculates that he has only seen her three times in the last year, five hours in all in the last eighteen months, though he did paddle her in a canoe down the Cherwell once. He tells his friend he is going to take the plunge and approach her father: 'The sooner I try the chance the better. But I shall have to talk to Murray first: for my father's illness and her having had tuberculosis are two very big rocks.'

When he writes to his mother, Edith does her own investigations into Rosalind Murray and wisely tries hard to put her son off in every way she can think of. Rosalind has written novels, published with her father's financial help. Edith replies to Arnold that she has now sought out one of Rosalind's novels: as a serious and clever woman Edith must have been appalled by such stuff, though tactfully all she says is, 'You mustn't be hurt if I say she has had her heart touched before.'

Beyond that, she tries to use Arnold's father's madness as another impediment: 'It is the tragedy of Father's illness that he who would have died to save you a heartache, should now be chief obstacle. Dr. Craig told you that to

Arnold and Rosalind (foreground) on a picnic

counterbalance the sensitive nerves which Father and I are handing down, you would be wise to choose a very even nerved, placid, strong mother for your children. I know so little of Rosalind herself but I fear that her parents are very nervous, highly strung and that there is much delicacy in the family.'

Next she tries another tactic, warning him about the class barriers between them. When she writes to him that she hopes Rosalind's social class will not be a problem, she implies, of course, that it will: 'They are democratic and should not shy away at a "middle class" son-in-law.' Edith was not wrong. Rosalind was a snob, and all her life she regarded Arnold as socially beneath her – and all his life he looked up to her as a blue blood of refinement. She indulged in fantasies that she truly belonged in the aristocratic milieu of her mother's mother, the Countess of Carlisle of Castle Howard, not in the middle class dreariness of her parents' Oxford academia.

A fateful engagement

Arnold approached Gilbert Murray for Rosalind's hand and Murray sent him to talk to his father's doctors to discover if his illness was hereditary. The reply Arnold relayed was that the doctor 'said I must never overwork or even do extra work, as my father's case did show I had a tendency to nerve-exhaustion though it was not a mechanically hereditary thing'. All this nerve-exhaustion was indeed prevalent among the whole lot of them, constantly taking to their beds for long periods with curious remedies. This epic hypochondria was, from their letters, much encouraged by overbearing women in the family and by doctors who made considerable sums out of proclaiming them all on both sides to be suffering indefinable but chronic maladies that needed their constant ministrations. If a doctor opines that you are ill and nervous and weak, you are quite likely to feel ill and nervous and weak.

Assured that his father's illness was not hereditary, Arnold was welcomed by the Murrays and permitted to approach his 'faery princess' in her Baker Street flat. When he did, in June 1913, 'She was absolutely taken by surprise and could hardly speak a word,' he reports to his friend. I bet she was, since in his hopeless gaucheness, apart from making sheep's eyes at her from afar, he had almost certainly said and done nothing at all that made her think of him as a lover. It was certainly a very short proposal: 'It lasted three minutes and then I came back to Oxford.' The first he heard was a letter from her mother saying Rosalind says no. Then came another letter from her mother a week later, just as peremptory: 'Dear Toynbee, Rosalind wants to see you again. Last Sunday she did not tell the truth.' And this time she said yes.

The Murrays may have tried to encourage her, but it was her own choice to do exactly what her mother had done before her – to marry a young and promising liberal don, a classics scholar with neither name nor fortune, but only his brains and future hopes to commend him. He was twenty-four, she was twenty-two. Her parents were surprised but pleased, Gilbert writing to a friend, 'Not the man we should have guessed, though we like and admire him greatly. Not particularly her sort, but an extraordinarily good sort. They barely knew each other and seemed to have very few common interests. Fellow of Balliol, radical and, as far as I can make out, a quite satisfactory free-thinker with no nonsense about the Absolute: tremendous strength of character. He was, for instance, caught by brigands at Phocis and just argued them down.' (No, I have no idea about that story from his many travels.)

If she thought she was marrying the model of her father, she was right in choosing a man destined to become a similar, or an even more prominent public intellectual and a surprisingly popular bestselling historian. But she barely knew him. If she thought she was marrying a man of the same charm, wit, fun and outgoing social warmth as her father, she had made a bad mistake. Arnold Toynbee was awkward, socially clumsy and emotionally repressed. But underneath that gauche exterior he had always harboured a secret inner conviction that he had greatness within him, a flame of ambition few might have guessed. Where did this hidden self-confidence come from? His doting mother Edith possibly, the mother disappointed in her own intellectual ambitions and shattered by her husband's collapse and removal from the family, who had poured all her hopes into her three clever children, but above all she invested everything in Arnold.

He was not obviously prepossessing, so why did Rosalind marry him? She later claimed it was on the rebound. All her life she carried the regret that she would and should have married Rupert Brooke, the love of her life, who was killed in the First World War: my father said this was fly-blown fantasy as she barely knew the young poet. He said she only nurtured that romantic tragedy later on as a useful contrast to unromantic Arnold. She made no bones about it, making it plain to all and sundry that this marriage was the great mistake of her life. It was certainly his great blunder too – but he never knew it and went on loving and admiring her imagined superiority long after she had left him. The greater her snobbery and sense of social superiority, the more craven his worship became. My mother, who detested her on account of her cruelty and rudeness, had plentiful stories to tell. During the Blitz Rosalind said she herself was able to bear the bombs with fortitude, because she was upper class, 'But poor Arnold, being so middle class, is too afraid and has to stay out of London.' (He had been posted by the Foreign Office to Oxford.)

Rupert Brooke, from one of Rosalind's photo albums

Rosalind plainly knew that she was making an error well before the wedding, as during her engagement she was writing an even more frightful novel than her last, called *Unstable Ways*, which she didn't finish until after they were married. Far from a young woman in love, here is a young heroine – Giacosa St Claire – yes, really – having to choose between three suitors. She settles on Freddy – a barely veiled and unattractive portrait of a dry classical scholar very like Arnold. She pleads with him to be passionate: 'If he would only take her by force, if only he would storm her citadel of criticism, if only his love were a less timid, bashful thing. He was too considerate of her, too gentle.' Indeed, Arnold was always timid and subservient to her. At the end of the book on the eve of her wedding Giacosa drowns herself like Ophelia, and jolly glad the reader is too.

But Rosalind and Arnold went ahead with their register office marriage and they honeymooned in Castle Howard with her grandmother. Her father Gilbert, who had been through exactly the same Castle Howard honeymoon ordeal himself, sent this message of warning for his new son-in-law: 'Don't let Arnold be frightened. But I do not believe there is any advantage in behaving like a worm.' However, to his new wife, a worm Arnold was and a worm he remained all their marriage. His self-esteem and assertiveness came to reside only in his writing, in his grandly epic vision of a universal history of all civilizations and the explanation of everything in his twelve mighty volumes of *A Study of History*.

High-minded would-be-goods make bad parents

Before going any further, see where Rosalind came from and wonder at the mystery of how she emerged as such a snob from parents with such a noble and high-thinking cast of mind. The Murrays stood for that strand of reforming radicalism that threads all through my family, so Rosalind was, I suppose, the one exception, the rebel against all those parental values, the only one in the family to reject that liberal inheritance. But if she was a terrible mother to my father, could she perhaps point a finger of blame at her parents too? Here are the Murrays, a would-be-good couple piously committed to be world-improvers – but that didn't prevent them being disastrously bad parents.

In search of them, I stand on Boars Hill, a hamlet three miles outside Oxford, imagining its great days. From here, Matthew Arnold wrote of Oxford as 'that sweet city with her dreaming spires', those spires that never dreamed for me. Here on Boars Hill lived poets Robert Bridges, John Masefield, Robert Graves and Edmund Blunden.

Right here where I am standing was Yatscombe Hall, where I would visit my great-grandfather Regius Professor Gilbert Murray (Companion of Honour, Order of Merit) on occasions chiefly memorable as a young child because he gave me a pound, which was forty times my usual 6d. a week pocket money: tip children well to make sure they remember you kindly ever after. And I do remember him as a warm, affectionate old man, good at making children laugh and playing tricks. He may have been in a constant state of political warfare with the powers that be, but he was at ease with the world and all around him. He had none of the awkward embarrassments of his twitchy son-in-law Arnold.

Here at Yatscombe Hall he had entertained Mahatma Gandhi, Albert Einstein and Lawrence of Arabia. His old friend, fellow abstainer and theatrical colleague George Bernard Shaw was a frequent guest. From here at Yatscombe Gilbert and Mary had conducted a thousand campaigns against the forces of conservatism. From here he had fired off reams of letters to ministers, newspapers and grandees in protest at almost everything. Here they took in refugees from both wars. From here every good cause was backed, every act of villainy denounced, every free-thinking, high-minded, high hope encouraged. From here too, admirably, whenever progressive hopes were dashed, they were forever revived and begun anew.

But the house I visited as a child has long gone in a series of disasters that might seem to him the perfect symbol of modern times, if he were here to see it happen. At some point after his death a fake institution called Warnborough College was launched in Yatscombe Hall, attracting American students with a pretence it was part of Oxford University, until the fraudsters were sued and forced to close. At some point squatters and caravaners moved in. At some point developers bought it, planning retirement homes. At some point in the many years of a long-running local council dispute with the developers, the place conveniently burned to the ground. And now four executive homes occupy the site, while an old theological college nearby has been sold to Beijing University.

I didn't think of this as a child, of course, nor as a self-preoccupied teenager, nor even later, due to all the incuriosity of youth about crusty old relations. But now I ask, where did Gilbert's high-mindedness begin, all that impassioned anti-Toryism that was bred into our every fibre, passed on to all of us, without question? I now discover that as far back as I can research, every ancestor fought the good liberal fight for progress, so bear with me while I take you even further back, to Gilbert Murray's origins. Just as I can find no useful trace of working class roots, nor can I find anything but radicalism and resistance to the conservatism that always ruled the roost, then as now – and it's no surprise to find its Irish origins.

Colonial roots, but radical

Most British families can trace some relative with connections leading back to the colonies where so many went to seek their fortunes. I grew up knowing Gilbert Murray had been born in Australia because my father harboured romantic ideas of outback origins, of the rough plain-speaking honesty of Australian life and an imagined family history of Waltzing Matilda's jolly swagmen, jumbucks, wallabies and billabongs. We all nurture our own origin myths: he liked that inheritance of an Australian romance, a rugged classlessness which Philip relished as one of his chosen self-images.

Needless to say, it turns out our Australian origins were not in the least swagmanish, or not in the way we sang 'Waltzing Matilda' swinging along on our walks down Suffolk lanes. My father enjoyed a devilish hint that convict blood might lurk in his veins on those days when he felt like terrifying us with a twitching, grimacing transformation into a psychopathic killer. In fact, as he probably knew perfectly well, the Murrays were neither convicts nor swagmen but belonged to that same class of professionals, academics, civil servants and administrators in Australia as most of his family on many sides always had. They sprang from that same historic clerk class of in-betweens, pen-pushers and black-gowned functionaries, mostly not landed or moneyed, but clever at relying on their education to land them comfortably on their feet wherever they went and sometimes comfortably-off wives.

I knew next to nothing of this Australian background but I find it all laid out in Duncan Wilson's biography of my great-grandfather. The Murrays were Irish, Gilbert's grandfather rewarded for fighting with Wellington at Waterloo with the post of Paymaster to the British forces in Australia in 1827. His son Terence, born in Limerick in 1810, was rewarded too, appointed to a remote frontier magistracy in the colony at the absurdly young age of twenty-one.

I am surprised to find that my great-great-grandfather Terence too has his own Australian biographer, Gwendoline Wilson, who records the rapid rise and plunging fall of his career. Off the ridiculously young Terence went to the bush, taking with him ticket-of-leave convicts as servants, many of them also Catholic Irishmen. As an early pioneer, he acquired a grant of land on the present site of Canberra where he raised stock. According to Gilbert's biographer, Terence 'exercised an almost feudal influence as local magistrate and general adviser over his tenants and neighbours, largely Catholic and Irish. Life on Australian country estates at this time was lonely, rough, and dangerous. Terence Murray had to be handy with his fists and with his gun.' But he was well educated. Building up a large library he 'read very widely, and with a deliberate and continuous effort maintained the high cultural standards he imparted to his family'. He became a notable figure, a rich stock farmer, the Speaker of the New South Wales Lower House, knighted for his services to the colony.

But despite all that conventional authority, his liberal views were extreme for life in the outback of those days. He was the first colonial politician to campaign against the transportation of convicts and against the death penalty:

he was President of the Society for the Abolition of Capital Punishment. He and his wife strongly supported the Society for the Protection of Aborigines and, according to his biographer, 'Sir Terence mixed with them freely and genuinely liked them.' He commissioned an academic to collect and preserve the local Aboriginal nations' languages. He named his residence Winderadeane after a resistance leader from one of the Aboriginal nations around Lake George.

But his wealth and land didn't last more than a few years. In 1865 he lost everything in a succession of droughts and floods, a loss made worse by 'his habits of lordly hospitality and generosity'. He went bust, and his estates were sold.

After his first wife died, he married the family governess, Agnes, mother of my great-grandfather Gilbert. Ah, I think, she is the humblest of direct ancestors I can lay claim to and maybe, with luck, this servant, this governess is working class?

But no. Agnes the governess was of solid middle class background, since she was well educated, if penniless, and was sent to Australia from England to seek her fortune. Her cousin was W.S. Gilbert, the lyricist of Gilbert and Sullivan operas. After the Murrays' brief wealth evaporated and the Canberra estates were sold, they moved to the Sydney suburbs, from small houses to even smaller ones where 'Sir Terence's melancholy, extravagance and his heavy drinking hastened his death.' Drink, you will find, features powerfully in my family histories, swinging from life-damaging drunkenness to extremes of temperance. I don't know if this is a genetic failing or generations reacting emotionally against each other, but since this family is laced with alcoholism, the science is unclear: a predisposition can be inherited, but addictions involve myriad human factors and multiple genes.

Agnes set up a girls' school to make ends meet, and she founded the Sydney Foundling Hospital, the first refuge for unmarried mothers and their children. Her girls' school was not a success, but after Terence died of drink and despair, it did well enough for her to sell it, raising just enough cash to set off back to England in 1877 with the eleven-year-old Gilbert. She rejoined her own family, where they lived in South London crammed together in a tiny house with no garden and many aunts. Resourceful, she set up another girls' school to earn their living, while Gilbert won the only scholarship to Merchant Taylors' day school, and then a scholarship to Oxford in 1884.

Gilbert's dazzling successes – but political failures

Winning classics prizes was the only way he could afford to keep himself at university, as his mother had no money to give him as an allowance. He scooped up combinations of prizes never before received by anyone, including one for translating much of Shakespeare's *Henry IV Part II* into Greek verse, which seems an odd thing to do. He won another for gaining a mark of 100 per cent in knowledge of the *Agamemnon*, which he knew by heart in Greek. It earned his keep, though his assiduous biographer has checked his 'battels' bill at St John's College, showing the cost of the food and drink he consumed. It was exceedingly meagre compared with most undergraduates.

Gilbert was a radical, a vegetarian and a strong atheist, and above all he was a champion propounder of lost causes. I'm glad to find he was for a while President of the British Ethical Union – now Humanists UK, of which I too have been President and am now a life Vice President. In Oxford Union debates he stood up for Irish Home Rule, founding an Oxford Home Rule Union, the issue that split the Liberal Party at the time: it was not popular and most Oxford Liberals took the other side. In a Union debate on the issue he was principal speaker against Lord Randolph Churchill, but he was of course defeated by a large majority. He proposed a motion calling for 'Higher education for the lower classes' (defeated) and another declaring 'War is out of date' (heavily defeated, again). Imbued with the ideas of John Stuart Mill and Rousseau's social contract, he was fiercely political at Oxford, as he was all his life. He put the motion to the Union, 'This House views with intense suspicion the rise of the capitalist classes in political power' (defeated, of course).

All his life he had a particular horror of cruelty to animals, which caused fierce disputes over blood sports. He claimed that as a child he had first become an atheist on contemplating the story of the Gadarene swine (where Jesus exorcizes a man 'with an unclean spirit' and casts his demons into a herd of pigs who charge over a cliff and drown themselves), which was, he wrote, 'So monstrously cruel to drive a lot of unoffending pigs over a precipice.' He never forgot or forgave an act of cruelty: Rudyard Kipling was a contemporary and a friend when young, whom he never quite liked. 'There was something in him that repelled me: he threw his stick at a cat.'

Another of his life-long causes was temperance, and he spoke at the Union on a motion in support of total abstinence (defeated again). He stuck to it rigidly all his life, reacting to boyhood recollections of his own father's descent into alcoholism and early death and Australian drinking habits that he abhorred. His older brother Hubert had arrived at Oxford from Australia, but joined a hard-drinking, hearty, anti-intellectual set: friends noted their extraordinary physical resemblance, but were struck by Hubert's 'uncouth' behaviour, so unlike Gilbert's grace, courtesy and beautiful speaking voice, with the good looks, said one friend, 'of a young Apollo'. Hubert took to drinking heavily: as we shall see, so did Gilbert's sons, turning wildly against their father's temperance. Again, how strongly drink features in my family on all sides, veering from teetotalism to life-crippling drunkenness.

From his first arrival at Oxford, Gilbert's reputation soared as he acted well, played sport well, cricket, rugby and rowing, in addition to his famous shower of classical essay and Greek translation prizes. He had many friends and was popular and well known, a witty raconteur with a gift for making people laugh, turning ordinary events into flights of fantasy. Both my parents always told of their delight in the pleasure of his company, even in old age, and as a child I looked forward to those visits to see him at Boars Hill. My father had spent much of his childhood staying with these grandparents, dumped with them as often as his mother could, and he always spoke lovingly of them. My father found his grandfather's company considerably cheerier than the chilly and unwelcoming home of his own parents.

Yet for all his affability and social ease, Gilbert was always set a little apart by his rigid moral scruples. He wrote of himself, slightly exaggerating, 'Few people like teetotallers, still fewer can tolerate vegetarians. In the ancient universities I frequent they don't much like Liberals and I am all these objectionable things. Furthermore, I hate blood sports.' Later, looking back on his life, he was full of that all too familiar ruefulness and regret that is the destiny of those on the left who find their optimism crushed time and again. A baffled incomprehension seems to have been shared by all my family – and yes, by all of us still – that the world insists on doing the wrong thing when the right course is as plain as the nose in front of its face. Gilbert wrote of his youth, 'My greenness was unbelievable. I believed passionately in the progress of man. It was perhaps not quite inevitable, but it only needed the removal of a few selfish and reactionary old people to make the world a new Garden of Eden, with more scientific gardening.' But despite generation after generation of endeavour, those 'few selfish and reactionary people' still seem to keep a remarkable grip on the reins of power and, worse, a grip on public sentiment, with an entitlement to rule that leaves the left forever insurgent.

The terrifying Countess of Carlisle

Gilbert Murray's marriage was all but arranged by his alarming termagant of a future mother-in-law. The Countess of Carlisle, daughter and then wife of Liberal

MPs, was a head-hunter of clever young men of radical Liberal opinion, whom she gathered together in support of the Liberal cause in her formidable salon. She was not in search of the well-born, but of big Liberal brains. She had heard of Murray's radical reputation and set out to recruit him to her Liberal Party circle. It was part of her duty, as she saw it, as President of the Women's Liberal Foundation. In his unfinished autobiography Gilbert records his first unnerving encounter with her and her aristocratic Whig world.

He was sitting on the banks of the River Cherwell one summer afternoon at a picnic organized by friends when an unknown but commanding woman approached him from behind and began to grill him loudly and severely. 'I hear you are a teetotaller, Mr Murray?' He replied, surprised, 'Yes, I am, do you disapprove?' Indeed she did not, as she informed him she was President of the British Women's Temperance Association. She went on to question him closely on other matters. Where did he stand on Home Rule and on women's suffrage and a number of other great dividing-line issues of the day? On all these he more than passed muster.

So she swept him up, together with a coterie of young Oxford radicals, and invited them to her great stately home, Castle Howard in Yorkshire, the mighty Vanbrugh palace, later used as the backdrop to a television adaptation of Evelyn Waugh's *Brideshead Revisited* (and more recently *Bridgerton*). The story of the Countess of Carlisle's own marriage and its break-up is remarkably close to Waugh's portrayal of Lord and Lady Marchmain's separation. What caused the split in Waugh's novel was Lady

Marchmain's extreme Roman Catholic religiosity, which propelled her husband out of the faith to escape from her to live in Venice with his mistress. What caused the Earl of Carlisle to flee to live in Italy with his easel and box of paints was Home Rule, the same issue that was splitting the Liberal Party. His mild liberal conservatism clashed with his wife's formidable campaigning radicalism, as the Earl went with the Unionists and the Countess was with Gladstone. Arnold Toynbee wrote that during the Home Rule debate she was sitting on the terrace of the House of Commons when a friend warned her that her vehement support for Home Rule was dividing her family, to which she replied loudly in the hearing of all around her, 'What's that to me?'

Castle Howard

The Earl and Countess of Carlisle

There was more to the Carlisles' separation, of course, than politics. The Earl of Carlisle, George Howard, was a painter and a friend of the Pre-Raphaelites, whose pictures he collected: William Morris, Walter Crane and Edward Burne-Jones decorated his London house. He was, by Gilbert Murray's account, a gentle and kindly man married to a virago, but their most serious disagreement was over his ferocious wife's harsh upbringing of their first son. The Countess's sister Kate was Bertrand Russell's mother and she agreed with the Earl, observing how severely the boy was treated by his mother. The fate of the Countess's children suggests she was a dangerous mother they all shied away from. All of them turned against her on Irish Home Rule. She had eleven children and she fell out with every one of them. Five sons died before her. Her eldest fought in the Boer War, which she was against. One was killed as *Times* correspondent at the Battle of Omdurman in 1898, one died of pneumonia in the Irish Guards, one died in Nigeria on colonial service and one was killed at Passchendaele in 1917. All, it is said, were very heavy drinkers. Alcoholism was rampant down the generations, but whether her extreme temperance was the cause or the result of this, I don't know.

The Countess was a Mrs Jellyby, putting distant causes before immediate family, preferring to do good to far-off campaigns rather than needs nearer to home. Her daughter Dorothy described her conversational powers as 'like a flow of lava'. Though I suppose I should celebrate her as a great feminist, ploughing her own furrow, pursuing her own passions, running the vast estate herself and apparently very well, there are not many likeable recollections of her to be found. My father remembered her as an old lady at the window throwing down just one chocolate to the children below for the pleasure of disapproving as they fought over it. Teaching children severe moral lessons ran deep in those Liberal families. My father as a small boy was invited to Lady Violet Bonham Carter's famous annual children's Christmas party. She, the well-known daughter of Liberal prime minister Herbert Asquith and politician in her own right, had strung up wrapped parcels of all shapes and sizes along a rope, blindfolded the children and sent them over to grab one. My father had positioned himself in front of the biggest – but it turned out to be the only one with nothing in it: that was his lesson on greed, she told him firmly when he cried.

The Countess of Carlisle was of that ilk, and perhaps her domineering ways were inherited. Her own mother, too, by all accounts, was another dogmatic whirlwind of a Lady Bracknell, who was Bertrand Russell's grandmother. In his autobiography he recalled her with nothing but dread: as a boy, after quizzing him on his reading, she proclaimed, 'None of my grandchildren is intelligent.' But she was one of the founders of the first women's college, Girton, in Cambridge, so no doubt she too was admirable as an early campaigner for women's rights.

Swept up by an imperious summons to stay at Castle Howard for three long weeks, Gilbert Murray described life there under the Countess's rule as filled with earnest discussion interspersed with much cricket. Despite the grandeur of the setting and the magnificence of the paintings on the walls, guests were kept to a strictly puritanical and spare regime, with no gluttony, luxury or sloth. Her principles forbade any show of wealth or indolence, and she herself rose to work at

*Gilbert Murray and Bertrand Russell (on rocking horse)
with Russell's first wife, Alys, 1903*

4 a.m. all her life. Breakfast for guests was at 8 a.m., followed by day-long discussions on the oppressed colonies under imperialism. There was, of course, no alcohol to speed the flight of high ideals. Years earlier when her husband had departed to Italy and she took over the keys to the great house, she had ordered the entire cellar to be cleared and thousands of bottles of wine to be publicly smashed and poured into the lake. When newspapers reported on this vandalism, she claimed the wine had gone bad anyway.

Gilbert seems to have withstood his first encounter with this daunting milieu. He wrote later to his friend Bertrand Russell that the way of life there had 'a combination of beauty and discomfort... discomfort is of the essence of the place', a testimony from someone who was not in the least used to much comfort himself. 'Conversation,' he wrote, might be 'deficient in subtlety' but it was 'magnificent in its force and directness, ranging over all fields of politics and ethics'.

As a child, I once met Bertrand Russell at his house in Wales where we were on holiday and my father must have taken us to meet him. With great mock solemnity he stooped to shake my hand: 'I am your ancestor,' the old man said, though as my great-grandmother's cousin, it turns out he was quite a remote relative. I was spellbound by him, relishing him as an ideal distinguished white-haired forebear, who treated a child as an equal. Here's an extraordinary stretching of time: Russell, born 1872, was the (secular) godson of atheist John Stuart Mill, born 1806, so in shaking my 'ancestor's' hand I was touching down these liberal generations a remarkably long distance.

The next time I saw Bertrand Russell was in the distance in 1962: at the age of eighty-nine he was being carried off by the police from sitting in the road at a CND protest. He was leader of the Committee of 100, who believed in civil disobedience for the cause: I was a fifteen-year-old secretary of Chelsea YCND who were moderates on the side of purely legal protest. He was sent to prison under an ancient Act passed in 1361 against inciting the public to commit breaches of the peace. Later the Committee of 100 fell apart, as anarchists bent on insurrection took over and Russell bowed out in that familiar old cycle repeated in every left, feminist or environmental group I ever brushed up against, split, split and split again. Tories row and segment but they never split, so power is forever theirs.

On that visit to Castle Howard Gilbert met the Countess's eldest daughter, Mary, and he fell head over heels in love with her. She was delicate and beautiful and must have seemed like a gentle breeze in the wake of her gale-force mother. I have a watercolour painted of her by her father as Princess Snowdrop. Gilbert wrote of Mary, 'She had all the idealism, the saintliness, the inward fire and also, like Shelley's heroines, a remarkable gift of eloquence. She had not been to university but spoke French, German and Italian and was deeply grounded in Mazzini's Duty of Man.'

Mary as Princess Snowdrop painted by her father,
the Earl of Carlisle

The Countess approved and encouraged the match, but the courtship was long, partly because Gilbert had to find a job to earn their living and partly because Mary had her doubts. These were not doubts about his love, but doubts about whether his moral seriousness matched her own high-mindedness, as she had been well trained in her mother's ways and views. She had taken the Pledge in her early teens, the temperance vow, and with her mother had stormed through the Yorkshire villages of the district under their control, ordering every pub to be shut down. She had been brought up to a life of duty, reading the proceedings of parliament to study the progress of the Factory Acts so she could join in the discussions at the Women's Liberal Foundation.

A long and moral engagement

There was much comical misunderstanding in letters between Gilbert and Mary, as she had no sense of humour and took his honest and self-deprecating wit at face value. They were both extraordinarily moral and determined to devote themselves to doing and being good: the important difference between them was in self-awareness. He understood the many layers of absurdity and difficulty in striving for virtue, while she was dauntingly lacking in self-mockery. In a letter to a friend he recorded, 'She says to me, "Are you devoted heart and soul to the service of humanity?" I can only answer "No: I am very selfish; when I do an unselfish thing it is chiefly from personal sympathy, not from high principle."' With her unwavering lack of doubt, she was suspicious of his brain as a dangerous place where subtlety or equivocation might undermine strength of purpose. He protested, 'You have under-rated my sober qualities as much as you have over-rated my brains.' She accused him of weakness, aimlessness and want of high ideals to which he replied, 'I was a soldier in the service of Man before I entered yours.'

They sparred and parried back and forth over two years, driving themselves into fits of that curious weakness, illness and nervous attacks requiring convalescence and sea air that seems to have been a frequent intermittent condition all their lives. The same crops up time and again in their family and with their daughter Rosalind and her husband Arnold, who seemed equally prone to nervous vapours. High-mindedness doesn't seem to go with physical robustness. Was this psychosomatic or due to repression or chronic depression? Was falling into periods of weakness just an effete cultural habit of those times or was it the strain of aiming to be so good beyond what the human frame could endure? Or this may just be how health was before penicillin, and we have forgotten quickly that people regularly succumbed to low-level infections of which we are now mercifully free. But in their letters, their Long Engagement begins to bear the strain of the dismal Arthur Hughes picture of that name, depicting a couple tortured and wasted at a tryst under a tree. Gilbert had written to Mary's father, the Earl of Carlisle, in Pisa, to ask for her hand but had not got off to the best start. He received a crisp reply: 'I observe that you have begun your career as son-in-law most successfully by sending me your letter without a stamp.'

Gilbert at Glasgow University, 1891

Then at the very young age of twenty-three, Gilbert was appointed as Professor of Greek at Glasgow University, which came with a handsome salary of £1,300 a year, and an even more handsome house. So they married, with Mary finally convinced – and rightly too – of the sincerity of his moral and political beliefs. But weddings bring out the primeval in families, summoning up old primal urges to display inordinate pride in class and status. Why else do families of all classes invest such painfully disproportionate sums in wedding extravaganzas out of all keeping with their incomes? The Countess was no different. However much she might have spent her life eschewing vulgar luxury and self-indulgent waste of money that should be given to the poor and good causes, she could not resist laying on the full aristocratic display of everything that she declared herself to be against. Gilbert wanted a modest event, but the Countess took great offence at his interference and Mary wrote to him indignantly, sinking so low as to pretend the lavishness of their wedding was in aid of the servants: 'It would be bad to think of poor working men robbed of their treat. It was selfish, dear, was it not, to forget that we both have our duties on that day?'

So they were married in December 1889 at the chapel of Castle Howard by Benjamin Jowett, liberal cleric and Master of Balliol, despite Gilbert's atheism. Eighty girls of the Friendly Society dressed in green and white were arrayed on the steps to shake hands, the estate workers lined the gallery inside while the Harrow School band played at the evening ball. At one point the couple were drawn in a coach by 'the crowd', who must in reality have been estate tenants who may have had little choice in the matter. An intricate trousseau was purchased as mother and daughter set aside higher things and were caught up uncharacteristically in the details of elaborately furnishing the college house in Glasgow, to Gilbert's alarm. He was embarrassed by being given too grand a gold fob watch by his mother-in-law, which he kept tucked deep in his waistcoat pocket lest university colleagues should see its extravagance. Worse, there was the question of his wife's title. Both Gilbert and Mary preferred that she should become Mrs Murray – but the Countess, against all her professed egalitarian principles, insisted she keep her courtesy title as daughter of an earl, so my great-grandmother was always known as Lady Mary Murray. A dowry came her way too.

It was the habit of the time for young aristocratic brides to be presented at court after their marriage: at least Lady Mary and her mother declined that honour. But was that out of democratic sensibility? No, I'm afraid not. Years later Lady Mary told my mother it was because 'such common people were allowed there nowadays'. Jacobin revolutionaries had their own savage answer: they thought there was no expunging the deep habits of power, possession, heredity and snobbery from the blood of the aristocracy or the bourgeoisie except by the guillotine. And the liberal bourgeoisie are always the first to be hung from the lamp-posts. Have I inherited any of these traits? The most important one, of course, is the primal urge to try to pass on to your children all the educational and intellectual benefits you had yourself. Yes, guilty as charged. Some parents try to break that privilege: William Miller has written an angry autobiography blaming his father, director, writer and polymath Jonathan Miller, for sending him to a comprehensive school where he says he learned too little, compared with his father's great wide-ranging and omnivorous intellectual curiosity and encyclopaedic knowledge learned at a private school. William sent his own children to private schools to compensate, but perhaps they in their turn will resent the privilege? Parents are forever in the wrong, as illustrated in the stories I tell here.

As well as his academic life, first in Glasgow then in Oxford, Gilbert Murray was drawn into the world of the theatre when he translated the great Greek plays into modern poetry, influenced by the flowery style of Swinburne. All his translations were in rhyming couplets, although the original Greek had no rhymes. It was part of his life's work to bring the ancient world alive to the modern, and though his translations now read as stilted and Victorian, they struck a remarkable nerve at the time. Hellenism, admiration for all things Greek, was in his mind combined with modern progressivism: the passions of the great tragedies, and the origins of democracy and philosophy came from a better world uncontaminated by Christianity. He regarded Euripides, especially *The Bacchae*, through the eyes of anthropology. As a humanist, he was much influenced by J.G. Frazer's *The Golden Bough*, the study of ritual, sacrifice, myth and religion that scandalized many by setting Christ and Christianity on a par with other primitive cults. Murray felt that the Greek tragedies were closely connected with Ibsen, of whom he was a great defender against conventional drawing room critics who found those plays too shocking and obscene: the word 'Ibsenity' was used by one critic. He wanted, he wrote, to spread 'the Greek spirit' to all who could not read the language so people could 'enter more or less into that peculiar way of looking at things, that extraordinary shrewdness and knowledge of the world, that child-like impulsiveness for wild hopes and idealism which seems to leave a certain stamp of genius upon almost any sentence that has fallen from an Athenian pen'.

Hellenism was fashionable at the end of the nineteenth century. Lord Leighton and other Victorian artists were painting absurdly lascivious and fantastical pictures of classical life, filled with drooping women in gossamer

Greek garments lounging erotically on chaises longues. None of this was at all in keeping with Gilbert Murray's high-minded endeavour to engage the public with progressive Greek thinking – but his ornate translations caught a spirit of the moment. Women were wearing Greek- and Roman-inspired dresses, and the fashion for Greek dancing lasted, alas, in dancing classes for little girls well into the 1950s, when at the age of six I suffered in an eau-de-nil 'Greek' silk tunic dress for 'Greek' dancing lessons in bare feet to the wafting warble of a lone flute. To be 'Greek' was to be free like Isadora Duncan's ghost, in touch with nature and the essence of things. It was a long-lived fashion, for there is a photograph of my mother too as a child in the same garb, looking similarly doleful. Satirists made healthy fun of this brand of Hellenism, with Oscar Wilde writing wryly of the fashion, 'Over a substratum of pure wool, such as is supplied by Dr Jaeger, some modification of Greek costume is perfectly applicable to our climate, our country, our century.' Gilbert and Sullivan satirized the fashion for Greek dress and dances in *The Grand Duke*.

Theatrical life

Medea, *Hippolytus*, *Electra*, *The Trojan Women* and others followed one after another in rapid succession to critical success and fame for Murray, though the plays were never quite money-makers for producers. Harley Granville Barker, the actor manager and Shakespeare critic, played in some productions, directed others and became a great friend. Sybil Thorndike, her husband Lewis Casson and Mrs Patrick Campbell also acted in the translations, and Murray had one play of his own produced as he was drawn into the theatrical world. George Bernard Shaw was already a friend and ally in many radical campaigns. Writing of him years later, Murray said, 'We were both teetotaller, both vegetarians, both great "world-changers" to use a recent key word of Shaw's, neither of us at all grumbly or unamiable.' They came to know each other very well, exchanging cheerful criticisms of one another's work.

George Bernard Shaw

Their friendship was close enough to survive the blatant and instantly publicly recognizable satire on Gilbert Murray and his family in Shaw's *Major Barbara* in 1905. Shaw had warned Murray and shown him the script in advance. When Murray suggested he write a feminist sequel to *The Taming of the Shrew*, Shaw replied, 'I can't. I'm doing a play called Murray's Mother-in-Law.' The opening scene begins with Lady Britomart, a virago of a mother berating her son, that was such a precise portrait of the Countess of Carlisle that Murray made him take out one line from the original script. In it Lady Britomart says, 'Never call me mother again!', the exact words spoken by the Countess to her eldest son, which could only have been told to Shaw by Murray. Shaw obliged and removed the line, but the veil of disguise was wafer thin. In the play, Major Barbara, daughter of Lady Britomart, is a young aristocratic officer of the Salvation Army, devoted to converting social outcasts to a better life. Her father, Andrew Undershaft, is a worldly arms manufacturer, separated from his wife, just as were the Carlisles. Barbara is engaged to Professor Adolphus Cusins, a young Australian Greek scholar who frequently quotes Euripides. He's a religious sceptic, but to win Barbara he is ready to help her salvation work. Major Barbara strives hard to convert the down and outs only to be disillusioned when they revert to their old ways. When the arms manufacturer wants to hand over his empire to the young scholar and his Salvationist daughter, there follows a thoroughly Shavian debate on God and Mammon, in which the utilitarian arguments of Undershaft win out over innocent idealism: manufacturing arms will make more money for their good causes.

In Shaw's first production Granville Barker played the Greek scholar. Murray wrote an only semi-playful letter to Shaw before the opening, saying, 'If you get Barker up like me, with spectacles and a moustache and a bald wig, it would have a kind of music-hall funniness for the few people who knew about me' but it would 'lead one on a wrong scent' for the meaning of the play. To his wife, Murray wrote more crossly, 'The caricature of me is rather tiresome. The man is not like me... I don't know whether they will get him up like me or not. But I am clear that, since duelling is not in fashion, there is no possible course except indifference. If I object, the incident will be more piquant.' To his daughter Rosalind he wrote, 'The caricature of me... is outrageously personal but not a bit offensive or malicious.' Shaw did get the character up to look like him, putting Granville Barker in a bald wig, but it is certainly an affectionate and only slightly mocking portrait. Lady Mary as Major Barbara emerges as far more charming and less severe than she was in life, and as for her mother, she did see the play but seems to have been utterly oblivious of her similarity to Lady Britomart: self-awareness was not her forte.

Struggles over (too much) money

Gilbert and Mary Murray may have had nothing to do with religion, the Salvation Army or arms manufacturing, but they were the perfect butt for Shaw's wit and the playing out of the clash between money and doing good, between unrealistically high principles and the everyday fallibility of all human beings. It was a struggle both Gilbert and Mary well understood, trying to live good and simple lives without luxury, giving away considerable sums, yet remaining comfortable members of the middle class, with some servants and rarely any anxiety about money. They shied away from excess or display, and they turned down an enormously grand inheritance.

When the Earl died, followed much later in 1921 by the Countess, Gilbert and Mary agonized over whether they had broken the spirit of inheritance tax law, though not the letter, by having accepted money from her long ago when they first married: they refused to hold property in their joint names as they saw this as an inheritance tax avoidance scheme. The Earl had broken up the Castle Howard estates on his death, the Countess taking over most of it. The title went to their dead eldest son's son, so title and Castle Howard went their separate ways.

When the Countess died the Murrays were horrified to find she had left the great house to them and they were appalled at the idea of living in such ostentatious grandeur. They instantly handed over Castle Howard to Mary's last surviving brother, while they gave their daughter Rosalind a pretty house in Ganthorpe, on the edge of the estate.

At the time Mary sat down to calculate what they needed, assuming his League of Nations work might stop Gilbert earning much. In her accounts she estimated their household spending at £1,200 a year, and donations for charity at £1,000 a year. That is certainly a generous portion to give away. They were left a piece of land in Cumberland, which Mary intended to hand over immediately to the Quakers for the relief of post-war famine in

Central Europe, but Gilbert urged her against this, for fear of their unpensioned old age – and indeed they both lived a very long time, he until he was ninety-one, she into many sad years of dementia.

Questions of class worried them, Gilbert most of all. In an exchange of letters with Bertrand Russell, who had written in praise of his *Bacchae* translation, he expressed his dissatisfaction with his life, the inadequacy of the pursuit of art or beauty in his poetic translations. He was strongly against the aesthetes, being by nature a moralist.

> I have a feeling – rather mystical – like this; that there is, really existent a Glory, a Heaven or God, of which we can get glimpses in many different ways – music, poetry, mathematics, heroic conduct etc., and that while I do not insist that all Common beings for any a priori reason must be able to have the glimpse somehow – that is mere religion or sentiment – still I should not be surprised to learn (from an angel or the Reuters Agency or the like), that my gardener or charwoman had been having vivid and intimate glimpses of it under my very nose, when I could see nothing.

There was just occasionally that casual envy of the imagined 'simple' working class life that crops up in George Orwell's writing, especially that scene in *The Road to Wigan Pier* where he describes an idealized working class family sitting contented by the hearth. Murray writes wistfully, 'In time past I have sometimes envied the working men who simply hail a stranger as "mate"; we dons and men of letters seem in ordinary times to have no "mates" and no gift for getting them.' Their youngest son Stephen, who became a communist, recalls that when he demanded the household took the *Daily Worker*, Mary agreed only 'as long as the servants don't see it'. (Though I have a hunch this might be a wishful-thinking memory of a rebellious son, since I have heard precisely that anecdote told of many households and in many families, and it doesn't quite chime with the Murrays' general attitudes.)

The puritanism of their home reached into every aspect of their lives. Murray, speaking to the Fabians, was concerned that socialism lacked a certain puritan ethic:

> I do not for an instant believe that the happier life which Socialism aims at will be attained by any slackening of the grip in which civilised man is accustomed to hold himself, by any loosening of self-control. There is a reaction against Puritanism at present in this country... But I cannot imagine a life that will be able to dispense with the Puritan virtues – to get on without courage, without fortitude, without power of sacrifice... Those persons who are really capable of attaining a great joy – poets, artists, discoverers or what one roughly calls heroes, are people who can and do renounce a vast quantity of smaller and commoner things for the sake of the great thing.

His wife tended to take this 'renouncing things' to further extremes, in giving things away, giving things up and eschewing pleasures. When Gilbert had an eye infection and she had to read to him, she was horrified by his taste for P.G. Wodehouse and detective stories. In a letter to a friend, he wrote, 'Lady Mary reads detective novels to me with an expression of outspoken contempt and occasional ejaculations such as "What is the good of this sort of book? No character study at all!" "A drinking book!"' True, it's hard to imagine a version of P.G. Wodehouse expurgated of alcohol.

The old Liberal world was fading away, and they loathed its last hurrah. Gilbert Murray so detested Lloyd George in and after the First World War that he refused to accept both a Companion of Honour and a knighthood from him. (He accepted an Order of Merit much later, in the next war.) The Murrays had been friends with Herbert Asquith before the war (their grandson, my uncle Lawrence, married Asquith's granddaughter Jean) but they had come to shun him: Gilbert referred to him as 'a roué and a tiresome flirt', knowing him to be not only a heavy drinker but also an adulterer, something neither of them tolerated.

Political lives

Mary by then had left the Liberals and joined the Labour Party. During the General Strike she made a point of walking miles to Boars Hill with the shopping rather than using buses manned by Oxford student Hooray Henry strikebreakers. For many years Gilbert stood time and again at general elections for the Liberals for the Oxford University seat, beaten every time by Conservatives. He spoke of wanting a merger or coalition between the Liberals and Labour, but never quite joined Labour himself. I discover that with a certain ruefulness. All my life the split between the anti-Conservative parties, the liberals and the left, has guaranteed right-wing hegemony. Efforts to join them in a 'progressive alliance' fail time after time. I joined the Social Democratic Party (SDP), splitting from an unelectable out-of-Europe and out-of-NATO Labour Party led by Michael Foot, and the hope was that we would beat Labour and force that coalition. In 1983, the SDP's first election, fought in alliance with the Liberals, I stood for Lewisham East. We almost did it, coming less than 2 per cent behind Labour, but due to the warped electoral system that enforces a Manichean two-party choice, killing off interlopers, we won virtually no seats. Had we overtaken Labour, then a unity on the left would have been within our grasp, but the damaging split goes on. At virtually every election the anti-Tory vote wins a majority: as I write, at the recent local elections all over the country, 85 per cent of seats had only one right-wing candidate, all of them Tory, while Labour, Liberal Democrats and Greens fielded two or three against them in all those seats. What my great-grandfather Gilbert Murray saw so clearly when he repeatedly stood for election remains just as painfully true now.

He was a strong supporter of trade unionism, involved in the Amalgamated Society of Engineers' strike for an eight-hour working day, sitting on a committee for their cause. He was involved too with the Workers' Educational Association, the setting up of Ruskin College, working with the Fabians and joining the Webbs' campaign for reform of the Poor Laws. He campaigned vigorously against the Boer War and all forms of imperialism. During the First World War he worked for the Ministry of Information which he called the 'Mendacity Bureau' and risked the friendship of many pacifists who opposed the war. Those friendships were redeemed only by his vigorous campaign in support of the rights and fair treatment of conscientious objectors, such as his friend Bertrand Russell who was jailed.

After the war he devoted most of his time to the setting up of the League of Nations and became the first Chairman of the League of Nations Union, but that noble endeavour failed in its founding purpose to prevent another world war. When the next war came, in what must have seemed to that generation such a short time between the two, the Murrays dedicated themselves to the cause of refugees from Germany, campaigning to let them into the country, taking a large number into their own home and protesting at the injustice of the internment in camps of so many who were fleeing from the Nazis. After the war when the League of Nations was re-founded as the United Nations, he remained President of the United Nations Association for many years, never despairing of the prospect of perpetual world peace.

Whatever the changing politics and causes of his times, in one thing he was unswerving. He was always scathingly and vituperatively anti-Tory, supporting whoever and whatever could best keep them from power. What he faced – how familiar! – time and again was defeat for the liberal/radical causes he espoused. In speaking about imperialism, he damned the jingoism of Cecil Rhodes and Rudyard Kipling's mistaken romanticism about the goodness of the English. 'It is not more cleverness that is needed in our (imperial) policy, but more sympathy and more sense of right and wrong; these men are stupid because they are wicked.' He was periodically pessimistic, an inevitability given the failures of so many cherished causes. Why do Conservatives almost always win, he asked?

In 1901 he was depressed by failure to prevent the Boer War, and depressed too to learn his elder brother Hubert, who had converted to Catholicism and drunkenness, had gone to fight against the Boers in South Africa. In a bleak and certainly not 'positivist' mood, he wrote in the *Positivist Review* about the repeated failure of liberal causes. He wrote with that grim clarity and honesty that only strikes those of us on the left when we are forced into confrontation with inescapable and abject defeat. He concluded bleakly of his radical Liberal wing,

> We are a very small minority, the extreme wing of a thoroughly weak and beaten party. An influential section even of this party would sooner side with our opponents than with us... We have been living in a Fool's Paradise, misled by the enormous prestige which has attached to the word 'Liberal' during nearly the whole of the last century. But there has been no time when the mass of the nation was genuinely and in cold blood Liberal. To expect a nation to be Liberal is to expect a great deal.

How Labour has always struggled with that dilemma. Is the public essentially and irredeemably conservative, as Tony Blair's New Labour believed? Can the public only be placated, appeased and fooled into a little light progress under cover of stern edicts on scroungers and criminals? Or can good leadership bring out the more generous and optimistically liberal side of human nature? I have to believe the latter or despair.

Rediscovering for themselves that 'Fool's Paradise' of Gilbert's upended one good cause after another espoused by my great-grandparents, my grandparents, my parents, my own generation and my children's – and yet reformers picked themselves up and started all over again. Why, when confronted by so many failures? Because the bigger picture that can only be seen from afar across the decades was also a story of success.

In his long lifetime, despite losing and losing again in one liberal endeavour after another, Gilbert Murray saw great social improvements: the dismantling of the empire he so detested, the rise of the trade unions that brought in Labour, the NHS and the welfare state, the end of corporal and capital punishment. He died in 1956: before the end of capital punishment in 1964 and the ban on corporal punishment in schools in 1986. No doubt he would have been astonished to know he would live until the age of ninety-one, after so many years of swallowing quack doctors' strange medicaments delivered with grim diagnoses of curiously ill-defined ailments. The fine old atheist should be buried in Conway Hall, founding home of the humanists, but he is buried in Westminster Abbey, a final and fitting ethical contradiction.

I wish I knew him with more than a child's eye, for he was a would-be-good without unctuousness, delighting a wide circle of friends with his (non-alcoholic) gregarious company and unswerving belief in the inevitability of progress.

5

Good People, Bad Parents

DON'T LET PARENTHOOD be anyone's only defining quality, for good Gilbert and Mary led a life of fine principle, valiantly swimming against prevailing reactionary tides in pursuit of social justice. But all this effortful goodness didn't do much good to their children.

It's worth recounting the fate of their children as a piece of social history – and a salutary warning against oppressive virtue, however radical and liberal in spirit. The Murrays had five children, two daughters and three sons, but only their youngest son seems to have emerged alive and likeable. My grandmother Rosalind survived, but poisonously.

She was their eldest, who was declared frail on various dubious medical diagnoses and was sent away with a nurse to a better climate for many months at a time to Switzerland and Italy at the ages of eight and nine, and frequently later too, in a way that seems incomprehensible to us now. I suspect they were more neglectful of their children than was usual, even for the bad-parenting habits of their day. It makes no sense to me. Their expectations of their children were probably impossibly exacting, morally, culturally and academically. I'll leave Rosalind, my unpleasant grandmother, until last, for you to judge if her character might be partly explained by her parents' odd blend of childhood neglect and high expectations.

Poor Denis

The Murrays' second child, Denis, they always regarded as a problem. Even at the young age of four his father wrote coldly of him, 'He is a charming boy in his way but I never feel confidence in his discretion or his affection. I feel on stand-off terms with him, just as one does with a school boy.' At four! They were horrified when a colleague gave him tin soldiers for his fourth birthday, war toys in a near-pacifist household. Gilbert gave lessons to his children, which seem to have been stressful on all sides: in my experience with both my parents and my children, lessons from parents are mostly a very bad idea. Denis was sent to Bedales School at the age of seven, which, though it had a progressive reputation, threw him out for teaching another boy to say 'damn'. (Surely he must have done something worse?) He was moved to another prep school, then shoehorned into Winchester College, where naturally they expected him to soar academically, especially in classics.

Gilbert faced the comically familiar problem of liberal parents sending their children to profoundly conservative establishments, demanding a good education yet detesting the cultural, political, military, religious and social ambiance of English public schools. They want to have their educational cake and eat it. That throws their children into a conflict with their public schools from day one, torn

*The Murray family. Gilbert is in the centre at the back,
holding Mary's chair; Rosalind is directly in front of Mary*

between fitting into the conventions of the place or rebel-
ling in honour of their parents' liberal views: it happened
to my father, it happened to me and I confess doing it
to some of my own children. This is what Gilbert wrote
about the culture shock of taking Denis to school for the
first time: 'We took Denis to Winchester yesterday. The
air was thick with rain and with the most crusted Toryism
that I have smelt for years. Mother and I lay back in our
chairs and gasped for some time. I managed to be very

polite all the time, but I contrived to tell a bishop he was immoral, while mother showed him that he was illogical. She also told the housemaster that if he could not get discipline into his boys without sending them to Aldershot for military training, he must be rather unskilful with boys.' Denis got bad reports, perhaps not entirely his own fault: his housemaster suggested he be removed from the school as a bad influence, due to his views on the Church of England, which were, of course, his parents' opinions. The housemaster received a rude letter back from Gilbert: 'I trust that the tone of your letter to me is due to temporary irritability and lack of self-control. If so I shall be glad to hear from you further before consulting the Headmaster as to whether the authorities whom you refer to as "we" share your sectarian objections to Denis' presence at Winchester.' Other objections arose when Lady Mary heard word of immoral goings-on and nearly removed him. However, Denis plainly reassured them, as Gilbert wrote to her: 'It was less serious than I thought. Nothing of that kind at all. It appears that two elder boys talked obscenely and Denis was thrown into intimacy with one of them because they were both in the infirmary together... I gave him a little sermon on the subject.' I get the feeling quite a number of little sermons were usual in that household, though not unmixed with imaginative nonsense games Gilbert played with them too, in the limited time he spent in their company.

Denis went up to Oxford but failed even to get a pass degree, though he was allowed to try twice. Letters from the college said he had been gated, or confined to college, 'for example's sake', and was often in trouble, mostly for drunkenness, though the Murrays may not have known that. Denis was sent to study engineering at Birmingham University, as he liked motorbikes, but he still didn't get a degree. Instead he went as an apprentice to an aircraft factory and started training for a pilot's licence, later taking his father up in a plane and encouraging him to buy himself a motorbike, which he did, to his wife's alarm. But Murray was plainly disappointed in his children, writing in one letter of 'the incapacity of the young to endure boredom or follow argument not immediately interesting. How will they get through life?'

At the start of the First World War, Denis joined the Royal Flying Corps and in early 1915 was shot down on the Dutch coast. Relatively unscathed, he was captured and kept as a prisoner of war in the Netherlands. As it was a neutral country, Lady Mary was allowed to visit him in Groningen prison, helping him with various escape attempts. They sent him a trench tool hidden in a parcel and Gilbert consulted a doctor about drugs that might make him, Juliet-style, seem ill to win his release. Lady Mary came away from a visit reporting how depressed and broken Denis seemed. She was distressed that 'he has given up teetotalism', as if this were a revelation to her. But all these escape plans came to nothing. He was released in 1917 with an authentic bad case of pleurisy. He had taken to drinking heavily and after the war had trouble finding any kind of work. When he died of drink and depression in 1930, Murray wrote with a chilling coldness, 'I did not see Denis often and had not many interests in common. But it is curious how the death of a child affects one like a wound.' Curious, perhaps, only to him.

Wild Agnes

Agnes

Their third child, Agnes, died young too. She went to Oxford, was a close friend of Vera Brittain's and got a third class degree, which disappointed her father who had decided she would be the academic success, having failed with his two eldest. She was by all accounts beautiful and charming, with many friends, but much criticized in her mother's letters for 'flirtatiousness'. In the war she drove ambulances in France where she was engaged to a young officer who was killed almost at once. Her parents regarded her as wayward and complained of her taste in men. Many letters have been destroyed or heavily censored. But this one survived, as Lady Mary wrote in frustration, 'What is she about now? I suppose it's all right, but these children are a terror. Each time I am brought up afresh against her men and her mode of life, I am puzzled and distressed.' When Agnes brought home a young Greek man she wrote, 'Why, oh why can't we have some ordinary right-thinking straight unmarried English gentlemen as playfellows?' Agnes died in the Auvergne in 1922 on holiday with her Greek lover, from acute peritonitis. Both parents rushed out when they heard of her illness and were there when she died. Lady Mary tried to persuade her eldest daughter Rosalind to come to her sister's deathbed, but she refused angrily, shocked at the immorality of Agnes's life, sending her husband Arnold instead. Rosalind made a great moral scene about Agnes's shame, which annoyed both parents who were distraught with grief at the death of their most loved child.

Wicked Uncle Basil

Their fourth child was Basil, thoroughly delightful and thoroughly badly behaved – known as 'wicked Uncle Basil' to my father, whose mother held up her brother as an eternal warning of her wayward son's certain fate. Basil was one model for his friend Evelyn Waugh's Basil Seal, in *Black Mischief* and *Put Out More Flags*, always in scrapes, troubles and debts of one kind or another. Or so my father said, though other models have been suggested. Arriving at Oxford in 1920, Basil was too young for the war, but the right age for the wild twenties generation. A friend of Waugh's, he was a part of that louche set described in the novels: as a result of wildness he only got a third class degree in classics and ran up enormous debts. Lady Mary wrote of him to Gilbert that it was not yet too late for Basil to mend his ways, 'once he realises how his mind is placed on inferior objects'. That forbidding sentence suggests how utterly out of touch they were with their children and especially with this new generation, for it was far too late to raise his mind from 'inferior objects' to higher things. Since the demon drink was again the issue, she worried to Gilbert that it was due to 'my brothers coming out in them', for they had all taken to the bottle and died of it. She worried it was genetic from both sides, bad drinking blood from both Gilbert's father and brother, and from Mary's dead brothers. It doesn't seem to have occurred to her that their own extreme teetotalism might be part of the cause. But she added, 'I don't think so much it's my brothers as me, too much money and insufficient discipline.'

After university Basil worked as a journalist and at one point had a job in the publicity department of the League of Nations, but by 1932 he was in heavy debt through divorce, not earning much while spending a lot. In paying off his debts, his parents ran into a financial crisis of their own and nearly sold their Boars Hill home. Basil stood for parliament in 1935 as an anti-government Liberal in Argyll. The next year in Oxford he was arrested at a meeting of Oswald Mosley's British Union of Fascists (BUF) at the Carfax Assembly Rooms. His nephew Philip, my father, was with him, distributing an anti-fascist newspaper, barracking and shouting 'Red Front!' At one point Mosley challenged anyone to shout it again and when Basil did, they were all set upon by the fascist stewards and were quite badly hurt. The BUF took out a summons against Basil for 'acting in a disorderly way at a public meeting and inciting other persons to do so'. Mosley won the case; Basil was fined £3 and £33 costs. The law coming down on the side of Mosley against the freedom of hecklers became a cause célèbre and Isaiah Berlin was among those protesting to the Home Secretary at this 'disastrous miscarriage of injustice'.

After this, Basil went to the Spanish civil war as a correspondent, broadcasting from the Republican side in Valencia. He died a year later, not of gunshots but of pneumonia. His father thought the war horrors he had witnessed 'Very terrible. I think they weakened his power of resistance.' He had been far fonder of Basil than of Denis, writing that he was 'always good-tempered and gay and generous in his outlook in the face of great trials, a great friend and companion to me'. My father used to say that his much-loved 'wicked Uncle Basil' had died in Gibraltar living with a Gibraltar ape, but this seems not to be true, or not on the record and certainly not reported to his parents. But now I find that the journalist Claud Cockburn in his memoir reports the same story, that Basil was bitten to death by his pet Gibraltar ape while lying in a drunken stupor in a Valencia hotel.

Stephen's rebellions

The Murrays' youngest child, Stephen, went to Oxford in 1927, studied law and managed to offend and alarm them in a novel way. He joined the Oxford Group, a booming Christian cult started by Frank Buchman, an American living in England. The Oxford Group led the way for a host of similar Norman Vincent Peale type American churches that attracted the rich by praising wealth as a sign of blessedness. 'Wasn't God a millionaire?' said Buchman in defence of his elite congregation and his own swelling coffers. The group was known by outsiders as the Salvation Army for Snobs, as it rejected the usual Church of England emphasis on social good works and the plight of the poor, in pursuit of personal salvation and the self. It could hardly have been better designed to disgust the Murrays, in both its religiosity and its dubious self-centred morality. However, Stephen soon married an Oxford Quaker, gave up the Buchmanites and he and his wife joined the Communist Party instead. This was, according to the Murrays, an improvement, but not much. Reading Stephen's *Daily Worker*, Gilbert exclaimed, 'By golly, what a paper!', not with pleasure.

Shortly before his death Gilbert wrote longingly about his two most loved, dead children: 'Curious those one misses, and those that just pass away. I miss Agnes and Basil a great deal – the naughtiest and most affectionate of our children.' In several writings Gilbert tried to understand why their children were such a problem to them and he wondered if having intellectual parents must be a trial to children. But I doubt it was the Murrays' intellect that was so daunting. What sent the children off the rails in one direction or another was more likely to be their parents' overwhelming and crushing moralism. The idea that every aspect of one's life should be devoted to doing good must have been oppressive beyond bearing. For all their atheism, that stern moral duty must have been as alarming as being brought up by a hell-fire preacher warning of an all-seeing God judging every minute of a child's day.

With that self-awareness that made Gilbert so likeable, he reflected late in life, 'I have been thinking how funny and how priggish Mary and I were when young, and half thinking of writing a reminiscence – in the 3rd person – of "A Victorian Prig". We were really nice young people, but so unlike the nice young people of today.' In truth, he was too self-knowing to be a real prig, whereas Mary was so priggish that in her world of absolute high- and low-mindedness she might not have understood what the word could mean. Nor was Gilbert really willing to relinquish Victorian values, still to the end disgusted by the amorality of aestheticism and by the Bloomsbury Set who did so much to demolish the remnants of Victorianism: 'Lytton Strachey, of whom I really had and have a horror, has had a sort of permanent bad influence,' he wrote in 1954. As for Basil, he diagnosed himself cheerfully as having 'a complete lack of repression' and an 'anti-virtue complex', which is perhaps what happens to the children of the overly virtuous.

Paragons of virtue are hard to live up to. Vegetarian, teetotal, donors of a large slice of their income to good causes, unmaterialistic, high-minded with relatively humble tastes, vigorous anti-imperialists, campaigners for all the great liberal causes – yet all but one of their children went to the bad in one way or another.

The alcoholism that did for Gilbert's Australian father and brother had also killed all Mary's brothers young and it consumed their sons too. Later it damaged my father and his brother as well.

Finally, Rosalind

Rosalind and Mary

I have left their eldest child, my grandmother Rosalind, to last. Was it partly Gilbert and Mary's fault that she grew up to be a disastrous mother in her turn? The eldest of Rosalind's three unhappy sons killed himself at a young age while the other two struggled with alcohol all their lives. These men blighted by drink may be victims of an inborn addiction, or each of them may have been self-medicating to numb their childhood suffering under phenomenally difficult parents. But nothing, I think, justifies Rosalind's destructive nature that wrecked the lives of those around her. By turns seductive and rejecting, she was sanctimonious and vain: in the end it emerged she was also a hypocrite of Tartuffe proportions. Only an extreme Freudian or a genetic determinist would absolve her altogether, but her own upbringing was strangely negligent.

She invented for herself a warped resentment that she had slipped down in social ranking, falling out of the aristocracy where she believed she belonged. That is the way of class idiocy. The only one of my antecedents who broke the long line of progressive, liberal and radical freethinkers, she turned Conservative, Catholic and fixated by ideas of blue blood, as wicked a rejection of her family and her husband as she could have devised.

Though she only died in 1967 I never knew her, which was her choice not mine. She regarded my mother as near-cretinously stupid for marrying her dissolute son, and praised her acidly for divorcing him as the 'only intelligent thing you've ever done'. On hearing of their engagement she said to my mother, 'I can't think why you want to marry Philip, but I suppose he has got "S.A."' That's Sex Appeal, a vulgarism that stunned my poor mother who pretended not to understand. Rosalind regarded my clever mother as a fool for marrying him, and then as wicked for divorcing him. Divorce was against the canons of her faith – until she wanted one herself and then the Pope obliged with a convenient annulment.

She was beautiful and she bitterly regretted marrying, as she saw it, beneath her in attraction, class and sensibility, far below her imagined level of emotional, aesthetic and cultural sensitivity. Though she was two generations away from the Howards of Castle Howard, like so many offshoots of the aristocracy, she was haunted by illusory notions of falling down from where she believed she belonged. Literature is full of such twigs from the trees of great families, foolishly indulging in blue blood pretensions.

As eldest child, at first her father used to say she was closest to his heart, though not by the time of his death. Initially Gilbert had harboured great hopes of her academically, but she never went to university, which all the others did, though none of them with much success. She was clearly closer to her father than her mother. Mary may have damaged her children early on, since she suffered what in retrospect seems to have been a serious case of post-natal depression. She writes in letters at the time of Rosalind's birth telling of uncontrollable crying fits. After having her first three children in quite quick succession she retired for a while to a nursing home with nerves. But then illness was Mary's speciality as she and Gilbert, with their fleet of homeopathic doctors, had endless complaints with strange remedies, such as 'peptonized cocoa' (the spell check likes this term as little as do I, but look, there it is in the Harrods catalogue of 1895). Their stern rationalism certainly didn't extend to a scientific approach towards medicine. Rosalind, from a young age, seems to have been the main victim of her parents' hypochondria. At the age of seven she was diagnosed by one of their many quacks as suffering 'rheumatism affecting the heart' that set her on a permanent path of childhood invalidism. Rosalind kept being sent abroad for recuperation for extraordinarily long periods of time on the flimsiest of diagnoses. In one letter her father writes vaguely that their two doctors 'Basso and Boon say it comes from either rheumatism or tuberculosis or anaemia and as usual cannot say which.' After a couple of years away at the ages of seven and eight, she was sent to a boarding school in the south of Ireland, goodness knows why so far. Then at fifteen she was sent away for a very long time to Alassio in northern Italy. One doctor said a month would set her up, but ominously Lady Mary dismissed this as 'simply foolish' and Rosalind was left there until 1908 when she was eighteen. Her father did sometimes go out to visit her and keep her company, and he often said he regarded her as his true intellectual companion, though mainly from afar.

Mary, on the other hand, may have been chilly towards her: she had judged Rosalind as a child as 'clever, cold and unloving' and later that Rosalind had 'very little tender thoughtfulness' towards her parents. It was said in the family that she was jealous of Rosalind's close relationship with her father, with whom she used to perform telepathic experiments. They amazed guests by how easily Gilbert Murray could guess whatever book Rosalind had chosen from a bookcase. His powers of apparently reading her mind were recorded minutely in the annals of the Society for Psychical Research, of which he later became President. Odd for a rationalist, but he stressed he did not believe in magical powers, but in semi-conscious or unconscious perception. He thought his success in these experiments with Rosalind – which on paper do look remarkable – might be due to an undetected hyper-hearing ability, so he was getting clues even though he was in another room far from where the book was being chosen by Rosalind. He suggested

'Hyperaesthesia, making the most of extremely faint sense-impressions, too faint to be consciously perceived at all.' Whatever the reason, they both believed there was a special bond of sympathy and understanding between them and on her twenty-first birthday he wrote to her, 'You have been like a companion to me since you were about eleven.' Well, up to a point, since she was sent away for so much of her childhood. But that closeness made her brand of rebellion against her parents later in her life especially painful to him, and the break with her more bitter than the various spectacular disappointments of his other children.

Rosalind started to write poetry and novels at a young age, her first book, *The Leading Note*, published in 1910 when she was twenty, with financial help from her father after it was turned down by two publishers. He showed it to John Galsworthy who wrote back in that deathless way I've often politely warded off unsolicited samples of journalism: 'most promising and interesting'. In the end Sidgwick & Jackson published it, with the Murrays putting up half the printing cost. It was a tale of an English girl in Italy in love with a noble Prince Kropotkin who most nobly refuses to take her back to Russia for fear of oppression by the Tsar: she said it was in the style of Turgenev, but I doubt Turgenev would have recognized it, though it had one or two encouraging reviews. She moved for a while among the outer fringes of a world of aesthetes, the 'Cambridge crowd' of whom the Murrays disapproved for their lack of moral purpose: beauty was not truth, nor truth beauty in their eyes. From a great distance, she fell in love with Rupert Brooke: she kept a 'poetic' photograph of a play they both performed in. Her second novel, *Moonseed*,

Rosalind

was an affected attempt at romantic dissipation about an English girl in love with a morphine addict, but she marries a (noble) Frenchman who turns out to have drowned his friend. It was worse than the first and, though published, it failed completely.

After that, she abandoned the Cambridge world of self-conscious decadence and plunged instead into quite another set, who upset her parents even more. She took up with a hunting, shooting, county set her parents regarded as mindless upper class oafs. But even worse, she herself started to hunt. To Gilbert Murray this was an unthinkable horror and he wrote her a ferocious letter: 'It looks to me as if hunting was a flag to wave: a sort of indirect way of telling us that your moral standard in life was different from ours, and that you meant to act on it. If so, I do wish you would choose another flag.' He went on:

> For some reason, either some special sensitiveness or because I saw so much cruelty to animals as a boy, I do happen to feel intensely about all 'sports' in which human beings associate their pleasure with the pain and death of weak animals. Such pursuits seem to me unpleasing in a man and, if you will excuse my saying so, rather loathsome in a woman. I mean they give me a feeling of physical disgust... It is a personal bitterness that the person whom, in some ways, I have loved most and been most intimate with, should side against me on the point about which I have the most 'message' or the clearest instinctive feeling. I fully realise that if you gambled or turned up with an illegitimate baby I should not mind nearly so much, though it would be infinitely more serious... About coming here, I was thinking of going away when you came. If you feel you don't want to talk things out, that you would sooner hunt than be preached to, I think it would be painful for us all for you to be here... Your loving Dad

She did keep hunting. Yet there was some kind of reconciliation, for although living in London, she was, alas, around enough at her parents' Boars Hill home to be spied by the shy young Arnold Toynbee at the Murrays' Sunday evening gatherings for classics scholars.

* * *

Rosalind and Arnold's wedding party at Overstrand, 1913

Rosalind and Arnold's wedding has a doleful look, but perhaps I project too much of what I know onto that formal row of family in one musty black and white picture. A year later their first son Anthony was born and the First World War broke out, which was to leave a permanent scar on Arnold's self-image, and, he feared, on his public reputation too. Ever afterwards he saw himself a little like the pained and guilty father in the wartime recruiting poster, 'Daddy, what did YOU do in the Great War?' In the patriotic passion of war fever, even his adoring mother Edith urged her treasured son to fight. Here's what she wrote to him: 'You've got to be a good, not an indifferent platoon commander and you've got to hope very much not to be killed but to help get the better of the Germans. Everything is against you; your poor physique, your consequent lack of high spirits and animal courage... But I'm not afraid that you would show the white feather or fail.'

He had been educated to admire the heroic as well as the philosophic ideals of the warlike Greeks and Romans. He felt an intense moral obligation to volunteer – but he was appalled at the prospect. He had a horror of military drill and team games at school, and he knew he could never join in the manly, jovial comradeship with other soldiers. Add to that, no doubt, inevitable fear. In 1915 he did volunteer, sort of. But he arrived at the recruiting office with a doctor's certificate stating that an attack of dysentery he had in 1912 would probably recur if he was exposed to harsh conditions. He hastened to write to his mother: 'Just a line to let you know that they have rejected me because of my dysentery; it is very bitter but undoubtedly right.' His biographer notes that dysentery never troubled him again. But the white feather problem for a fit twenty-five year old was embarrassing. He wrote a book, *Nationality and War*, explaining the complexities behind the assassination of Archduke Franz Ferdinand at Sarajevo, taking a pro-war but liberal view: 'The only way to convince Germany that war is not in her interest is to beat her badly and then treat her well.' It was rudely reviewed in the *Oxford Magazine* with the brutal remark that the author would be better employed at the front than writing such stuff. Thereafter he was taken into the government information department and deputed to write reports for the cabinet.

In 1916 conscription came in, and Arnold presented himself to the military again. But the first doctor he had approached refused to give dysentery as an excuse, so he went to a second one, who neither saw nor examined him, and who his biographer suggests was recruited by Rosalind to furnish this useful letter for the recruiting office: 'I feel sure your diarrhoea (plague) would begin again as soon as you were exposed to damp and cold and undue fatigue.' Plague! That one word must have done the trick. Arnold pretended in public to great shock at his rejection: 'I was very much surprised as I gathered they were accepting everybody,' he wrote disingenuously to his mother. Later as the need for cannon fodder accelerated, he was twice called up and twice again evaded the draft, but by this time he was exempted with letters from his Foreign Office employers certifying that he was doing essential war work. His biographer writes, 'In later life Toynbee often dwelt on how the dysentery he contracted from drinking from a contaminated stream in Greece in 1912 saved his life in World War I, and the debt he incurred through his own survival to those who had died in the trenches. Yet if he had been willing to join the army he could certainly have done so. From October 1914 onward, he had a secret to hide.'

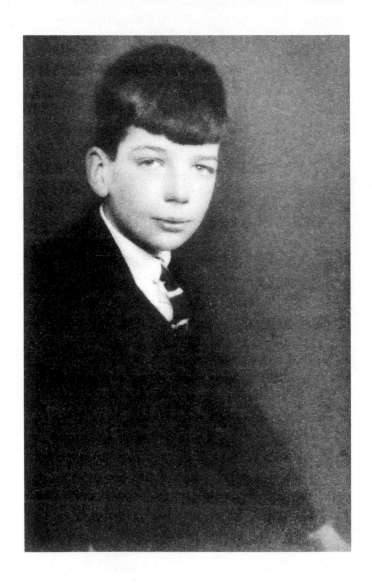

6

Philip the Child

WHY WAS MY father as he was? Rosalind is the simple answer. Unfair, I usually think, to over-blame mothers, but I put her in a special class of her own. Maybe the drink was in the family genes too, with all Philip's maternal uncles dead of it young, his great-uncles too, his brother blighted by it, his Australian great-grandfather ruined and dead of it. That hardly seems random. But he blamed his mother – and surely he was right, for she labelled him wicked from his earliest childhood so that he believed in his essential sinfulness. She carved that guilt into his soul when she rejected him and cast him out.

Philip was their second son, born in 1916, who all his life held onto the idea of the first six years of his life 'in vague half-mythical memory' as 'happy and free'. A pretty little boy in a smock looks out of the photographs, nicknamed Fatmouse by a mother who seemed to him as loving as he was. He passionately adored her, writing later how he and his brother Tony, two years older, regarded her with awe, 'our own Good Judge, my wise and loving mother'. 'All that period of my youngest childhood is filled and suffused with love of my mother. She seemed a wise, strong and tender giantess, holding my hand or swinging me high above her head.' It took him many years to accept 'the thought she might be wrong in anything she did or said'. But wrong she certainly was.

As he tells the story, everything changed with the birth of his brother Lawrence, six years younger. It was not just the jealous imagining of a displaced child, for family, friends and her parents later confirmed to him 'how my mother transferred much of her overt love from Tony and me to the third-born son'. Philip was thrown into a turmoil of misery and naughtiness. He wrote near the end of his life, 'I was made captive of these emotions and remained their captive for forty years. I was propelled from childhood into late middle age unremittingly bedevilled by that more and more distant withdrawal of my mother's love.'

His much-loved elder brother Tony was already a day-boy at a local North London prep school. When Philip, according to his mother, was causing rumbustious trouble at home, he was sent to the same school but as a boarder at the unusually young age of six, as a punishment. Although it was near where the family lived, he was not even allowed home for weekends.

This was not a figment of my father's Freudian imagination. Reading the family letters of the time, Arnold's biographer confirms the story.

The effect on Philip was traumatic. Being bustled off to school at the age of six, almost immediately after Lawrence's birth, seemed like an outright rejection by his mother. Philip reacted by showing off in every way he could think of. When precocity (and Philip *was*

Philip, Lawrence and Tony

precocious) failed, the obvious way to get attention was to misbehave. He accordingly fluctuated between frantic efforts to win his parents' admiration and bouts of provocatively outrageous behaviour. The pattern lasted all of his life, and made him a truly extraordinary person.

There it was, the childhood damage that he recognized and understood, yet could do nothing about.

He was expelled from that first prep school and from five others, including the tough Dragon School in Oxford. He was packed off away as far as possible to some Dotheboys Hall in Scotland called Dalhousie Castle. In one of his first novels, *School in Private*, he describes the horror and bullying of 1920s prep school life. His elder brother Tony's reaction to the removal of their mother's love was to withdraw into himself, for which Philip loved and admired him all the more for his 'courage, pride and icy self-control'.

How was Arnold and Rosalind's marriage going? It was all spelled out in public in 1922 as Rosalind was, alas, writing another novel soon after her third son was born. *The Happy Tree* was an even more thinly disguised portrait of an unhappy but beautiful and sensitive aristocratic woman who grew up in a fine mansion (which she did not), with her refined cousins. Her boorish husband is a professor of epigraphy who works too hard at the Admiralty, who tried to enlist in the war but was found unfit. He is mean with money and so are her hard-hearted relations who refuse to pay for a nanny for her three children. Unsurprisingly, publishers were not in hot competition to print this stuff, and so poor Arnold himself put up the guarantee with Chatto & Windus to print it. It was reviewed a little but not well.

Had Arnold read this attack on himself? Yes indeed, and he proclaimed it very fine, as he licked the boot that kicked him. 'I am very excited about Rosalind's new book,' he wrote in a letter. 'There is such mastery in it – she can make you feel and see quite exactly what she wants. Whether it be popular is another thing, but I know it good.' To my astonishment, when I bought an old copy through Abe Books, a magnificently bound and tooled leather edition arrived with gilded lettering, an edition of a grandeur beyond anything produced for any of the plenitude of books written by many others in the family. The novel still harped on about Rupert Brooke and ends with the immortal words, 'I was happy when I was a child. I married the wrong person, and some one I loved dearly was killed in the war – that is all.' And quite enough it is too.

Arnold, Lawrence and Philip

Arnold remained in thrall to her but, dominated by her contempt, he withdrew increasingly to his study and his work, in pursuit of admiration in the great world beyond. McNeill, Arnold's biographer, says quite rightly, for my father remembered it well, that he 'did not know how to play with his sons any more than he had been able to play with his schoolmates'. My father wrote, 'He simply had no understanding of children and young people and no great interest in them either. My two brothers and I attracted his attention largely as nuisances. How clearly, even now, I can see his head poking out of the window of his study, his face a mask of nervous irritation, as he sternly reproved us for making too much noise.' And how often 'he kept telling us how expensive we were to bring up'.

The idea for Arnold's mighty history of all civilizations came to him as an epiphany, walking along Ebury Street in London when he said he was suddenly blinded by an all-encompassing vision of the shape of everything. As this modest and apparently self-effacing man set to work on it, the idea swelled in dimension and grandeur in its ambitious universality. Rosalind dismissively called it his 'nonsense book' thereafter, never sharing his intellectual interests: humbly that's what he came to call it himself at home. His theory was that civilizations rise and fall by 'challenge and response', responding to exceptional trials with an upsurge of progress. Decline was never predestined, but civilizations fall due to their own moral failure and loss of social cohesion. 'Civilisations die from suicide, not murder' and our fate is always in our own hands. Its colossal success propelled him onto the front

cover of *Time* magazine. He was invited to give the BBC
Reith Lectures and for the rest of his life he globe-trot-
ted to the four corners of the earth lecturing and being
awarded honours. I was with him when he was given the
Order of the Rising Sun by the Japanese, always their
hero for predicting the inevitable rise of the East. At
home he was made a Companion of Honour, but was
secretly disappointed he never won the highest prize, the
Order of Merit conferred on Gilbert Murray.

But these accolades came with savage attacks from British academics: this brand of history was out of fashion, especially with the right. It was Hugh Trevor-Roper who punctured him, a young Oxford don making his name by launching a lacerating attack, personal and poisonous. Calling it 'philosophy mish-mash', he accused Arnold of posing as a prophet, mocking his near-religious belief in mankind and civilization's ultimate purpose. The *Daily Telegraph*'s editorial called it 'vapory Buddhism', detesting its anti-nationalism and anti-colonialism as insufficiently patriotic. It is indeed imbued with liberal optimism, which hardly sprang from his own generation's experience. His final volume ends by defining civilization 'as an endeavour to create a state of society in which the whole of mankind is able to live together in harmony, as a member of a single inclusive family. This is, I believe, the goal at which all civilisations so far known have been aiming, unconsciously if not consciously.' By the time he reached his last volume in 1961, he still saw hope all around him: 'The relatively rich minority of the human race has now recognised that it has an obligation to make material sacrifices in order to assist the relatively poor majority.' This was a remarkable leap of optimism for a man who had been a despairing Foreign Office delegate to the Versailles peace conference in 1919, walking out in disgust at the spectacle of world leaders' revenge on Germany that he rightly predicted would lead to another world war. Consider too how he chronicled disappointment after disappointment in the Survey of International Affairs he wrote for Chatham House each year. Yet to the end he embodied liberal idealism at its most innocent, never losing faith in the essential goodness of humanity and the inevitability of progress.

He left the upbringing of his sons to the untender mercies of his wife. Cast out by his mother at the tender age of six, after Philip had been expelled from one stern prep school after another, Rosalind confined him to a reformatory in Kent, Seal Hart Farm, for delinquent boys. But by pure luck, not her thoughtfulness, this turned out to be the one happy time of his childhood as he fell into the kindly care of a woman he remembered with great love all his life. He searched for her many times, until by extraordinary chance, at the age of sixty, he found her through a friend of a friend, at a time when he had fallen into another of his prolonged and agonizing depressions. He wrote in his diary, 'Apart from the simple joy of finding her again; of sharing such ancient memories; of experiencing that strange and rich conjunction of two far-separated times – more than all these, my meeting with Connie has redeemed my child-hood.' His mother, until her death ten years earlier,

had still insisted I had been an impossible small boy; almost a perverted monster.

But not only did Connie talk of our past together with obvious delight; she wrote me a letter soon after that first meeting in which she told me that I had been 'a delightful little boy, mischievous, imaginative and affectionate'. The words amazed me; but as I gradually absorbed them I felt as if my mind had been cleared of a black fog which had hung there so long that I was no longer aware of how much it was darkening the present as well as the distant past.

He adds, 'Not that my depression marvellously lifted, but at least a new light was shone in the darkness.'

Running away

Later he was sent, unhappily, to Rugby. In his book *Friends Apart*, he describes how he came to run away to join the renegade fifteen-year-old Esmond Romilly, who had escaped from Wellington College. He didn't know the boy, but Esmond was already notorious and glorious by repute to any unhappy public school boy. Romilly the school runaway had started up *Out of Bounds* magazine designed to pull down the public school system. Philip wrote to him 'to pledge my fervent co-operation and to promise I would act as the magazine's agent at Rugby school'.

This underground anti-public school magazine had an improbable mission to cause an upper class youth revolution. It proclaimed itself against fagging and corporal punishment and 'against Reaction, Militarism and Fascism in Public Schools. We attack not only the vast machinery of propaganda which forms the basis of the public school system and makes them so useful in a vicious and obsolete form of society; we oppose not only the semi-compulsory nature of the OTC [Officers' Training Corps] and the hypocritical bluff about "character-building". We oppose every one of the absurd and petty rules and regulations which would be more applicable to a kindergarten than to boys between the ages of fourteen and nineteen.' In truth, the public school sons of privilege, forever destined to inherit England in every generation, were probably the least fertile ground for igniting the revolution.

At school Philip resigned from the OTC and, he writes, 'I began to wear a hammer and sickle in my lapel' but this 'passive gesture began to seem more and more inadequate'. Before running away he wrote a valedictory message to his housemaster saying 'that I could no longer endure the selfishness of public school life and that I intended to work at a Toc H settlement'. Toc H, founded in the First World War trenches by army chaplain Tubby Clayton, had once offered a Christian soldiers' rest hostel in Belgium for all ranks to mix together, as 'an alternative for the "debauched" recreational life of the town'.

Now it ran clubs for underprivileged boys in the East End, where my father with some other Rugby boys helped out – shades here of that same university settlement movement. He writes of these excruciating Toc H meetings of boys of opposite social classes with revulsion at 'the blind self-satisfaction of these middle-class boys'. They used the word 'blogs' with which they outrageously dismissed all those who were too poor to afford a public school education. 'Blogs' was plainly the equivalent of the current equally repellent word 'chavs': Princes William and Harry once held a chavs party at Buckingham Palace where all their friends turned up dressed in a grotesque parody of an imagined Essex style.

My father was good at self-mockery, and looking back at his schoolboy diary of the time he laughed at his self-dramatization of that day of escape: he had written, 'I have taken the most momentous decision of my life. May God be with me!'

He found Esmond Romilly at 4 Parton Street, a street by Southampton Row in Bloomsbury, now long gone. It was a People's Bookshop, 'an archetype of all the Workers' Bookshops I was to know so intimately in the next five years'. He notes the solemn red-backed classics of the Marx-Engels-Lenin Institute and 'the Soviet posters of moonlit Yalta and sunlit tractors – the whole marvellous atmosphere of conspiracy and purpose'.

That was his first meeting with the remarkable, tempestuous Esmond Romilly who was Winston Churchill's nephew by marriage: his mother Nellie was Clementine Churchill's sister. My father writes of his first impression of Esmond: 'He was to be, I already suspected, my pitiless leader' who although younger had already charted an unrelenting course of rebellion. He was at war with his family, with his background and with 'the whole entrenched world he had left behind him'.

At this period he was at the height of his intolerant fanaticism, a bristling rebel, against home, school, society... the world. Though he described himself as a 'Communist', his anarchical self-sufficiency had nothing in common with the proprieties and heavy discipline of the Communist Party. Indeed he was as much an *enfant terrible* to those sober pundits of King Street, Covent Garden [the Communist Party HQ] as he was to the headmasters of public schools. In 1934, Esmond was a terrifying figure. He was dirty and ill-dressed, immensely strong for his age and size; his flat face gave the impression of being deeply scarred and his eyes flared and smouldered as he talked.

Esmond

All my childhood I listened to stories of Esmond Romilly and fell in love with him at a young age. When I ran away from my boarding school, I wished I were running towards his revolutionary hideout. Though I had never met them, he and his wife Decca Mitford were forever the tearaway rebels of my dreams, fearless, reckless, careless, determined, purposeful, romantic and brave beyond anything I would ever have risked. I never had that streak of downright daring. And, I see now, nor did my father, quite.

By that first evening, he is beginning already to lose his nerve. Over supper in a café in Theobalds Road that runaway evening, Philip panics as he realizes school prayers would have begun with his absence noticed. 'Oh my God why have I done it, why had I ruined myself, branded myself for life as a black sheep?' He would, he writes, have 'returned, abject, by the next train but for my greater fear of this dictatorial boy. For I had succumbed to him entirely and even in my panic I maintained a bluff imitative manner, swearing with him, smoking and making plans for the future.'

Over the next days, as Grub Street characters came and went in the back bedroom of the bookshop, delegates arrived from public schools: 'Ledward of Charterhouse – no bloody good... Pilkington of Lancing – he's done some useful work.' Three boys from Eton had resigned from the OTC and one panicking headmaster had expelled a boy for distributing *Out of Bounds*. 'Esmond infected me with his apocalyptic faith in the imminent downfall of the citadel.'

Within days they came looking for Philip.

A formidable and business-like lady suddenly appeared before us like the delegate of another age and another world. 'I've come to ask', she said, 'whether you have seen Philip Toynbee', and her eyes shrewdly perused us. A look of almost violent frankness appeared on Esmond's face, and when he spoke to her his voice was warmly co-operative. He had never heard the name, but if there was anything he could do... I sat and watched the lady, hoping that my face was as blank as Esmond's, but aware that a timid voice was crying out for self-disclosure, for surrender, punishment and safety.

This envoy was his grandfather Gilbert Murray's secretary, and she had not been deceived. She returned to make her report to the family.

Beaten up by Mosley's Black Shirts

The next day provided what I had lacked before, emotional justification for my escapade. Sir Oswald Mosley held a monster meeting at Olympia. In the afternoon we bought knuckle-dusters at a Drury Lane ironmonger, and I well remember the exaltation of trying them on. We flexed our fingers. 'A bit loose here', 'Not very comfortable on the thumb'. We were expert knuckle-duster buyers.

We seethed with the anti-fascist crowd down the cul-de-sac beside Addison Road station, at one moment carrying between us a great two-poled crimson streamer, dropping it at the next to escape from the hooves of the mounted police, shouting fierce slogans against the long, protected column of fascists.

One-two-three-four
What are the fascists for?
Lechery, Treachery, Hunger and War.

[At Olympia] in every open space, at the end of every row, stood black-jerseyed stewards with hands on hips, complacent and menacing. The seats had been full for many minutes before hidden trumpets sounded a fanfare, and the Leader strode into the arc-lights. He was flanked by four blond young men, and a platoon of flag-bearing blackshirts followed in their wake. The procession moved very slowly down the aisle, amid shouts, screams and bellows of admiration, amid two forests of phallic, upraised arms. Sir Oswald held one arm at his side, thumb in leather belt: the other flapped nonchalantly from time to time as he turned a high chin to inspect us.

He had stood on the rostrum for at least two minutes of this din, before his own arm rose, formidably, to impose silence. And then... not the commanding single voice, but a sudden blasphemous interruption from behind us. It was shocking and incredible, as if a scene had been made at a coronation.

Hitler and Mosley mean hunger and war!

Hitler and Mosley mean hunger and war!

I turned just in time to see three young men and a girl standing side by side, their alarmed defiant faces turned towards the ceiling. A moment later the stewards had closed in on them and they had sunk out of sight in a storm of black bodies and white fists. The girl screamed and it was this which brought Esmond and me to our feet. We ran up the stairs and threw ourselves on the stewards' backs. I remember the coarse rub of a jersey against my cheek, before I was thrown over from behind and pressed against the boards. Someone had caught my arms and twisted them behind my back: I was dragged up from the floor and propelled to the stair-head. A glimpse of faces below me, yearning upwards for their victim and I was tumbling down the outer stairs. Arms whirled like windmills, thudded on my head and back, and I was again in the wide corridor which was thick with blackshirts.

Esmond and I had been separated and I was terrifyingly alone down there, among the weaving, punching, merciless enemies. Tearful, bruised and broken, I was at last thrown out into the street, to be picked up by communist organisers of the interruption and taken to a provisional first-aid post.

But those 'bloody and dry-eyed heroes' were not weeping as they witnessed 'my sobbing humiliation. I left as soon as my minor injuries had been attended to.' Once away from that embarrassment, he recovered his nerve as he ran and sang 'along Hammersmith Road; I sang up Kensington High Street and across Hyde Park Corner. For I believed I had struck my first blow for the revolution and that the revolution itself must surely follow.'

He found Esmond back at Parton Street, already at his typewriter composing a story about it. 'We sat for hours in the bedroom, recounting tirelessly, but not competitively, the details of our adventures. And our first hopes became more apocalyptic than ever. Surely we had heard already the first mutter of machine-guns in the suburbs of a brooding Petrograd, and tomorrow... I fell asleep to dream the whole adventure as it should have been.'

For myself growing up, I demanded my father tell me these stories time and again. How I envied his 1930s generation, fighting the Mosleyites, off to the Spanish civil war, in innocent days when communism was credible and fascism a clear and present danger to be fought with every sinew. The world looked simpler, ideals shinier, hopes of revolution untarnished, beliefs believable, spirits undaunted, the good old songs stupendously rousing. My father never glamorized his years in the Communist Party but I grew up nostalgic for his youth and in love with Esmond Romilly from all the stories my father told of him.

Beating a retreat

But Philip was not the rebel he wanted to be: like me and like most people, he was not cut from that heroic cloth. The grey and rainy morning after the Mosley punch-up, Esmond handed him an envelope.

> My housemaster's letter could not have come at a more propitious moment; it sped like a dart into one of the many gaping joints in my armour. He wrote that I had taken a thoughtless and selfish step, and that the harm I had done to myself and others could not be undone. This was a crisis in my life and he besought me to come to my senses. He would arrive at Euston that afternoon and he asked that I should meet him there and return with him to Rugby.
>
> A crisis in my life! Oh, the mad and criminal act that I'd committed! But was it too late? Would they take me back, now, if I promised that never, never again...?

He turned tail and fled back, despite Esmond standing over him, glowering. But 'In my panic to submit, I was impervious even to his snarled and outraged contempt.' Revolution, even against school and family, let alone the mighty state, takes exceptionally stout-hearted bravery.

As is the treacherous way of the ruling public school, he might as well have stood his ground: despite his grovelling recantation, as soon as his housemaster brought him back, Rugby called on his parents to remove him. The school had to make a public demonstration of him to the other boys, some of whom waved goodbye: 'Good luck, Toyners, good luck!'

His parents were summoned rapidly back from Berlin 'to greet their expelled, humiliated son'. When his mother packed him off to the monks of Ampleforth Abbey, he was not allowed to join that school, regarded as too dangerous a bad influence on those Catholic boys. He was kept absolutely apart in the monastery. She told him that if he worked hard and got an Oxford scholarship, 'I would be allowed to continue the normal education of my age and class, but if I failed, I was to start working for my living in the New Year.' Though of course then as now, private schools were a tiny niche, no one he or his family knew would ever have considered state education, an unknown realm.

He was banned from communicating with Esmond ever again. But of course he kept in touch, following his exploits from afar 'with envy and admiration. I could not forget the shame of my abject submission to the world which he was flouting.' *Out of Bounds* continued for a few issues, copies smuggled in to him at Ampleforth, one edition containing his own first ever printed article, a report of the Olympia meeting. 'I read them from my monastery with a violent regret for the rebellious life which I had won for a moment and lost so abruptly.'

He won the scholarship to Christ Church, and went off to get drunk with Esmond, so drunk they tipped up dustbins and banged on Esmond's mother's door in the small hours: Nellie Romilly instantly called the police, who threw them into the cells at Bow Street station. Both sets of parents turned up appalled at the magistrates' court next morning. Philip's mother called Esmond 'rotten meat', while Colonel Romilly told the papers his fifteen-year-old son was the one who had been led astray 'by an older cousin'.

With typical snobbery, Rosalind told Philip that 'I had evidently been born out of my class, which gave me gleeful satisfaction. I was glad to think I belonged not to my apparent background of scholarly distinction, but to the traditional race of outcasts, tramps and bohemians.' But he adds honestly, 'Yet it always proved I was too timid ever to do more than make frantic lunges into that world.' There it is, the fate of we bourgeois leftists, too firmly entrenched in the world of privileged security to really take flight and abandon everything. I never have. Esmond Romilly was an extraordinary exception.

Back in the fold, Philip found himself invited to Castle Howard among a bundle of Whiggish liberal second cousins, where he fell in love with Laura Bonham Carter, granddaughter of Herbert Asquith, Liberal prime minister. 'What I best remember about the first breathless evening is a dinner in the Canaletto room...' Ah, the same Canaletto room that had so astonished both his father Arnold and his grandfather Gilbert in their first invitations to this palace. After some – but not much – dallying with my father, Laura later married Liberal leader Jo Grimond in this tight little old-fashioned Liberal world fast fading away from power. They were, my father wrote, 'Worldly but high-minded, intensely political but traditionally familiar with the arts, intellectual but often frivolous, I saw them as fascinating and doomed.'

Though as a child he had sometimes spent holidays in a cottage in the grounds, he had never stayed in the castle itself, so he reports the usual indignities of inexperience, a teenager lacking a black tie or pyjamas, as a servant unpacked and laid out his shabby clothes. This Edwardian country house life might have been losing political power with the collapse of the old Liberal Party, 'But I could see no sign of material decline, for this pretty Georgian house seemed mellow and prosperous. There were ponies in the stables, several servants, protracted and delicious meals. I believe it would have entirely pleased me if it had not been for the agonising ambiguities with which I was surrounded... Here, as in Parton Street, I was in a strange place, attached to a world which I admired but could not understand or properly belong to.' This might be mildly disingenuous. No black tie? But as he was chaotic with clothes and possessions, he may have been genuinely ignorant in the ways of grand stately home life. But he was on his way to Oxford now and Oxford Union debates in their full absurdity of tails and traditions.

Visiting Castle Howard

Once when I was nine he took Josephine and me on a camping holiday, where he seemed to be in search of his roots, for he started with a tour around the flatlands and fens of Lincolnshire, in Swineshead and to Gedney Drove End, a lonely spot out on the Wash. He was looking for ancient gravestones and parish registers of Toynbees who settled there, he thought, after arriving with marauding Vikings to impose the Danelaw down England's eastern side. Then we travelled north to Yorkshire to see Castle Howard, and we gazed in amazement from afar at this magnificent yellow stone Vanbrugh confection. He knew the grounds well as he had played there as a boy, and he told us to pitch the tent round the back of the mausoleum in a far corner of the park where the bodies of centuries of Howards lay. He terrified me by lying down in an empty vault and whooing out ghostly noises in the dark, noting the coffin space was too short for him: 'You'll have to cut my feet off to fit me in here.'

A thunderstorm that night was so ferocious it whipped the tent off us and blew it away across the fields. While we were trying to retrieve it in the pelting rain, across the lawns and beyond the ha-ha, we saw torches heading our way. The current owner was his cousin George Howard, a man my father barely knew. He was not the Earl of Carlisle as the title had descended to another branch of Howards, my father explained. Cousin George took pity on us and invited us into the house for the night. Dripping wet we steamed in front of a great fire until shown into a room with a colossal four-poster bed, with damask canopy and velvet curtains. Josephine and I sank into the deepest feather bed that enveloped us almost to suffocation, but we left early next morning, uncertain if we would be welcome for breakfast.

The next time I visited was just a few years ago as I started out on this book, on holiday, buying a ticket to gaze in awe at its paintings and sculptures, its halls and galleries. But I was embarrassed, caught out like Elizabeth Bennet at Pemberley ogling my distant ancestry, when one of the volunteer guides not only recognized me from appearances on television, but knew exactly by what degree I was related, with a typical guide's encyclopaedic knowledge of the Howard family tree. 'Come over here,' she said, and took me, blushing awkwardly, to a room to see a painting of my great-great-grandmother Rosalind, Countess of Carlisle. 'Quite a character,' she said. 'She was called the Radical Countess,' and she told the old stories of her women's suffrage campaigning and her temperance fanaticism, smashing those thousands of wine bottles, closing down all the local pubs and those mortal rows with all her six sons, five of whom predeceased her, mostly taking to the bottle. She looks deceptively calm and angelic in that portrait by Dante Gabriel Rossetti, with a tepid expression like all Rossetti's fashion-plate perfect faces; he gives her a tinge of red hair, more Rossetti's than hers, and he seems

Rosalind, Countess of Carlisle,
by Dante Gabriel Rossetti

to have avoided portraying her true character or the fiery expression in her eyes. I looked in vain for the famous Canalettos, but they were sold off long ago. I walked out to see the mausoleum where we had camped; still plenty of empty slots there, but not of course one for my father. He is buried by the banks of the Wye in the Moravian churchyard in Brockweir.

7

Philip at Oxford and at War

THOUGH IT FEATURES so strongly in my family history, I have no feeling at all for Oxford, no sentimental attachment, quite the reverse. Revisiting it gives me slight shivers of some indefinable alarm and a strong wish to escape. I have regularly turned down invitations to speak at the Union, at colleges or Labour meetings, to avoid the bleakness of standing on the platform at Oxford station late at night reminding me in some intangible way of unhappy times I can't quite fathom.

Not so my father. His Oxford was another era, another world, and it was as distant from mine as it was unrecognizably far removed from those far-off groves of academe inhabited by his grandfather, father and his two scholarly aunts. Philip's Oxford was a ferment of hot 1930s politics. Undisciplined in most things until then, under the stern authority of the Communist Party he submitted to its rigours and regulations that were more severely demanding than any of the public school Officers' Training Corps drilling that *Out of Bounds* had denounced. He delighted the party with his election as the first communist President of the Oxford Union. When I first met Denis Healey, he told me my father had recruited him into the party at Oxford at that time.

There was always the distant call of the wild, the possibility that Philip might have taken the other road, rejecting the easy Oxford path for a less privileged life, but he was painfully aware of his failure of nerve to break away. Esmond turned up in Oxford one day looking for Philip, and that gave him a jolting reminder of what his life might be like had he dared to follow his friend and forsake his social background, education and family. Esmond was selling silk stockings door to door.

Following their arrest at the hands of Esmond's mother, because he was still legally a child Esmond had been sent by the courts to a boys' remand home for a while. Now released and angrily shunning any contact with his family, he was earning his living as a travelling salesman. My father wrote, 'One of his purposes in coming to see me was to ask for all the names and the colleges of all the girl undergraduates I knew. We talked for half an hour before he hurried off to Somerville and St Hugh's with his case full of samples. Without hoping or wishing to imitate him, I admired him more than ever in his new and unexpected role.' Extraordinary as his earlier rebellion had been, 'it was even more remarkable that he should refuse to submit even now, even after the collapse of *Out of Bounds*, after his distressing weeks in a remand home. Rather than surrender to his parents and return to the normal and easy life which was always available to him, he was hurrying from one commercial hotel to another, touting on doorsteps and working on commission.'

In his book *Boadilla*, Esmond describes how his privileged, if truncated, education left him unfit for most work.

I have always found selling fairly easy, as I am naturally inclined towards exaggeration and have often been criticized for an over-willingness to talk and go on talking. Having been educated up to school certificate stage at a famous public school (Wellington College), having left rather rapidly and suddenly, and decided it was preferable to support myself by my own labour, having no specialized knowledge of any kind, and not being troubled with an over-quantity of honesty or scrupulousness, it was, I suppose, inevitable that I should soon be selling somebody something. I belong to that very large class of unskilled labourers with a public-school accent.

Confronted on doorsteps by resolute parlour maids, this brazen seventeen year old would announce 'Captain Romilly!' My father writes: 'It was impossible not to admire him, or to feel a shame-faced envy for a life so different to my own.'

Esmond was not a party member, but a 'free-booting ally on the flank'. He used to mock Philip for his unswerving loyalty to the party line.

He liked to make me stumble through my paces on the Moscow trials of 1936 and 1937, knowing very well that I was far more uneasy about them than he was... he made a fool of me over the devious party line of rearmament. In fact he was never, in any sense, a 'contact', and even if I had succeeded in my half-hearted attempts on his independence, it is likely that the Party would have refused to accept him as a member. Good communists always spoke of him with the shuddering distaste of a nanny referring to the rough street-urchin playmate of her charges.

Philip had kicked against family and school, but he accepted a far stricter discipline from the party, because he had voluntarily chosen it.

Here's an episode that makes my heart sink at how little changes, how little society progresses: he was involved in the events at the Cutteslowe Walls that had Oxford trade unions and left-wing students up in arms together over a town issue, a disgraceful event but one that frequently still happens now with developers' new estates. In North Oxford a new development was designed with one half for the middle classes and the other half as social housing. Philip writes, 'To prevent any contamination of the first by the second, brick walls had been built right across the central road of the estate dividing the respectable houses from the rest. This meant that while the richer were able to use the road, the poorer had to make a wearisome detour to reach a bus-stop.' Several times campaigners, among them Philip's friends, used a steamroller to knock the walls down, but they were rebuilt and stayed there for the next quarter of a century, not demolished until 1959 when the council managed to make a compulsory purchase of the strips of land they stood on. These same social-deterrence walls are still built now in new apartment blocks that have 'poor doors' at the back for the social tenants, smart front doors for the private owners only. New playgrounds are built for private homeowners' children while blocking access for the children of council tenants, happenings that still erupt into the pages of the *Guardian*. That same deep English social class divide never surges up more fiercely than over the need to preserve property values for homeowners from proximity with lower class neighbours.

Life on the left was hard work, none harder than for Communist Party members. Here's Philip's diary entry for 25 January 1937: 'Morning – round colleges interviewing contacts. Lab Club lunch till 3; Union Committee till 4.30; Secretariat till 6; Cell till 7; Lab Club Priv. Business meeting 8 to 10.45.' He adds, 'I claim this as a record day!' At evening socials they sang a rueful song:

> Dan, Dan, Dan!
> The Communist Party man,
> Working underground all day.
> In and out of meetings,
> Bringing fraternal greetings,
> Never sees the light of day.

He was not a clandestine member, but one of the few who represented the party's public face, 'a small iceberg peak above a submarine majority'. Indeed, he didn't even know who the underground members were. My history tutor at Oxford, the daunting and dazzling Jenifer Hart, was an Oxford contemporary and a friend of his, so when my father came to visit me at my college, St Anne's, she invited us both to lunch. Philip joked and told stories about his old communist days while she listened with sceptical nods of amusement. But when he had regaled us for some time with his old party tales of derring-do, she finally revealed,

Philip

rather quietly, 'Philip, I was a party member too, but while you were making a lot of noise in public, I was a mole.' He was at first astonished and then rather crestfallen.

She had joined in 1935, and afterwards she won the highest place any woman ever achieved in the civil service exams. She went to work in the Home Office, where years later she rose to become a principal, working for Permanent Under-Secretary of State Sir Alexander Maxwell on defence regulations and the police, but by the time she reached those heights, she said she had long since left the party. She, like my father and so many others, walked out in disgust at the Hitler–Stalin pact in 1939. But they had both of them stomached the Moscow 1936–7 show trials brutally satirized in Orwell's *Animal Farm*, over which Esmond had taunted Philip, leaving him uneasily making excuses he didn't believe. I have no way of putting myself in their shoes, returning to the political mood of those days when they lived in fear at the rise of Hitler and alarmed that the English establishment would never stand up to fascism. Consider Beatrice and Sydney Webb's visit to Russia resulting in publishing in 1935 their excruciating eulogy 'Soviet Communism: A New Civilisation?' For the reprint of that Fabian book in 1937 they even removed the question mark. Would I as blithely have overlooked Soviet atrocities, eyes tight shut for the greater good? I fear I probably would.

It says something about the hopelessness of the spy-catchers that Jenifer Hart could talk so openly, as she did to us on that day, about being a Home Office mole in the run-up to the war, without it ever reaching MI5's ears. It wasn't until 1983, when she had no doubt spoken once too often and loudly about her communist past, that she faced a sudden brutal newspaper exposé. They accused not only her, but her lawyer husband who worked in MI5 in the war, of passing wartime secrets to the Soviets. They hadn't, they sued and they won an apology. But as with my father's close friendship with Donald Maclean, he was shocked to find he had been clueless about those who had been secret members, while he had paraded his party credentials in public.

The moles would have been lucky to miss the excruciating round of party meetings, but they also missed the parts of membership my father most enjoyed. His vacations were spent travelling to international meetings. He was delighted to be assigned to work with unemployed communist miners in the Rhondda Valley, where he returned frequently to live and organize, joining their strikes. There was less time for his grander private life, though as he was still pursuing Laura Bonham Carter he would drop back into that other world from time to time: the all-knowing party didn't object. 'My purely "bourgeois" life was not forbidden to me or even disapproved of – it was a principle that we should work in whatever class we belonged to.' But the party was a tough task master, 'authoritarian and possessive', and 'it practised dishonesty almost as a principle'. He was pleased with the genuine comradeship, though 'I was always uneasily aware that large and precious areas of thought and feeling were being not only disregarded but angrily denied'. The party used him to make public speeches and to do 'contact' work, interviewing any member of the university who had ever expressed communist sympathies. He was a good recruiter, as Denis Healey recounted. He would tell his converts the Communist Party was 'able to satisfy every need and adapt itself to every individual. This was the nearest I came to emulating Esmond with his silk stockings.' In one term he recruited fifty people, but 'The weakness of my method, which had been to offer everything to everybody, was only disclosed a few months later when forty per cent of my disillusioned recruits had left the Party again. I was not aware of deceiving them when I urged that all their problems would be solved by joining us. I believed there was room in the Party for everyone.' He writes of the painful boredom of interminable meetings, 'But I greatly enjoyed my unembarrassed visits to the

Rhondda. I enjoyed the strikes at the Oxford factories, the slogan-shouting marches through London, the international conferences and the whole lively atmosphere of purpose and intrigue.'

Socially, he veered from one world to the other, at one point leaving a Wiltshire stay with the Bonham Carters for a Welsh miner's cottage in Tonypandy. 'The contrast delighted me. Though I was heavily conscious of the tail-coat and white tie hidden in the bottom of my suitcase. The suitcase lay for the whole of my ten-day visit, under the bed which I shared with a seventy-year-old pensioner, and I felt that the tailcoat was like a corpse which I was hiding there from the anger of my new comrades. When I knew them better I realised that they would have laughed to find it.'

Not quite fighting in the Spanish civil war

The romance of the Spanish civil war lasts on through the generations, as does the heroism of those who joined up with the International Brigade to fight for the Republican cause, the democratically elected government under attack after a coup by General Franco's fascists. Hitler and Mussolini armed Franco, while the pusillanimous British, French and Americans stood back and failed to support the Spanish democratic government: the passions it stirred came from a fear this was a rehearsal for fascist invasion across Europe that would be greeted by appeasement not confrontation, as indeed at first it was. Back in Oxford in the winter of 1936,

Philip's chief work for the party was setting up Spanish Defence Committees. 'Although this was probably the most useful and effective of all my activities as a communist, I was continually aware that Esmond's role was the nobler one.'

Esmond had pretended to go on a bicycling holiday in France, but headed straight for Spain, where at eighteen he was the youngest recruit to the International Brigade. 'A letter arrived from him in November to tell me he was already fighting in the outskirts of Madrid. It seemed very typical of his bluntness, but also of a sort of inverted romanticism, that he wrote most vividly about the smell of the dead.' It was not the policy of the party for Oxford student communists to leave to fight in Spain; 'There was a great deal of uneasy muttering about the guilt of safety which nearly all of us shared. A few slipped away to Spain. Soon we had our own hero, John Cornford, a fanatical Cambridge communist who was killed in the early months of 1937.'

Philip was eventually sent to Spain by the party, but only as leader of a student delegation, not as a fighter. 'I felt so wildly excited and yet so wretched at being a student delegate.' He arrived in time to learn news from General Kléber, commander of the International Brigade, of the disastrous battle of Boadilla in which most of the English volunteers had died. He found that Esmond was one of only two survivors of the English group, but he had been sent home on sick leave with dysentery, charged with the terrible task of visiting the families of the dead to bring them the bad news. Esmond arrived back sobered and talked of the International

Column's disorganization, rivalries, 'harsh mutual criticism, disgraceful retreats, cold, uncongenial company and the rapid fading of romance'. Some of that is bitterly recorded in Orwell's account of fighting and the in-fighting in his *Homage to Catalonia*. When asked, Esmond refused to make recruiting speeches, but nonetheless he was determined to return once he had recovered. As for Philip, he was due to report back to a large and earnest meeting at Conway Hall, but by the time it was his turn to speak he was so drunk he lost his notes and was booed off the stage.

Decca Mitford bursts onto the scene

It was a few weeks later that Esmond first met Decca at the house of a mutual relation. They were second cousins but had never met before. For those who have managed to stay unfamiliar with the extraordinary Mitford story, despite its frequent retelling, Decca was the sixth of seven children of eccentrically reactionary, foreigner-hating Lord and Lady Redesdale. They denied schooling to all six daughters, letting them bring themselves up at home where they invented their own world and childhood language. Life in their semi-stately Oxfordshire home was made famous in the comic novels of the eldest daughter, Nancy Mitford. Their shocking politics made the family notorious. Diana Mitford married the fascist Sir Oswald Mosley and spent the war in prison. Unity Valkyrie Mitford went to Germany before the war where she fell in love with Hitler: she shot herself in the head on the outbreak of war, a bullet lodging in her severely damaged brain, though she didn't die until 1948. In an extraordinary event at the start of the war Hitler had her sent back to her family on a stretcher through the lines across frontiers. The youngest daughter, Deborah, married the Duke of Devonshire and became the chatelaine and manager of his mighty Chatsworth estate in Derbyshire.

Decca, the sixth child, had turned the opposite way, when she became a communist from a young age and she stayed hard left all her life. All this remarkable family history Decca has described herself magnificently in her book *Hons and Rebels*, which tells of her elopement with Esmond ten days after first meeting him.

As Esmond was Winston Churchill's nephew, the escape of these two scions of the aristocracy to Bilbao was headline news. In a sign of the power of aristocratic titles, Foreign Secretary Anthony Eden, at her parents' urging, diverted a destroyer to fetch them back. Her father had her made a ward of court as she was under age, and he threatened to put her into a home for wayward girls. Under orders, the ship's commander inveigled them on board, but as Decca writes, 'It was all to no avail. Esmond pointed out to the commander of the destroyer that he had no legal right to hold us: penalties for forcible abduction can be severe. The argument proved to be persuasive, and we were put ashore in France. We settled in Bayonne where after a good bit of turbulence, as airline pilots put it, we married in June 1937.'

These stories I knew from earliest childhood. I grew up in love with Esmond and Decca, envious of their daring through reading their books, *Hons and Rebels* and *Boadilla*, many times over and willing myself into their adventurous lives. But I had never met Decca until, to my excitement, she burst in on my life when I was fifteen. She had arrived unannounced in London from her many years in America, with her American son Benji, who is my age. Though a life-long friend of my father's, she didn't know me but she telephoned me out of the blue and swept me out to the theatre and dinner with them. The play was an awful light comedy by William Douglas-Home called *The Reluctant Debutante*. The arts were not her thing and she often had an odd nostalgic taste for English upper class things, despite her escape from all that. From then on, she was my adult friend, my new non-godmother who I adored, as did my children when she often came to stay, though later we frequently argued about politics.

For several summers I went to stay on her Scottish island, Inch Kenneth, off Mull, amid scenes of wild games, songs and uproarious absurdities. She was the kind of compulsive rule-breaking fairy godmother any child would yearn for, outrageously generous and badly behaved. She had clever wheezes for avoiding paying for train tickets or for long distance telephone calls: if she called she would reverse the charges, giving herself a name that contained the message – so the call could be refused, no charge paid, but message received. When she left some shoes behind, she made a call in the name of Mustafa da Shoos.

Her little island, less than a mile long, with its white cliffs and secret coves with sandy beaches, had been left by her mother to all her daughters except Decca, who was cut out of her will: Decca was so angry that she bought out her sisters' shares, being by then a successful writer. Her mother's Inch Kenneth house was damp and decrepit, with shades of Miss Havisham hanging over the dusty four-poster in the main bedroom: Decca never removed her mother's possessions, which included a wind-up gramophone and Unity's records of German marching songs with swastikas on the covers.

Philip first met Decca when she and Esmond had returned from their elopement to live at 41 Rotherhithe Street, both of them working for an advertising agency. Philip describes his first visit to their house: 'I took a tram for miles along the Jamaica Road from the Elephant and Castle and then I was lost among the dark wharves and warehouses of Rotherhithe. When I asked a muffled stranger the way, he said, "What ship do you want, mate?" and I knew I was in authentic Esmond territory.'

It wouldn't be Esmond and Decca territory now. I walked along there recently, but 90 per cent of Rotherhithe buildings were destroyed in the Blitz, the bombers targeting Surrey Docks. The street is rebuilt, the old cheap and shabby housing replaced with expensive modern homes now that most of the docks have been filled in and re-developed, desirable dockland flats selling at high prices.

Decca writes about first meeting Philip: in him 'were combined all my favourite characteristics; he was a gifted and very funny raconteur and a perfect target for teasing, one who readily joined in the laughter against himself. But there was the serious dedication to the causes Esmond and I held paramount; anti-fascism and the eventual triumph of socialism. His amazingly versatile love-life and the high drama with which he invested his accounts of its fluctuations, were an unfailing source of wonder and amusement; as good as going to the theatre, Esmond said.'

Philip moved in with them for a while after graduating and their roistering life included laying waste to aristocratic houses they had manoeuvred their way into visiting. There was the bohemian life of Fitzrovia and Soho too, the nights in upper class David Tennant's Gargoyle club with its Matisse-painted walls, and the seedier Colony Room, with Muriel Belcher perched on her stool, the French pub and much carousing with figures of the literary and artistic world, where, Decca said, Philip was known as 'Plunger Abrams' for his inevitable plunges into something or someone before the evening was over. This was the self-confident world of a relatively closed intellectual coterie.

Frank Pakenham, a Catholic socialist earl, had founded a small left-wing newspaper in Birmingham called the *Birmingham Town Crier*, and he appointed Philip as editor. One of its purposes was to rally the people against the Munich appeasement and to bar the city to its most famous son, Neville Chamberlain. 'Birmingham has spoken!' his front page proclaimed to all of its twelve hundred readers. Alas, it had not. 'A week later Neville Chamberlain was given a Roman triumph through his native city.' And so it usually happens, time and again, as blindingly obvious good causes crash to the ground with the public inexplicably on the wrong side. Hard not to whisper to oneself Brecht's wicked irony in his poem after the East Berlin rising of 1953:

Wouldn't it
Be simpler in that case if the government
Dissolved the people and
Elected another?

For the left, the British people have been a disappointment more often than not. For those of us trying and failing to represent 'the down-trodden masses', this keeps coming as a perennial shock. These days the left is impudently branded by Conservatives as an out-of-touch 'metropolitan elite'. That word 'elite' has become the portmanteau insult of our times – shamelessly hurled by the Etonians in charge against those they call the 'liberal establishment', an imaginary caste squeezed out of almost every sphere in their scorched earth 'culture wars'.

Before war broke out, Esmond and Decca set off for America. They were not escaping war, as Esmond was quick to join up as soon as it was finally declared. The draw of America and its supposed classlessness sent them on their way, fleeing stifling Englishness. Decca had come into £100 from an aunt on turning twenty-one, enough to buy an £18 boat ticket for each of them – and one for my father if only he would join them. They planned a lecture tour trading on America's imagined unabated fascination with the English upper classes. The Romillys picked topics for themselves, Esmond to talk on his uncle Winston Churchill, Decca to speak on the life of a debutante, while they had Philip down for a lecture on 'Sex life at Oxford University' and 'Arnold Toynbee, Historian, but First and Foremost, Dad'. He ducked out, he said, intimidated by the thought of being

Esmond, Decca and Philip at Waterloo

alone with them for so long, swamped by their overpowering personalities: there is a photograph of him bidding them sad farewell at Waterloo station.

Joining up for war

When war broke out, my father writes, 'I was misguided into proposing myself for a commission in the Brigade of Guards.' He had been levered into the Grenadiers by his father-in-law, a professional soldier – but he was quickly expelled for sliding down banisters naked and drunk, failing inspections and other trouble. 'After my unsuitability had been demonstrated to them, I was transferred to the Intelligence Corps,' again deeply regretted, wishing he'd joined the infantry instead of the 'unrewarding inhumanities of intelligence'. I wish I knew more of his time in the war: I know he learned some Russian and some German, as he used sometimes to stand on a haystack or a farm gate in Suffolk and declaim great rousing Hitlerian or Stalinesque speeches, though my sister whispered he was only counting from one to a hundred.

He was stationed with an infantry regiment in Bridlington on the Yorkshire coast and that is where he last saw Esmond two years later. Esmond had enlisted and served as a navigator with the Canadian air force, which was stationed in Abingdon, Oxfordshire. On leave, he came up to Bridlington to visit my father who writes, 'He was a little ashamed of his commission and explained he had accepted it only because it had been forced on him. He

Philip the soldier

disliked it partly because to wear an officer's uniform was, for him, like parading the mark of the beast, and partly because he was afraid this artificial distinction might be used to separate him from his friends who had remained in the ranks.' Esmond was horrified to find that now they were stationed in Britain they came under RAF regulations, which included no use of Christian names between officers and men: Esmond and his fellow Canadians walked out of the lecture that delivered these very British strict social class separation orders.

Philip took him on a crawl round local Bridlington pubs he had been frequenting, where Esmond was shocked to be reminded of everything he most detested about the English life he had escaped. In those days there was rigid social segregation in pubs between the public bar (cheaper beer) and the saloon bar for classier custom-ers: army regulations said officers were banned from using public bars, with privates and non-commissioned officers barred from the saloon, to prevent fraternizing between the ranks. My father always broke the rule and made public bar friends; it was the same when I was a child: if I was looking for him in pubs he was never to be found in saloon bars. The very act of anyone choos-ing to use a saloon bar warned him of their political proclivities and the likely insufferable conversation of those who chose to pay more to preserve their social status. Later in life, in his own local Brockweir pub on the Gloucestershire/Monmouthshire border, too small for two bars, he joined the working class Buffaloes, an ancient pre-welfare state self-help fraternity like the Odd Fellows, that collected money to help any who fell on hard times. He liked their motto, 'No man is at all times wise.'

That Bridlington evening Esmond regaled my father and his pub friends with imitations of his uncle, Winston Churchill, 'ironic but with genuine admiration'. I have often puzzled over how my parents' generation knuckled under to military life, none more unsuited, I would have thought, than he and Esmond. But everyone did. Anthony Powell's descriptions of his characters' unrecognizably altered lives during the war in his epic *Dance to the Music of Time* gives one of the best accounts of how people of my parents' background adapted to serving in the forces, to discipline, authority, boredom, petty-fogging rules and officious minor tyrants, because that's what saving the country from fascism demanded. 'In spite of opposition to social distinctions of rank... Esmond wasn't "against" the Canadian air force as he had been against public schools and the upper classes. When he passed high-ranking officers he saluted them, although he derided the principle of saluting.' Wartime meant an armistice in the revolution and they shared 'a practical recognition of the irrelevance, in these circumstances, of the old standard of revolt for revolt's sake'.

On this, Esmond's last visit,

he talked freely about the possibility of his own death, his fears and his illogical confidence. He recognised that pilots had to believe that they could survive entirely by their own skill: he himself believed that his skill as a navigator would safeguard him from disaster. He supported this difficult act of faith by a pure superstition: he had improbably survived at Boadilla and therefore, though he knew the chances against his survival at this time were no more than ten to one, he was assured that he would improbably survive again.

That evening in 1941 they stood, drunkenly, on the shingle of Bridlington beach watching bombers fly over the town on their way out to sea.

'Two days later a friend of mine in the officers' mess at Bridlington gently showed me the paragraph which announced "a nephew of the prime minister was missing from a raid over Hamburg."' Esmond left behind Decca with a baby, alone in America, where she lived for the rest of her life – and he left forever a profound sense of loss

Decca and Esmond

among all his friends. What would have become of him, what would he have done, how would his remarkable life have rolled out over another half century? Could he have held onto his optimistic faith in the inevitability of socialism?

My father by then had married my mother, Anne Powell.

8

My Mother Anne

IN THE BEGINNING I owe my existence to the word 'puzzled', or so my father said. I use it quite often, rolling it around on the page, enjoying the way its shape and sound sit in a sentence. We were on the train from Liverpool Street on one of the Cob Cottage Fridays when we went home with him every other weekend. We always ran for that train, clutching our attaché cases and comics and we were always early. My father had a life-long recurring nightmare about missed trains so we always ran for them in a panic and we were always at least half an hour too soon, sitting on our cases watching the steam engines letting off their billowing clouds of smoke and black coal smuts up into the great glass roof of the station.

On the train we sat, as always, in the bar where he had his 'train friends', regulars who drank together commuting home each evening, chummy, beery, joshing, loud, reactionary 'train friends' who made our hearts sink as we pulled out of Liverpool Street, past the gigantic enamel advertisement for Virol. We tried to persuade him to sit anywhere else except the bar, with its battered and stained railway wood panelling and its reek of smoke and beer. But it was always the bar, same seat, same train, same commuter 'friends', some getting out at Chelmsford, some at Marks Tey. On this particular Friday evening he was talking to us, not to them for once. He was reminiscing into his beer, telling us about marrying our mother. He said: I was a bit drunk when I proposed, just a bit one over the eight. So next morning I went round to see Anne and I said, Look, it's impossible. How can we? I have no money, no proper job, no prospects, how would we live together? We'd better forget it. Do you mind most awfully? Anne looked at me and she just said, 'Well, I'm puzzled.' That was all she said. It was that one word, 'puzzled', that got me. I said, Oh to hell with everything, I love you, let's get married!

And so they did.

Philip and Anne

* * *

Who had he married, when she bowled him over with that one word 'puzzled'? My bold mother Anne wasn't a good chooser, or not in worldly or conventional terms, not if she was looking for a stable provider, a solid stayer. But that wasn't her. She chose two utterly different husbands, both dangerous, but with these qualities in common: their riskiness, their enthusiasms, their intellectual fervour and their unpredictable aura of thrill. Never dull. My father, the writer and journalist, my stepfather, the philosophy professor and aesthete, were, of course, both strongly of the left, anything else unthinkable. Both were troublesome to me in their very different ways but I wouldn't be without the outlandishness of either in my childhood.

My mother was only eighteen so Philip and Anne needed her parents' consent. What on earth made blustery Colonel Powell agree? Nothing about my father can have looked like a good prospect, not even a middling prospect. He was quite transparently bad news, you would have thought, but they reckoned he'd be killed shortly in the forthcoming war and so they agreed to let them have a little married time together before he would be gone forever, like so many in their own generation. The Colonel had fought in the trenches of the previous war and he assumed that even more young men would be massacred this time round; the machinery of death with bombs and gas had been honed to perfection over the last twenty years. So they said yes, and what's more, they would give my mother some money. How much? I don't know, but enough to make my father's meagre and intermittent Grub Street earnings stretch to renting a flat and hiring a cleaner. Besides, said my mother, her parents liked Philip. Everyone liked Philip. He was warm and affectionate, and it helped that he liked her parents and he made them laugh, all of which are winning attributes in sons-in-law. When they reckoned he wouldn't be alive long enough to worry about his future finances or the longevity of his liver, they miscalculated. My father's military ineptitude ensured he never saw active service, never came within distant earshot of gunfire, just like Arnold before him, who never even got as far as joining up, let alone fighting in the First World War, to his shame for the rest of his life.

Debutante hell

Anne in Sussex Square

My mother Anne had just completed the season as a debutante. She came out, had a ball at Claridge's, was presented to the King in white gloves and ostrich feathers and detested every moment of it, as did her perverse mother. Every day of the season from Easter to the August start of grouse shooting there was an arranged lunch, tea, dinner and ball, with Henley, Ascot, Goodwood, the Oxford and Cambridge boat race and all the rest of it. This was the marriage market for a narrow circle of girls and young men approved from official lists exchanged between mothers, chaperones and duennas, also obliged to attend every one of these events to guard their charges. Before the season began Anne was taken by her mother to Paris to have dresses and ball gowns made for her: you could not be seen in the same dress often, nor the same dress as anyone else, and the fashion houses kept lists to make sure no one bought identical clothes. My mother told of sitting in the private showrooms of the grand dress-makers – Molyneux she remembered, pronounced by the English upper classes as Mullynukes – where a personal *vendeuse* would model the clothes one by one, to be ordered in the size and fabric to suit. The cost of this gigantic new wardrobe was, she said, staggering. To her discomfort, Coming Out meant being assigned a lady's maid of her own to look after the clothes, and to wait up till all hours to undress her. My mother found her presence so disconcerting she kept sending her away, letting her off for the night, to the irritation of the housekeeper.

My grandmother Barbara found the season and the marriage trade as tedious as did her daughter, but in that milieu, it was *comme il faut*. She wouldn't have known what else to do with her two daughters, although it cannot have been a habit for long in her less than aristocratic brewing family. Barbara was a first generation debutante, from parvenus briefly on the up. Her family, the Pryors, were trade, a branch of the brewers of Truman's beers, hardly blue bloods. But the English upper class has thrived over the centuries by assimilating new money into its ranks, wiping clean inconvenient humble origins in a trice. In Spain the aristocracy was forbidden by the court from marrying anyone but those of the lineage of their own kind and forbidden to work, which helped hasten their decline in the seventeenth century, in-bred and impoverished, barred from necessary cash transfusions from the up and coming. The British aristocracy always kept a canny eye on the main chance.

Her mother Barbara

Barbara, tall, auburn-haired, ram-rod backed and slender as a bean pole in her many patterned tea-gowns, smoking sixty cigarettes a day, playing bridge every evening with friends with names like Binky and Poots. That's as much as I can remember as she died of a sudden stroke caused by smoking when I was six. Before the war they lived in a colossal house in Hyde Park Gardens, the same street overlooking Hyde Park where the Churchills lived, with a panoply of servants from chauffeur and butler to cook and maids. Barbara was a Catholic, a faith inherited from her French mother, and she sent my mother to day school at the Convent of the Holy Child in Cavendish Square. By chance, it's a building I often visit as the old nunnery is now

Barbara

home to the health think-tank, the King's Fund, so I look up at its Jacob Epstein figure of Madonna and child over the entrance and think about my mother going to school each day through that same archway. But my grandmother was a rebellious Catholic and on many Sundays she would march her daughters furiously out of the church, bristling with disapproval of ultra-conservative sermons. Once her children grew up, she stopped going to church at all.

So far, so conventional, but my older cousin Emma Tennant, the writer and novelist, who remembered her well, wrote in her obituary of my mother for the *Guardian* that Barbara joined the Communist Party in the 1930s and was an ardent member of Victor Gollancz's Left Book Club, whose yellow-jacketed books littered the house. How oddly that sits with the Paris fittings for Molyneux dresses. I suspect Emma embellished the story by making her an actual communist, but even so, why on earth would a left-winger marry my grandfather Colonel Powell? That perplexed my mother, who detested her father.

Colonel George No Name

The Colonel was a Conservative to the core, even briefly an MP for Southwark South-East in the 1931 National Government when any idiot could be elected even in this solid Labour seat. In that landslide Great Depression election 430 Tories won seats so they must have scraped

The Colonel

the bottom of the barrel for candidates. My mother remembered, with some embarrassment, that he had taken her, aged ten, on an election parade down the Walworth Road, she wearing a smart emerald green matching coat and hat, leading a dachshund sporting a 'Vote Colonel Powell' tartan coat. The Colonel was, not surprisingly, removed at the next election when the seat returned to its rightful Labour owners. He had not, as far as I can see, ever spoken at all in the Commons: no doubt with 429 others on his side of the House, it was hard for him to catch the Speaker's eye. If he had, I doubt he would have had anything much to say.

Pause here for Roy Jenkins' social class

An odd quirk in Roy Jenkins' capacious mind was an ability to remember, it seems, every MP ever elected since the dawn of time, the way other people learn cricket scores from *Wisden* or football teams back to the invention of the game. I was taken aback once when he suddenly said to me, 'Your grandfather, Colonel Powell, Tory MP 1931 to '35, Southwark South-East, wasn't he? Grenadier Guards, I think?' I was frankly ashamed to confess that I had this ex-Tory MP as a close relative, something I had conveniently forgotten all about.

But this polymath, Bletchley code-breaker, bon viveur, biographer and beacon of civilization, Roy Jenkins himself makes a fascinating study of class-consciousness, both his own, and other people's view of him. He is one of the politicians of my lifetime I most admire – I chose him for my contribution to Radio 4's *Great Lives* programme.

The social reforms he steered through Labour cabinets as Chancellor and Home Secretary made more radical change to people's lives and public attitudes than any other single political figure. Against the instincts of most in a socially conservative Labour cabinet, he ushered in reforms to permit abortion, divorce and LGBT rights, and the abolition of birching, theatre censorship and capital punishment, one man causing that heroic advance in tolerance and freedom. He is famous for saying, 'The permissive society is the civilized society', which like so many other famous sayings he may not quite have said, but certainly meant.

As for his class, he was brought up in South Wales, son of a National Union of Mineworkers official who later became Pontypool's MP and Clement Attlee's Parliamentary Private Secretary in 1945. His family were upwardly mobile, as they had a servant, not quite working class enough for some in the Labour Welsh valleys, as Roy rose from grammar school to Balliol College, taking that well-worn path from an Oxford PPE degree to MP. By the time I knew him he seemed immensely grand, orotund in speech, though with the same Germanic rolling R's as Colonel Powell and an acidly sharp wit. His taste for cigars, claret and duchesses was much mocked: the first Tory poster attacking the Social Democratic Party, the idea for which he was the originator, featured a row of claret bottles as an insult to him. Though so clever himself, I wonder if he was oddly glamorized by quite stupid smart people because of his own relatively humble origins. Some said his father had aspirations: when he went to prison briefly for actions in the General Strike, the family were so ashamed it was kept a dark secret, not vaunted as a badge of pride.

Roy's distaste for the dictatorship of democracy came from his many skirmishes with Labour's Bennite left that sought manipulation of every lever of power by claiming superior democratic legitimacy. When I was elected to the National Committee of the new SDP, founded from a Labour Party split by the departing Gang of Four – Roy Jenkins, Shirley Williams, David Owen and Bill Rodgers – in 1981, there was an instant divide between Jenkinsites and Owenites that began with its very first constitutional issue on that question of democracy: should the leader be elected by OMOV, one-man-one-vote, of all members (Owenites), or only by the very small band of twenty-nine SDP MPs (Jenkinsites)? Like all parties, this one was split into those two factions right from the start, but although I was strongly of the Owenite tendency – he was for women's quotas for selecting candidates and committees while Jenkins was a poor party leader – Roy Jenkins stands out as one of the most admirable progressive figures of our time, and he remained a friend. But there's no doubt notions of class held him back: his assumption of slightly comical upper class manners and voice and his taste for upper class company was a drag anchor on his reputation and his political fortunes in the world of Labour and the liberal-social democratic left.

Barbara and George again

Back to my maternal grandparents: what was left-wing Barbara doing marrying a dull colonel of such a different political and intellectual bent? She had the money, the intelligence and the looks, so what did he bring to the party? My mother often wondered that but never dared ask her. It's just possible that his experiences in the First World War may have damaged him in ways that meant my mother never knew the better man he may have been when her mother married him.

The Second World War was liberating in unexpected ways to all manner of people if they wanted to be liberated, including some women in the upper classes. While some simply moaned about the servant problem and sulked at what they feared (wrongly) to be the passing of the *ancien régime* – for others like Barbara, the war opened new doors. She did not, like most of her class, take to committee and charity work, bossing others around, organizing things and making an officious nuisance of herself. Instead when war broke out she chose of her own accord to work in a munitions factory somewhere in the far western outskirts of London, rising early to catch the dawn bus, puffing away at cigarettes on the top deck, her hair wrapped up in a bright 1940s Rosie-the-Riveter style turban. She used to bring back occasional small parts and widgets to explain to my mother what it was she was making: she was not compelled to do war work, but she loved the factory and, never having worked before, was proud of her pay packet: a wage of one's own is even more liberating than Virginia Woolf's room of one's own. Their gigantic house in Hyde Park Gardens was abandoned and sold when war broke out and Barbara and George moved to a flat. Their servants were commandeered for war duties and the car was put up on bricks with no petrol. Abruptly their whole way of life was dismantled in less than a year: only a year earlier she had been bringing out my mother, her younger daughter, in the last London season before the war. I don't know why their money dwindled considerably, perhaps just spent or gambled, but they never lived such a grand life again after 1945.

Within every social class there are finely graded sub-divisions. My mother was not high in the pecking order of debutantes: not only was her mother from the brewing trade, but her father's ancestry was a mystery, a blank. Lieutenant Colonel Evelyn George Harcourt Powell, known as George, had all the trappings of upper-classness – except money or a proper birth certificate. How he came by the name Powell, who his father was, no one knows. He and his elder brother Harcourt went to Eton and into the Grenadier Guards, but who paid and with what? They only had a short birth certificate with just their mother Lily Powell's name, a scandalous rarity in those days, as indeed it remained a mark of illegitimacy right up to the 1970s. The secret was a 'guardian' who sponsored them, an unknown benefactor who was probably their real father. My cousin the Hon. Emma Tennant pretended to think the 'guardian' we presume to be their father must be royalty: Lily must have been one of Edward VII's mistresses, she said, and she tried to dig into Lily's past, but without success. That would make George a fitz-royal, and us bastard royalty too, she claimed, but I laughed at the absurdity. That is the commonest fantasy for every family born the wrong side of the blanket. Whatever the truth of his parentage, as a child I always thought the Colonel was German because he rolled his R's with a thundering Germanic gurgle at the back of his throat, though he talked proudly of our Welsh origins, and the name Powell being Welsh – without telling anyone how he acquired that name. His face was as round and bloodshot red as Colonel Blimp's and he walked with a silver-headed cane and played canasta when he came to our house. That was my child's eye view – for what it's worth, which frankly isn't much.

How odd that the Colonel went through life without his children ever asking about his father or his childhood, but so many families are stuffed with rich secrets never spoken. One thing was plain, he had no money, and a Guards officer's pay couldn't even cover the cost of his tailor-made uniforms required for every occasion and every colonial climate. He certainly couldn't pay his mess bills and keep up the style expected of a gambling, racing, London club man, bowler-hatted at all times in civvies and cashiered if ever falling seriously into debt, unless he had a Pater to pay up. Marrying money was essential, so marrying rich and clever Barbara was the only intelligent thing he ever did. Barbara's beer money kept him in the unsustainable manner to which he had been brought up, unfit for work of any kind. Once out of the army in the late 1920s, only his brief spell in parliament could count as work.

His elder brother did the other thing – married a dancing girl and the story goes that he was struck out of decent society forever more, condemned to a French demi-monde in Le Touquet. My mother only heard of him when she was grown up, and then she was shocked at her father's social ostracism of his only brother on account of no more than a bad marriage. No doubt the simple fact of penury was enough to sink brother Harcourt out of sight. Maybe George didn't want to be touched for a handout by his brother, and so his exaggerated moral disapproval of the dancing girl may have been financially convenient. There but for Barbara's money go I, George may have thought, as he cut his brother adrift.

The Second World War was certainly not liberating for George: my mother was full of stories of his piggish selfishness, which was, she said, typical in many families in the war. The Colonel would commandeer the household's small butter, egg and meat rations as a droit de seigneur, saying men needed to keep their strength up. Incidentally, my mother used to tell many stories of people's bad behaviour in the war. She used to say the war was a great eye-opener on character, revealing some people's unexpected generosity and other people's meanness over rations. Some stood by a firm moral refusal to use the black market, while others eagerly profited from it. Some friends proved uncharacteristically brave, but others surprisingly cowardly. She gave one example of a dinner she and my father had with Cyril Connolly, the literary critic, and his wife: when an air raid struck, Connolly plunged straight into the only safe place of shelter, abandoning his wife and friends. Afterwards, heaving his large frame out of the small cupboard under the stairs he apologized with the quip, 'Perfect fear casteth out love,' neatly reversing the biblical sentiment, which almost made his behaviour forgivable.

Shame in the trenches

Before we consign Colonel Powell to the oblivion where he belongs, my father used to tell one story about him that might soften my view of him. He was a professional soldier, straight into the Grenadier Guards from Eton. (He often had us parading round the room singing the Grenadiers' regimental song, 'Some talk of Alexander, and some of

Hercules... With a tow-row-row-row row-row for the British Grenadiers!') But in the first war his career was blighted.

He never quite recovered from being buried alive in a trench after an explosion, lost for over a day and nearly suffocated until he was dug out by his batman, the odd name for an officer's servant. He emerged with severe shell shock and had to be invalided out for a while. He went back to the front, but at some big battle, I wish I knew which, when the whistles blew and every officer should have waved his pistol and led his men up the ladders and over the top, he refused. Either he couldn't or he wouldn't, but he didn't and so his company lived to die another day when all around them men were mown down. My father, generous-spirited, says George told him it was not cowardice but he was overcome by horror at the carnage and he would not lead his men to their certain and futile deaths. He was not court-martialled; it was hushed up and he stayed in the regiment, where after the war he was comfortably posted to Windsor where they lived until the late 1920s. Officially, nothing more was said about his failure to fight.

Except, so my father said, for what was murmured in the Guards Club of an afternoon. The Colonel went to the club at Hyde Park Corner most days to play cards, which, being not excessively bright, he played very badly and lost sizeable sums after a bottle of claret at lunch. But if, by chance, once in a while he started to win anything approaching what he lost most days, the other officers would start to whisper the name of that battle around the table, louder and louder, until George had to put down his cards and slide away in shame.

So my soldier grandfather emerged as shamed by the First World War that he had fought in as was my other grandfather Arnold, who had ducked military service altogether with a spurious sick note, leaving him forever tormented by the deaths of friends who took his place.

Wartime honeymoon, saved by a French hat

How did my so well-chaperoned mother meet my disreputable father towards the end of her coming-out season? He gatecrashed a debutante ball, smuggled in by a friend, Ivan Moffat, a fellow communist and later a Hollywood screenwriter. That's how my mother met him, as he stood out tall, rumpled and comical, the plainly unsuitable one in this sea of suitable but unspeakable young men. Of course, he was in and out of that upper class scene from his Oxford connections and his friendship with the grand old liberal world, his brother Lawrence marrying an Asquith and his own lost love for a Bonham Carter, even while under strict orders from his Communist Party martinets.

They were married in 1939 in September just after the war had begun, a quiet Paddington register office event with no nonsense, she in a hat and fur coat made of skunk, a fashionable badger-striped luscious fur we played with all our childhood, dressing up as wild animals. In the one and only wedding photograph taken by the *Yorkshire Post*, Philip's hair is uncharacteristically smarmed down with Brylcreem, though nothing else about his lumpy nose or craggy face could ever quite look smooth. Goodness knows why – they both looked back on it with incredulity – they decided to take a late honeymoon in Paris towards the end of May 1940. In the Café de Flore they spent time

My parents' wedding day, 1939

with old friends and new, including Giacometti, Tristan Tzara, the Dada impresario, and Donald Maclean, among other artists and writers. They had set out in what was then the phoney war, confident the Maginot line would hold: they were not alone in this act of insanity, when many others were snatching French holidays. But the Maginot line didn't hold and suddenly German tanks were rolling through the Ardennes towards Paris. Trains and boats to escape were full and the price of rare tickets was exorbitantly beyond what little cash they still had left. I imagine scenes of panic as described by Thackeray in *Vanity Fair* in Brussels on the day of Waterloo, frantic people bargaining for horses with the price of carriages sky-high, the grandest on their knees to grooms, their dukedoms for a horse.

My mother thought she remembered that her mother had some money in a French bank, an account she had kept for paying for all those now useless Paris ball gowns the year before. Perching a small and elegant hat with a veil on the side of her head with a pearl hat-pin, Anne called on the bank manager. In her perfect French – she had spent a year in France when she was sixteen – she begged him to give her the money, though she had no chequebook nor proof that she was her mother's daughter. *Prenez, prenez tout!* he said with a shrug and a smile. Otherwise the Germans will take it all, so why not give it to my pretty young lady in her fine hat? And he handed over enough francs to buy them tickets on the last boat out of Saint-Malo to Southampton before Paris fell. And so that money saved them when many others were trapped. I still have that crumpled hat in the children's dressing up box.

On their return, my father rejoined his army unit, and my mother went back to her job in the fire service where she worked as a switchboard operator. She slept in metal bunk beds through the long nights between shifts, barked at by an overbearing senior fire officer but relishing such indisputably useful work and the company of the other women as they answered calls and summoned out the fire engines in the Blitz. Later she worked as a barmaid serving beer to De Gaulle's Free French army.

How we left-wing middle classes hate the sound of our own voice

So what does all this say of any use about the nature of class? Setting out on these explorations of my own family,

I am suddenly less certain that they offer a useful social story. Except, go back to where I began and everyone I ask has a family story to tell that is always a tale of class, of social rises and falls and of nice distinctions. No story makes sense without admitting the importance of money, the having and the not having of it. Class and money are at the heart of everything, the context for everything, wherever a family perches on the social spectrum. My mother broke free of a social milieu on which her parents only had a tenuous hold, by marrying two unconventional men, both intellectuals, both emotionally difficult, neither with a penny to their name. Yet whatever choices we make, we are never quite free of our background and our upbringing. Certain emblems remain: she would never ever wear any scent that wasn't French nor touch custard or mayonnaise that was not homemade.

Despite our own ineradicably middle class habits and voices, she also bred in us an aversion to all such social class presumptions, the braying voices, the rudeness to servants or waiters, the snobbery, or the use of mock cockney accents to imply the stupidity of the working classes. In the year she was a debutante *Me and My Girl* was the hit show in the West End: she shuddered with distaste at the spectacle of drunken debs and their partners, towards the end of late night balls, lining up to sing the musical's hit song 'The Lambeth Walk' in fake cockney accents in their ball gowns and dinner jackets, ending with 'Oy!' and cocking a thumb. Being a posh left-winger is a tricky business, walking across a minefield every step of the way. It often means revulsion for those who may look and sound like your own kind, but who are most definitely of the opposite political tribe. So when we had coffee in the café at Peter Jones or went to the theatre, we would listen to the unabashed loudness of upper class accents opining for all to hear, broadcasting their awful views, with a very particular abhorrence of being mistaken for one of their ilk. My mother had an ear so finely tuned to snobbery that she would wince or snap very easily at those expressing casually obnoxious views.

She had a particular loathing for Nancy Mitford's elaborate classifications for what was U (upper class) and Non-U (vulgar or lower class), a confection of snobbery that became a great publishing sensation in 1956 in her collection *Noblesse Oblige: An Enquiry into the Identifiable Characteristics of the English Aristocracy*. Give the English half a chance and they relish defining the verbal and behavioural tics that mark out their secret social class codes, so hard for outsiders to break into because they are nonsensical.

This work by the Hon. Nancy Mitford, eldest of the famous five Hon. Mitford sisters, author of mildly comic novels about eccentric upper class families the model of her own, became a bestseller. Her sister Decca, who had fled all that by living in America, chose to remain true to herself with no pretences: for all her life she never changed a scintilla of the modulations of her extraordinarily exaggerated and by then old-fashioned, cut-glass upper class accent.

As for that particular brand of condescension to the lower middle classes, my mother also detested John Betjeman's 'How to Get on in Society' satire on lower middle class gentility, which my sister once recited because she thought it was funny, before she was sharply corrected and told it was pure snobbery.

Phone for the fish knives, Norman
As cook is a little unnerved;
You kiddies have crumpled the serviettes
And I must have things daintily served.

My mother was easy to tease, willingly laughing at her own class sensitivities. My brother once said as a joke, 'Mum would never say toilet, she'd think it was common.' I teased back, 'Nonsense! She'd think it even more common to use the word "common" or even to think that anything or anyone could ever be "common".' And she had to laugh at the truth of the contortions needed to avoid being mistaken for the most repellent members of our own social class, angels on pins, treading along a tight-rope, hating the snobs who mocked what they considered to be lower middle class habits. Her own escapes from our class included working as a school bus driver for many years, and as a volunteer for charities getting extra money to the poorest families in crisis in West London.

Much more than this about my dearly loved mother you may not get, only glimpses of this kind here and there in the story, for I miss her so much and her presence is so ever-present, so much a part of myself, that I find I am no more capable of capturing and shrinking her into a few neat lines of crisp definition than I am of describing myself. I see her in a gesture I make, in a way of clicking my tongue when concentrating, in how I roll out pastry or wash clothes by hand, in a sideways glance at my reflection in a shop window when my half-glimpsed face gives me a momentary flash of her expression. I hear her in quaint phrases of hers that fall unexpectedly out of my mouth and I sense

her in the many possessions of hers around my house. Since her death and my father's, with my stepfather, step-mother and my older sister all dead, there is no one left to remember lost times, events and places. My dear twin half-brothers, my mother's sons, are six years younger so they don't remember some things. My other younger three half-siblings, Philip and Sally's children, I share fewer memories with. Besides, each one of us will view the same events through wildly different lenses, so all we can do is recount what we think we know, as best we can.

Philip and Polly at Cob Cottage

9

Philip the Father

MY BATTERED OLD pram in khaki paint was rattling along down the hill, my hands gripping the sides as Josephine ran along behind laughing. 'Look, no hands!' said my father and he let go. The pram hurtled on, bouncing over stones with him chasing after, but no chance of catching the handlebar before it tipped up into the ditch, propelling me out onto my head. I screamed and yelled, as I always did. They picked me up and patched me up, tried to pull my woolly bonnet over the bump on my forehead so my mother wouldn't notice and sang songs all the way home to cheer me up. But as soon as I saw my mother I started howling all over again, 'Papa bump! Papa bump!' My sister and my father looked at me outraged at my betrayal and Josephine gave me a pinch. Do I really remember? I think I do, I think it's my first memory and my father used to swear those were my first words, but perhaps it's only a collective memory, told and retold. I feel its resonance because my father and my sister were the wild ones, the brave and the daring, while I was the weakling, the cry-baby, the snitch and the tell-tale.

That was the lane from Yafford, the house in the village of Shorewell on the Isle of Wight where I was born in the famously bitter winter of 1946–7, when the doctor who came to deliver me had to be brought by the local farmer on his tractor through snowdrifts that rose higher than the first floor windows and lasted until March. My mother worried I'd never survive the freezing nights with one weak bar of a post-war rationed electric fire. But then she thought I'd never survive the pregnancy, when her rows with my father were so ferocious, loud and unceasing that she thought I was bound to be scarred by what I had heard from within. But I was robust and placid as second children often are. It was Josephine, four years older than me, who took the full force of the tempestuous ending to their marriage. My arrival was forever linked in her mind with those rows that led to the later divorce, as if I were the cause. Her golden era, her paradise lost was the four years before I was born, remembered or misremembered, but never the same again and I was to blame. Her annoyance with me did me no harm, trotting along behind her, hoping she might once in a while play with me, but I let her take the brunt of whatever came our way. And she did, brunt after brunt, as eldest children do, making her own trouble for herself as she went. As soon as I was old enough to think about it, I was glad of the divorce. I had been lucky to escape Philip as a full-time father, better by far to have him as a fascinating, dangerous, difficult and – mostly but not always – enjoyable and loveable part-time parent.

What were our parents doing renting that draughty old house on the Isle of Wight towards the end of the war? J.B. Priestley was living nearby and he was something of a mentor to my father who by then had published two novels. Somehow he had persuaded my parents of the charm of the island. They were escaping from London bombs perhaps, but more urgent was the need to avoid London life where my father was always drunk. From then on he recognized he was only sober in the country where he could write in peace – so long as he stayed away from company. The width of the Solent would keep him from trouble, that was the idea. But he would be off on the ferry, leaving my mother alone for long stretches in the cold house, far from friends and family. He'd be away to London to earn money writing articles, drinking and carousing, notorious for it, creeping back shame-faced and pitifully hung-over 'like an old Tom cat', my mother used to say, to confess abjectly to all his sins, including plentiful unfaithfulness with whoever he could lay hands on. Worse still, he would arrive with a flotilla of assorted friends or recent pub pals, expecting to be fed and catered for in those rationed days of an austerity more severe than during the war itself. That's what their rows were about.

Philip and Anne with Josephine and me at Yafford

Tall, rangy, shambolic-looking, a rumpled and pock-marked Gary Cooper, as Decca Mitford described him in *Faces of Philip*, the memoir she wrote about him after his death. Philip was exciting, frightening, funny, frolicking, fearless and a fearful father. Writer, literary critic, campaigner, he tended towards the extreme in everything he did, with new passions taken up, new causes espoused, projects for personal improvement – or, far worse, projects for the improvement of members of his family. He wrangled perpetually with inner demons that finally conspired to sink him for many years into the depths of the darkest depressions. His child-like qualities made him a great companion to his children, the wild inventor of extraordinary games and adventures, inhabiting stories that lasted for years. Hours spent stalking in the woods to capture each other's flags were both petrifying and the best of wild games. Ponham was his mythic world of threat and promise, ruled over by a frightening woman of that name, with a shark pond and dangerous bad boys called the Disobedients. He invented Ponham stories as a child for his elder brother Tony, who in turn tried to invent one back, a place he called Doncaster: Philip was furious when he discovered it was a real place. For us, my father reinvented Ponham. Barley was the good man, but unpredictable. We could be marching along a Suffolk lane holding hands with Barley, but watching his face carefully all the time: at any minute his lips would curl and twitch, transformed in a flash into Ponham and we would run away in terror. Fascinating and terrifying, at least to me, the cry-baby, I both adored and feared him. Imagine having Just William as a father, with all its perils and delights, exhilarating and

Philip

unpredictable. Deadly serious some of the time – in his intellectual life, in his writing, literary reviews, political passions – but Just William as well.

I had bad nightmares staying in Cob Cottage, no great surprise: he used to tell me a story in the dark at bedtime, say goodnight and shut the door. But after a while, lying stiff in my bed, I would hear breathing and ghost groans from the cupboard: he hadn't shut the door or left the room at all but had crept into the wardrobe. Sometimes he hid in another cupboard under the beams wearing an old cowled grey dressing gown, pretending to be an ancient long-forgotten aunt.

Sometimes, as the house was small, I slept on a mattress on the floor in a corridor and I had a horror rats would come in the night and climb on my face. His teasing plan to keep the rats off the bed was to build a staircase of books beside my pillow that led to the top of an enamel bucket with a piece of cheese in the bottom. 'Don't worry, any rats will climb the stairs to get the cheese and fall in the bucket.' I lay there in terror listening for the pitter-patter of rat feet up the staircase of books, waiting for the loud drop into the bucket that never came. Cruelty? A friend reading this said it was 'abusive', but if so, it wasn't intentional aggression or bullying, just his boyish idea of fun. I was often terrified of staying in that house, dreading the dark and the night, but although my mother begged him not to frighten me, being fearless himself, he couldn't quite take my night-time terrors seriously.

Other reasons to be afraid in Suffolk included any walk that veered anywhere near Colquhoun and MacBryde, real life evil spirits. In a cottage with a creaking lean-to studio, these two painters, the two Roberts, were drinking themselves into paralysis, both past the brief peak of their post-Cubist fame. I would try to rush my father past, or tiptoe by whispering shh, but all too often their studio door was hanging open and they would lurch out. The wolfish, lantern-jawed Colquhoun, rude, violent and sneering, would make a push and a shove to drag Philip in for a drink. Mostly, but not always, my father resisted, but it always meant a long harangue and an aggressive argument, slurred abuse and sometimes a grab at me in a not quite mock-playful knocking about. They were the dregs of Fitzrovia, Fitzroy Tavern, French pub, Colony Room, Gargoyle club and Queen's Elm in the Fulham Road, that well-worn writers' and artists' pub crawl, inhabited by

Francis Bacon, Lucian Freud, John Minton and scores more. But these Roberts were among the casualties, the ones who didn't survive that hard-drinking life. By now they were barely painting but rowing with anyone they could find.

I spent enough of my early, barely grown-up years in those same haunts, daunted by Muriel Belcher on her high bar stool, intimidated by Jeffrey Bernard in a bad mood at the Coach & Horses, fascinated by the satanic darkness of Lucian Freud. I baby-sat for the ferocious Henrietta Moraes's outrageously badly behaved children in the Chelsea studio where Minton had hanged himself. My time in that world was when I lived briefly before university with Johnny Moynihan, son of painter Rodrigo Moynihan who, Johnny claimed, had fleetingly been my mother's lover. But Johnny, who took me to 1966 World Cup matches, really only impressed me because he had been married to the admirable, exotic, elfinly beautiful Diana, who had since married writer, art critic and jazz singer George Melly. In this short detour around my brief teenage encounters with the tail end of my father's Fitzrovia world, I have to say I was emotionally inoculated against it by my early phobia for blind drunkenness. My father was bad enough, but Colquhoun and MacBryde were in another league.

As for my father, typical was the time we ran out of petrol – or we might not have run out of petrol – in the old Ford Popular with its one windscreen wiper and a crank handle to get it started. On the journey across Suffolk my stepmother Sally had kept saying, 'Philip, we need to stop for petrol,' and he kept saying, 'Don't worry, we'll get there.' 'Then go slower, so we use less petrol,' and he would say, 'No, we'll go faster to get there before the petrol runs out!' until the car ground to a halt. 'It's NOT the petrol!' he said crossly, starting to turn the crank. 'Yes it is!' she said. 'No it's not, I'll show you!' and he took out his matches and held one over the open petrol tank to show her there was still some in, while we screamed in the back of the car, my stepmother too. But there wasn't any petrol, so we didn't get blown to pieces.

Or the day out in Cambridge. He was heading for E.M. Forster's seventy-fifth birthday feast at King's College, taking along Josephine and me to be left free for a Cambridge day, with pocket money for chips, Vimto and a trip to the cinema on our own. Checking on Forster's birth date, I must have been seven and Josephine eleven. The day began so well, singing all the way, my father in the highest spirits and his musical voice mellow and fine. He would sing 'Wobbly' songs from American trade unionism, our best one inducing loud shouting and giggles:

> *Alleluyah I'm a bum,*
> *Alleluyah bum again,*
> *Alleluyah give us a hand-out*
> *To revive us again.*

Or that parody of a Salvation Army hymn,

> *You will eat, you will eat, by and by,*
> *In that glorious land above the sky.*
> *Work and pray,*
> *Live on hay,*
> *You'll get pie in the sky when you die*

and we bellowed out, 'It's a lie!'

There was the runaway slave song, 'Down in the Cane Break', there was 'The Red Flag', and 'The Internationale' in French:

C'est la lutte finale
Groupons-nous, et demain
L'Internationale
Sera le genre humain.

The saddest song that still brings tears to my eyes tells of an old Southern couple come to the railway station to collect their Confederate boy's coffin.

Don't handle it so roughly, boys,
For that's our darling Jack.
He left us just as you are now
Look how he's coming back.

Other songs he chose to suit his good voice, 'Blow the Wind Southerly' and 'I Know Where I'm Going', both from his Kathleen Ferrier 78 record, played on the old wind-up gramophone, as Cob Cottage for some years had no electricity. There was always 'Waltzing Matilda', for his Australian heritage, romantically casting himself as the jolly swagman with his tucker bag.

Bowling through the Suffolk countryside, we played games and whooped it up. In Cambridge we waved to him as he departed through the gateway of King's College, free for a day to do as we liked, Josephine cheerful and willing to tolerate my company. On some days she would make me walk several paces behind so she could pretend I wasn't with her, but not today. I remember the film we saw, memorable partly because we rarely saw films and partly because it was like us. *Little Fugitive* was about a boy called Joey who runs away after his big brother plays dead, tricking Joey into thinking he has committed fratricide. When we came out of the cinema it was cold and dark, a January late afternoon, and we hurried along back to King's. But there was no sign of our father. We hung around a long time by the gatehouse until plucking up courage to enter the forbidding porters' lodge. The irritable porter looked down at us and said he'd never heard of him, had no idea, and went back to reading his paper.

We waited and waited in the street outside, stamping our feet in the biting Cambridge east wind. At last, there he was, heading our way across the great expanse of the mighty front court, but our hearts sank. He was zigzagging along, stumbling as he went. When he was drunk, he was a stage-drunk, glassy-eyed, twinkling with a daft smile and you could almost see the cartoonist's stars circling above his head. If he wasn't your father, you might think it was funny, as he was an affectionate and affable drunk, not the violent quarrelsome type. No problem, no problem at all, he said, fumbling for his car keys in his raincoat pocket. Everything's fine, just fine. It took time to find the car, time to open the door and time to get the keys into the ignition. Then time to climb out again, find the crank handle, fit the handle into the hole in the radiator and even longer to kick the engine into life. Josephine and I huddled freezing in the back of the heaterless car.

Then up came kindly Angus Wilson and his life-long partner, Tony Garrett, who had been at the Forster feast too, also heading back to Suffolk, they to their Bury St

Edmunds home and we to the remote hamlet of Lindsey. Philip, don't drive, they said. Please don't drive. Come with us, or one of us will drive your car, please. But drunks don't listen to reason so off we went, his foot down at a whistling pace, or as fast as an old Ford Pop will go in the rain with only one windscreen wiper. As seen from crouching on the floor in the back, the car veered from side to side of the road, telegraph poles looming up in the headlights to right, then left, hedges and ditches clunked into, verges bumped over, farm gates grazed, houses rising up out of nowhere in the dark, and me whimpering wretchedly. I knew it was serious because Josephine was for once terrified too, huddling down and clutching me, whispering, 'Shh, you'll put him off his concentration.' Judder, judder, bump, bang, splutter, until finally the car stopped in the middle of the road. Out of petrol. And then up behind came the headlights of Angus and Tony's car. They had followed us all the way, expecting to scrape our bodies off the road. Instead they took us home with them to Bury St Edmunds for the night. Of course I sneaked on him to my mother when we came home to London, Josephine kicking me under the table and shaking her head angrily at me. Our outraged mother went straight to the telephone to shout at Papa and ask our stepmother Sally how on earth she could ever have let him drive us to a feast when of course he would get drunk?

Divorce and after

My parents' divorce was oddly amicable, staying friends for life. Twice a week my father came to tea with us in

Pelham Crescent, for an hour between his *Observer* office in Tudor Street, Blackfriars, and the Liverpool Street train back to Colchester. My mother always had crumpets and Gentleman's Relish anchovy paste for him. There would be games and jokes with Josephine and me, but we knew he'd really come to see her, not us as he'd spend most of his time talking to her, to our annoyance. He pined for her for years after they separated, would tell us stories of happy times, confirming all my sister's remembrances – or false remembering – of things past. After the divorce my mother had moved from the Isle of Wight back to London to marry Richard Wollheim, the young philosopher.

Now I don't know if this story is true, but John Gale, great journalist but maybe a great fabulist too, told me this when I arrived to work at the *Observer*. My father had told him how Richard and my mother fell in love. Philip had brought Richard to the Isle of Wight, recovering from a heartbreak. It was icy cold, and my parents could hear him in the night weeping in his bedroom, so Philip went to find him and brought him back to their bed for comfort and warmth. But the bed was small, my father moved into the spare room – and that was that. Or so my father claimed indignantly to John Gale. But my mother was by then certainly in search of escape from the Isle of Wight and him.

My father had found a billet at the *Observer* as a foreign correspondent. I had always thought – and I think my father thought – that his father had secured him the job, worried at his son's state of mind after the marriage broke up. Arnold wrote frequently for the *Observer*, so my father assumed it was he who had pulled strings with the owner/editor David Astor. Astor was a famously whimsical and usually brilliant

Josephine and me with our mother and stepfather

employer of passing acquaintances and old friends. Deep into psychoanalysis, he specialized in anyone who seemed emotionally fragile or in need: at the time, staggering away from the divorce, Philip fitted the bill. There it was, the wound and the bow image he often used about himself and his own suffering, the image of the artist as Philoctetes, the man with a suppurating wound and the compensating bow that slew untruth. 'The great thing about the *Observer*,' my father wrote, 'is that all you have to do is show your wound. They never ask to see your bow.'

Astor made non-university-educated Terry Kilmartin literary editor in thanks for Kilmartin saving his life in the war. After Astor had been machine-gunned inside his car, Kilmartin had picked him up under a hail of gunfire by the roadside in France in 1944 and carried him away to safety. As it happened, Kilmartin was a great literary editor and he stayed on for life. Astor made his butler the *Observer* office manager after he had been found in the master bedroom one afternoon with the housemaid: Astor felt he had to be removed from the household, but he didn't like to sack anyone.

However, it turns out that it was not direct nepotism that secured my father his much-needed *Observer* job, as I later discovered it wasn't my grandfather who recommended him to Astor. Not long ago the *Guardian/Observer* archivist unearthed a letter from George Orwell to Astor written in 1949 from Cranham Sanatorium where he was dying from TB as he was finishing his last book, *1984*. 'I think Philip Toynbee is a good idea. I don't know him well but he seems to be quite gifted and politically OK... I believe he drinks a bit, ie not soaks steadily but is easily knocked out after a few drinks – however I don't suppose that would affect. One advantage of having Toynbee is he would bring you into contact with younger writers.'

Comrade Donald Maclean

So my father was hired and was sent off to report on Palestine in 1950 for the *Observer*, far away to recover from the divorce. Based in Tel Aviv and then Cairo, from there he sent us postcards telling of riding in camel races. I thought he couldn't ride but a picture of him racing a camel has suddenly appeared. He certainly did engage in epic drinking races with his old friend Donald Maclean, with whom he stayed. He had no idea that Maclean was a spy, and was genuinely astounded when he defected to Moscow in 1951, as were all those who worked with him or knew him. My father had good reason to think Maclean was strikingly unlikely to be capable of keeping such a secret: in one day-long bout together they drank six bottles of Gordon's gin between them and that's why, it emerged later, for a while Maclean's code name with his Russian handlers was 'Gordon'. He was Counsellor at the British embassy, ranked number three, dignified, respected, a successful Foreign Office high-flyer by day, but a demonic drinker by night whose wildness took even my father aback. My father writing about him years later talks of their first meeting when at Oxford in the late 1930s where Philip was the first communist President of the Union, and the three years older Maclean had already started work at the Foreign Office. (A digression: Matthew Spender, while researching his excellent biography of his father Stephen Spender, finding that my father, a friend of Spender's at Oxford, was one of several men simultaneously having an affair with Inez, Spender's first wife, also unearthed how Philip succeeded in his unlikely election as communist President of the Oxford Union in 1937: the Conservatives voted for him out of repugnance for their own candidate, Randolph Churchill.)

By the time Philip met him again in Egypt, Maclean had long been proclaiming loudly that he was no longer a communist. Philip writes that he was 'rather disgusted' when Maclean said flippantly he now preferred to 'serve the ruling class'. Philip describes how at one of their first meetings they spent the evening as they did many others over the years: 'We were at the Nest together, that easy-going Negro night-club of the pre-war years, and later still, as the sun rose over the park, we were swimming side by side in the Serpentine, still fully clothed in tails and white ties.'

If ever I met anyone who said they knew my father it caused in me a familiar sinking feeling: a drunken tale was bound to follow, but usually with a bit less charm – maybe sick in the soup, fallen under the table or vomiting out of the taxi window. 'So funny! So wild!' people would say and I would nod and smile wanly. On my first day at the *Observer*, Alf on reception, who had been there since time began, leant across the counter and said, 'I hope you're not like your dad. I hope you don't pee in the lift.'

Philip racing camels in Cairo

In Cairo my father and Maclean went on spectacular benders which sometimes included nights when my father would have to pull his friend away from throttling his wife, Melinda. But these binges came to a sudden end when one night they had crept out of the house for a drink and ended up at 3 a.m. smashing up the apartment of a secretarial assistant to the American ambassador, neither of them remembering how they got there or why. It was Maclean who did the smashing, as my father stood there reeling and laughing as his friend lifted a gigantic mirror and threw it into the bath, breaking not just the mirror but the bath. After these binges, with all the discipline of a spy, my father records Maclean's ability to pull himself together and walk, immaculate in a white suit, into work to take command of his department next morning, however much drink and however little sleep he'd had the night before. The Foreign Office was apparently as ignorant of Maclean's Jekyll and Hyde life between office and bottle as they were of his spying activities. But this last time there was no disguising the trashing of the ambassador's secretary's flat. Melinda persuaded the Foreign Office that Maclean must be suffering from a nervous breakdown and he was sent back to light duties in London. On the brink of detection as a Russian spy, the next year he defected to Moscow, to my father's astonishment. How could a man so drunk keep such a secret? Or was the drunkenness the only way he could live with such a secret? Much has been written about the Cambridge Five spies, none of them ever arrested, as three slipped away to Moscow while the two grandest, Anthony Blunt, Surveyor of the Queen's Pictures, and John Cairncross, intelligence officer, were allowed to strike a deal and carry on with their lives in England, so as to save the face of the secret service.

My father came back to London in 1951. I was only four, but I remember it well. He rang on the bell for the first time at my mother's new home in South Kensington and I opened the door. A tall man with an immensely thick gingerish beard, dark glasses and a battered straw hat asked in a guttural foreign accent if he could speak to Mrs Anne. 'I am most interesting in taking away with me a little girl called Polly with the pigtails, right now!' and he grabbed me and swung me up in the air, pretending to run off with me as I screamed in terror. My mother arrived behind me with a loud sigh, and said, 'Oh Philip, put her down, you're frightening her!' Josephine, who had been hesitating, unsure if it was him, now dashed out and grabbed him round the legs crying, 'Papa, Papa, you're back,' like Roberta in *The Railway Children*, while I clung to my mother.

He brought us black velvet Palestinian boleros embroidered in gold thread, which we wore with black tights and black velvet caps our mother made for us. We were the two Princes in the Tower at Lady Violet Bonham Carter's charity children's fancy dress party, for which my father had brought us two invitations from the *Observer*. We weren't even runners-up in the fancy dress contest: no one knew who we were supposed to be as the two princes were never seen together, the elder refusing to stand anywhere near the younger. As well as the newly grown beard and the boleros, my father also brought back from Palestine another surprise, a new wife, Sally Smith from Shaker Heights, Cleveland, Ohio and Antioch University, whom he had married in a whirlwind at the Tel Aviv American embassy where she worked as a secretary: as was the disgraceful way for women in the US civil service, she was fired from her job for marrying. As to whether she could have had the remotest idea what kind of life and world she was marrying into, almost certainly not. Nor might she have known of the deep scars his mother left on him.

What Rosalind did

In case anyone thinks my father exaggerated his mother's malign nature or the damage she did him, here are some final revelations about her. My father remembered her overwhelming power: 'How could anyone stand firm against the vast resources of that will? I never heard her admit a mistake.'

Her dislike of her two older sons led to tragedy. Her letters reveal the flavour of her distaste and irritation with both Tony and Philip, while doting on her youngest, Lawrence, who she called 'the nicest and happiest little self'. When my father swallowed a pin, she wrote, 'It seems so typical of him to make the most inconvenience and upset everyone that we can't help feeling very much annoyed with him.' In the same year she wrote, 'Poor Philip of course has developed impetigo, a skin disease commonly found in the slums I believe – and very contagious.' Philip shocked them before his final expulsion from Rugby when they were summoned to the school where he was accused of 'dirty talk'. Tony was sent to Winchester but under a cloud of disappointment for failing to get a scholarship, which meant his fees had to be paid by Rosalind's parents. Arnold and Rosalind complained their eldest was 'sulky and withdrawn'.

In 1932 Rosalind converted to Roman Catholicism, which was even more shocking to her rationalist parents than her hunting had been. She could hardly have chosen a better poisoned dart to aim at her father's heart. All her childhood Gilbert had made anti-clerical jokes, calling Christmas 'Mithras's birthday', reciting limericks about bishops with much mockery at the Old Man up in the sky, very like my own anti-clerical upbringing by my father. But Gilbert was determined to behave in a civilized way, not to split with her, and he declared himself on 'terms of frank argument if not agreement'. Later she wrote a book publicly attacking him and his unshakeable atheism in *The Good Pagan's Failure*, a wearisome Catholic tract in which she exults in obedient servitude to a totalitarian belief. But her most severe argument with her parents was over their disapproval of her harsh treatment of Tony and Philip.

Her flight to Rome was a way to signal the effective ending of her marriage. Lawrence was still young enough to be swept up by her on the road to popery, but Tony and Philip, aged eighteen and sixteen, with strong atheist and socialist views of their own, were entirely shut out of their mother's unexpected new religious life.

My father was shocked, but hid it by mocking her. He recounts in his published diaries, *Part of a Journey*, how when coming home for the holidays, 'there would often be a new crucifix hanging on some wall or other. Once I confronted a particularly large and demanding version immediately opposite the front door and I paused with my mother beside me, and struck an attitude of quizzing connoisseurship. "Who's it of?" I asked; to which she answered, "A friend – to some of us."' Humour was not in her, let alone about the sacred.

At about that time adolescent Philip wrote of his parents in his private diary, 'She has a fixed idea of herself which nothing will alter. "I am good" and that's enough to keep her going for life. In point of fact she's a snob, rather a fascist, an isolationist and by no means a Christian. I'm terribly afraid I don't like her.' He calls her habit of calling someone '"quite a humble little person", literally unpardonable. Daddy, I've come to believe, is basically right-minded, but abjectly weak. His horror at a very ordinary detective film today was laughable, if it hadn't been such a devastating reflection on all his works.' For all Philip's patronizing youthful tone, he was right about his parents.

My father was a versatile and agile tease of his mother. I particularly enjoy the story he used to tell about how thoroughly he trounced her once. When he was about fifteen his mother arranged an exchange with a German boy called Kurt. As so often with exchanges, they had nothing in common and my father detested the boy, who it turned out was a Nazi sympathizer and a member of the Hitler Youth. Soon after Kurt arrived he suddenly announced to Arnold and Rosalind that he had to go home to Germany immediately, without any explanation. Once the boy had gone, Philip confessed to his parents that he had got rid of him by telling him that Toynbee was a Jewish name and they were a Jewish family. Arnold for once laughed, perhaps equally glad to be rid of him, but Rosalind was incandescent, less for Philip's naughtiness than out of mortification that anyone should think her Jewish.

Hers was not a mild religion, but an aggressive piety, imperious, declamatory and doctrinaire with all the passion of the convert. Arnold's reaction was a tit-for-tat suggestion that she should seek psychiatric help – from the so aptly named Dr Payne. She did, but the doctor declared her sane.

Tony's short life

Tony sank into a morose state the year she converted, and he failed at Winchester so badly he had to be taken away from the school. With no prospect of university, he wanted to join the Indian army, but instead he was sent to Germany, hoping to get him into a German university. It seems extraordinary to us now that anyone with no Nazi sympathies would want their child to study in Germany in the years of Hitler's triumphant rise, yet it seems to have been as common as studying in France. Tony's relations with his parents went from bad to worse. He developed a fascination for guns and kept a large gun collection. Neither parent seems to have had either sympathy or understanding of him. 'He has been doing no work at all this summer and showing no interest in anything else,' Arnold wrote to his mother. Rosalind wrote, 'He says himself that he is not interested in anything and that revival of the firearms mania is only an attempt to fill a vacuum.' So she sent him to Dr Payne too, with no obvious good result, except she was gratified when the doctor earned his fee by telling Rosalind how much Tony loved his mother, but couldn't express it. Tony was packed off to Germany but he alarmed them when he took up with a duelling fraternity and joined in a demonstration against the Treaty of Versailles. He was not, however, for long seduced by German nationalism.

Nor was Arnold, but while his son was in Germany, he had a two-hour interview with Adolf Hitler in 1936, a record of which he sent privately to Anthony Eden, the Foreign Secretary. Hitler had asked to see Arnold, knowing that he had always been an opponent of the Treaty of Versailles and that in his League of Nations work he always thought Germany should be given back some of the lands confiscated. As ever, naïve in his optimism that no one wanted war and that people are essentially of good intent, Arnold reported back that he thought Hitler had no ambitions beyond return of these territories. Hitler succeeded in persuading Arnold peace might be preserved. Later, once war was inevitable, he put all his hope in a future 'United States of Europe to hold Germany down', which was an early aspiration for the European Union.

Tony had come back from the University of Bonn ferociously anti-Nazi, and so any thought of his returning there was impossible. Instead, he decided he wanted to go to Russia and join the Red Army so as to be prepared for the war that he saw as the inevitable final conflict between communism and fascism. This seems an entirely extraordinary event, bizarrely unlikely, but it happened. Arnold agreed to help him with his Russian ambitions – perhaps eager to send him somewhere. He used his Foreign Office connections to arrange an interview with the Russian ambassador in London to see if the Red Army would take him. Arnold and Tony went together to visit Ambassador Ivan Maisky who greeted them politely, but told them very firmly that foreign volunteers were not accepted. It seems quite inexplicable that Arnold can ever have thought the intensely paranoid Soviet government would permit foreign 'spies' into the Red Army. It is another aspect of Arnold's optimism that he always thought all reasonable people could work together.

Tony did excel in languages and in Germany had learned not only German but several Slavic languages and some Persian. He took the exams for the Consular Service, passed and was sent to Peking to learn Chinese. But after a short time he contracted a fever that damaged his heart and he was sent home. Reassigned to a desk job in the Department of Overseas Trade in London, he threatened to

Tony

resign, but his parents ordered him not to, in no uncertain terms. Arnold wrote, 'We have sent him an ultimatum. He would be practically unemployable. I hope we shall head him off,' and they did. But Tony sank into a depression. As war was breaking out, a love affair came to an abrupt end and he shot himself on the day Hitler invaded Czechoslovakia. He was twenty-four.

Philip was so overwhelmed with grief he thought of killing himself too and he never recovered from the loss. My mother said he often woke in tears in the middle of night after dreaming of Tony. In Philip's last diaries at the end of his life, Tony still frequently appeared, the one member of his family he loved completely: he devoted a whole volume of his verse novel to Tony's life and death. As a child I often tried to imagine this missing uncle, my father's deeply mourned brother, but I can get no better idea of this unhappy, directionless young man or how he might have been as a grown man. Oldest children take the hardest impact of difficult parents. Like my father, Tony was blighted by his parents, both impossible in their different ways. Arnold had unreasonable academic expectations of his children, unable to comprehend or be much interested in anyone not devoting every minute of the day to the life of the mind. Rosalind's chilling, vain and self-absorbed autocracy did dreadful damage to all three sons, leaving one dead and two severely alcoholic, all contorted by their very differently intense relationships with her. However, my father became a good writer and my uncle Lawrence a good painter.

Rosalind's unholy divorce and her deadly secret

During the war Arnold had been stationed by the Foreign Office in Oxford (where Rosalind accused him of cowering away in fear of the Blitz) and they had been mostly apart. In 1942 his office was to be relocated to London where she was living, and they would be back together all the time. That prospect finally decided her, and she left him. Returning by flying boat from a mission to America, Arnold came back to their London flat to find her gone, without having had any notion she was about to leave him. Picking up signals was not his forte, so it came as a crushing shock. He begged, pleaded, bargained and, oh dear, he even wrote her poems:

> *Flitting dryad, sleeping hero,*
> *Urgent muse, elusive goddess*
> *I have loved you beyond measure.*

But all to no avail. He even turned to the family psychologist, Dr Payne, whose treatment of Rosalind, Tony and Philip had been so singularly fruitless. He wrote to Rosalind to say Dr Payne was trying to cure his 'psychological immaturity', but also to no avail. Rosalind was eager for a divorce, but her faith was an obstacle. The wonder of Rome is that all inconvenient things can be fixed, all rules can be overcome. Or at least, what couldn't be done for Henry VIII could be arranged for Rosalind Toynbee. She wrote to her Catholic adviser, Father Columba of Ampleforth Abbey,

> It now seems certain that our marriage was not valid, and that I shall get an annulment before long, without

even having to go to Rome. The ground is one that you were first to suggest – that I was not baptised when our marriage took place... It has been an almost bewildering relief to me to find that, after all, the feeling that I have had so long of never having been really married to him, was almost certainly justified... To me all this makes it seem much more clearly God's will that we should separate – that we were not meant to go on together, but I doubt if Arnold will see it so.

God's will was always miraculously well aligned to Rosalind's.

God no doubt looked benignly on her relationship with Richard Stafford, an ex-Dominican monk with whom she lived for the rest of her life. She used to boast ostentatiously to her family of the elevated nature of the religious and devotional life she led with Richard, their time filled with meditations and contemplations of the divine. As she was dying, Arnold reflected sorrowfully that Richard Stafford 'is the only person who has come up to her expectations. He is like an adopted son.'

As a grandmother, Rosalind was as sternly religious and censorious as she was of her sons, outraged when one of my cousins got pregnant when young, and was living for a while 'in sin', despite later marrying the child's father. Without deigning ever to meet me, she radiated her disapproval of me from afar, relayed indirectly here and there, based on stories within her Yorkshire Catholic circles that overlapped with the Catholic mother of that first young lover of mine. Everything she heard confirmed her very low opinion of my father's progeny, giving her even less wish to meet me. The grand Catholic world is a waspish little set.

When Rosalind died in 1967 Arnold was floored with grief, though he had by then been long married to his devoted academic researcher, Veronica Boulter, who had worked with him since 1920 on *A Study of History* and at Chatham House. Yet he was still in thrall to Rosalind, still her worshipper, still in fear and awe of her, writing that he 'felt towards Rosalind more as if she were a goddess than as if she were the human being that she was. I must still have some of this feeling left, because I can't imagine how Death can have had the audacity to take her.' Oh, the poor sap.

It wasn't until five years after her death that the scales finally fell from his eyes. My father had already discovered the truth one drunken evening spent comforting her ex-Dominican monk, Richard Stafford, just after Rosalind's funeral. Richard blurted out to Philip the passionate intensity of their relationship, no, not just religious but wild and

Arnold and Veronica with Sally at Cob Cottage

ecstatic sex. It's not the sort of thing a mother's lover should tell a son, but he went further and gave my father her private diaries, filled with graphic descriptions of Rosalind and Richard bathing naked in a lake, and much, much more. My father was shocked to the core. The idea of older people enjoying unrestrained sex always appals the generations below them: when every other inconceivable obscenity is available at the click of a mouse, sex among the old remains a last taboo. But what really horrified my father was his mother's gargantuan hypocrisy, along with the many other reminders in the diaries of her snobbery and self-righteousness. That night, as they got drunker, when Philip had read more than enough, he and Richard threw the diaries in the fire and they were destroyed. He told his brother Lawrence the truth but they kept their father Arnold in the dark. But finally five years later, still obsessed with the memory of Rosalind, Arnold asked Jean, Lawrence's wife, what she thought had been the nature of Rosalind's special relationship with Richard. Jean is so honest and direct she could never tell a lie – and so she told him the truth. She told him it was plain that Rosalind was already having an affair with Richard when she left Arnold and living in sin when she applied to Rome for her virtuous annulment.

How did Arnold react? His wife Veronica wrote to my stepmother saying this had brought back to him, bitterly, Rosalind's atrocious behaviour over the death of her sister Agnes.

It brought up again a most traumatic experience Arnold had when he had to accompany Lady Mary to a remote village in France where Agnes was dying: she had gone there with a young Greek man with whom she was living, and was overtaken by acute appendicitis. Medical help came too late and she died in great pain. The thing that has now struck Arnold to the heart is that Rosalind was quite implacable in her attitude to Agnes: her mother nearly broke with her because she would not express sympathy. Arnold's first reaction was how could Rosalind have condemned C [my cousin], but soon this memory of Agnes swamped even that from his mind.

My father wrote to Arnold to try to comfort him in his anger and anguish.

I too felt extreme animosity towards Mummy when Richard blurted the whole thing out: most obviously of all, I longed to have her back so that I could confront her with this. She had marvellous qualities which were recognised by all sorts of different people who knew and loved her. But there must have been something terribly wrong with her deep inside her own mind and heart. Something which inevitably destroyed all her relationships when they made any real demands on her... My own feeling is that Mummy was capable of a greater – indeed a more ludicrous – degree of self-deception than anyone I have known.

Lawrence wrote to his father, 'Now that one sees her more in perspective, the view is a great deal less pleasant and I do find this traumatic.' His reaction to the disclosure was to lose all at once not only his faith in his mother, but in the Church she had swept him into as well.

Arnold suffered a severe stroke two years later that left him unable to communicate, read or write and he died after six months in a nursing home in York. The effect of marrying into a twig of the aristocracy was to imbue in him a lifetime's sense of social inferiority. How sad that despite his vast depth and breadth of knowledge across all civilizations, the absurd notion of inherited class and blue blood haunted him. His critics – Hugh Trevor-Roper especially – accused him of Titanic intellectual arrogance with his universal theory of history, but possibly he reached for ever-greater heights of intellectual ambition as a compensation for the sense of social class inferiority Rosalind impressed on him. A red mist of indignation may distort my portrait of my distant and hostile grandmother, but I can find no balancing qualities to soften into forgiveness.

10

Rhodesia: Many Painful Political Lessons Learned in One Brief Episode

IN JANUARY 1966, with most of the year to wait before going to Oxford, I was working in my cousin Emma Tennant's boutique, The Yellow Room behind Sloane Square, when someone invited me to a party – who or where I can't remember. I wish I could say that at the time I was filled with a burning mission to go and work in Africa, but my sister was out there already and nothing of the kind was on my mind, as I was writing a novel and having an affair with a television reporter.

At that party I fell into conversation with an animated, rather vehement man in his mid-forties, who turned out to be Peter Benenson, Catholic Etonian lawyer, founder of Amnesty International: I had helped run a letter-writing Amnesty club from my boarding school, schoolgirls writing to distant governments to petition for the release of political prisoners, collecting money to send to our adopted prisoner's family. His face lit up. Ah, you're one of ours! He meant that in every sense. He said he was putting together a delegation in a hurry to go out to Nigeria, where a violent coup had just ousted and murdered the first post-independence prime minister, Sir Abubakar Tafawa Balewa, leaving him dead in a road-side ditch.

Sir Learie Constantine, a famous West Indian cricketer, distinguished lawyer and friend of Nigerian lawyers, was leading the team, but he needed someone to go as his secretary. 'Since you're going to Oxford, you're obviously up to this job!' Astounded, I said I didn't think I was: no shorthand, two-finger typing, knowing nothing what-ever of Nigeria. 'Nonsense, you're leaving in two days!' That's the fine old British way of recruitment on which the empire was built: if you're the right sort, you'll do. With deep misgivings, I agreed, for who would turn down such an adventure?

What were we supposed to do? Find out what had happened to any political prisoners who had disappeared in the coup, Benenson said. The team included a sinister man, Commander Cunningham, as like a spy as ever my untrained eye could imagine. He lurked and he whispered, and he carried everywhere a large suitcase full of money from which he paid for everything by cash. Everything about this mission was chaotic. We stayed in the grand Federal Palace Hotel, Lagos, Sir Learie holding court in the downstairs lounge contacting old lawyer friends who stopped by for a drink while I took notes. But no one was any the wiser about what was happening, or if they were, they weren't telling us. Sir Learie's company was a delight, remaining unperturbed by the complete pointless-ness of our mission.

*The Amnesty delegation to Nigeria. I'm standing beside
Sir Learie Constantine, the West Indian cricketer and
lawyer, and Commander Cunningham is on the far
right holding his jacket*

This was not an ordinary Amnesty-style expedition, I
soon realized: having been a grassroots member, I knew
what Amnesty did, and it wasn't usually this. I thought
about the coins we had scraped together at school to send
to prisoners' families, and wondered if some of those
collections were paying our Federal Palace drinks bill.
(No, but more of the money later.) I sat at the phone in my
room calling every ministry in the phone book, every name
or contact I could find from anyone we met, trying to get
interviews, while noting down each attempt so as to have

something to write up for our very thin report: I rightly feared we would have nothing at all to show for this trip. Finally my one and only feat was to gain us an interview at the Ministry of Protocol. We trooped in and Sir Learie did his best to elicit any information on anything, with absolutely no success. No, we were told, there were no political prisoners. What had happened to the people from the deposed government who had disappeared? The junior protocol minister was polite but said he knew nothing, which was probably true.

When it was plain nothing was to be done, and we were about to head back to Lagos airport, a surprising telegram arrived for me from Benenson: 'Proceed to Salisbury', the capital of Rhodesia, renamed Harare after independence. Commander Cunningham gave me a bundle of money – though not, as it turned out, quite enough – and I set out on a series of flights, hopping step by step down Africa. My first cheap flight took me to Cameroon, where Josephine was. (More of that later too.) But no one had told me I needed visas in every country along the way: I was stuck for days in a run-down shanty hotel in Elisabethville in the Congo waiting for permits, eating nothing but bread rolls, saving every penny for flights.

By the time I reached Salisbury, I was alarmed to find my Amnesty predecessor had just been expelled, so I was on my own. All I had was the address of the office. I knew nothing, clueless, with only a hazy idea of what I was supposed to do for the African prisoners interned in the camps of Ian Smith's brutish Rhodesia Front regime.

There was much more I didn't know. I knew nothing about Amnesty's internal conflicts at the time, or that Peter

Benenson was in the throes of a near-nervous breakdown and that I was at the sharp end of what was in effect a free-booting rogue expedition of his own.

I was just excited to be there, right in the middle of what we on the left assumed would be Britain's imminent invasion of Rhodesia. Surely Harold Wilson would put an end to Ian Smith's illegal Unilateral Declaration of Independence (UDI), declared just three months earlier? A squadron of the British air force was rumoured to be nearby, just a short hop to the north in Zambia. Surely this tuppenny tinpot dictatorship would collapse the instant British paratroopers landed in Salisbury? As colonies across Africa won their independence, Ian Smith had demanded Rhodesia's too, but only as a white apartheid state with its whites-only parliament elected by a whites-only electorate (with a few token seats for obedient chiefs). This was the colony that could never be released without a democratic constitution. Former Tory prime minister Alec Douglas-Home had pussy-footed around with the Smith regime, suggesting compromises such as the 'improvement of the political status of Africans' for a gradual handover of democratic power. But the incoming Labour government laid down the law firmly: 'No independence without majority rule.'

Rhodesia had just 300,000 whites holding down a black population of four million, with little land and few rights. Smith appealed to the Queen to stay as monarch to his Rhodesia still in the Commonwealth: she refused. Surely now freedom for the black majority was inevitable and Labour would make it happen! This was an early and bitter lesson in political disappointment, disillusion and, looking back, possibly in realism too. Labour had a shaky four-seat majority, with an election approaching in a few months: Britain would never, said Wilson, go to war against 'our kith and kin'. That was, of course, white kith and white kin only.

I found the Amnesty office locked but a note was poking out just under the door. The World Council of Churches down the corridor said they had the Amnesty office key. They had been keeping an eye on the office, and they opened the door for me, where I found filing cabinets with all the gazetted names of those arrested and kept prisoner in Smith's internment camps. There were names and addresses of their families and further files of the dwindling number of lawyers willing to take cases on prisoners' behalf. And, said Jack from the World Council of Churches, he was holding a large sum of Amnesty's money in their account. What should he do with it, he asked? This was alarming as the money came with no particular instructions, no provenance, explanation or scrutiny as to how it was to be spent.

Down the corridor were offices of many international organizations of various kinds. I made friends with Rhodesian liberals struggling to survive against the Smith reign of terror, including the redoubtable Eileen Haddon, writer and founder of the Legal Aid and Welfare Fund, whose husband Michael was jailed for three years, and Judy Todd, daughter of a former Rhodesian prime minister, Garfield Todd. Later she was arrested and eventually fled to come and stay with my family in London for a while. I made friends with many black Rhodesians secretly involved with the Zanu and Zapu parties, already fighting in the bush, but it was a serious risk for them to be seen by the Smith authorities consorting with white liberals. The bravery of these fearless resistors was phenomenal at a time when people vanished overnight for writing or speaking against UDI. Black people vanished for doing nothing at all.

Garai and Runako turned up in the office, about my age but worldly wise and acting as runners and contacts for the freedom fighters, advising, explaining, translating and helping me. If ever we heard planes overhead, we would run together to the window to see if at last here was the RAF arriving under Harold Wilson's orders.

Within days of opening the office, long queues of people appeared, squatting in the corridors from early in the morning. They were the hungry wives and children of imprisoned men needing support: I would hand out money to them every week, after checking their husbands' names in the fastidiously gazetted official weekly lists of internees. Ian Smith's officials, Nazi-style, were punctilious about keeping administrative records of their imprisonment without trial regime. Did I have any idea what I was doing, where the money was going or how it should be accounted for? No. I was at sea and just hoped for the best.

Looking through my mother's papers for old photographs for this book, I was surprised to find she had kept a letter I wrote her from Salisbury, sent back with someone travelling to London. I am grumbling about Benenson suddenly turning up unexpectedly: 'He just breezed into the office the other day, just as I had completely reorganized everything and efficiently introduced a proper filing system. He lifts up piles of invaluable papers and messes everything around without finding anything and jumbles the whole place up. He walks around telling everyone here about Rhodesia as if he owns the place.' I describe my job:

> I sit in my office, send forms for people to fill in, give money to the people who most need it, write to headmasters of schools asking them to remit fees of the children whose fathers are under restriction or detained. I write letters to Amnesty all over the world arranging money transactions and if possible get money sent straight to landlords and find clothes for children. I am also the Prison Education Committee, all one of me, and I see that people in prison or restriction can carry on their education through correspondence courses and buy their books for them and go and visit them as often as possible, and see their wives and children.

I am glad to see a few words in the letter understanding what it is to be white under apartheid. 'The thing is not to get too sentimental. You have to realize it's a transaction and although they're friendly, which is nice, it can never mean that much.' Oppression oppresses every relationship. 'Another problem is the Zapu/Zanu conflict, as each side claims you help the other side more. The camps are divided into the parties, a clever piece of manipulation to make certain the two parties will grow in hostility to each other.' I tell her sanctions are having no effect, whatever Harold Wilson claims – and I tell her facetiously, 'Organize troop mobilization immediately! Do write. Desperate for news.' Reading this now I wonder if I am over-egging this portrait of my super-efficiency, but in all honesty I no longer remember all the details of my work with prisoners' families to know if I was really as well organized as I was trying boastfully to make myself sound in that letter home.

From hints, from words let slip by Benenson in cryptic phone calls, after a while I realized the money came not from the carefully collected funds of small local Amnesty groups, such I had collected at school, but from Harold Wilson, via George Wigg, his spy master. It was hush money, but I didn't immediately understand that, as among my Rhodesian friends, we were at the time naïvely optimistic that Wilson's air force would come swooping down any day now and liberate the country, for whose racist society Britain was undoubtedly responsible.

To invade and remove Ian Smith's regime seemed the very least reparation Britain could make for the creation of this late colony, for licensing its detestable founder Cecil Rhodes, for the pilfering by the white settlers of all the best land, and eighty years of pitiless British colonial oppression. Kith and kin? Not mine. I admit to a supercilious loathing for the Smith-backing white Rhodesians: stupid, boorish, bigoted and arrogant, late-comers to Africa with not even a veneer of that old colonialist pretence of a little noblesse oblige towards Africans. These Rhodesians, many quite recently settled, looked up to South African whites as a superior social class and they inflated their own self-esteem with an extra dose of contempt for Africans. 'Whites Only' signs were multiplying everywhere, as Smith wanted Rhodesia to match South Africa in everything, wooing the country to back him in this emergency of his own creation. Whites Only buses, benches, bars and shops proliferated – and even where there weren't signs, segregation done by bullying was worsening by the day. But South Africa was wary of bringing down international retaliation and so it was reluctant to supply the oil Smith urgently needed. Only a few token barrels were rolled across the Beit Bridge over the Limpopo border by a group of white Rhodesians, for purely publicity reasons.

In the streets I saw elderly black people shoved out of the way on pavements by strutting young white thugs, growing more assertive and extreme under the tensions of international isolation and the beginnings of a guerrilla war. Sanctions were a weak weapon, another lesson I learned. Imported goods were increasingly unavailable in shops, no Cornflakes, no cotton reels, nothing British or American branded, including no TV shows, leaving the one channel reliant on a few frequently repeated *I Love Lucy* and *Bewitched* re-runs. But sanctions caused no real hardship for white Rhodesians.

Only a prolonged violent uprising, known as the Bush War, brought Ian Smith down. It was not until 1978 that his Rhodesia Front regime was removed, brought to humiliation at the negotiating table – at a horrifically high cost. An estimated 20,000 people were killed, almost all black guerrillas and civilians, with just 1,120 white forces and 468 white civilians dead. Could swift intervention by Britain at the start have prevented that long war? It was won not by white saviours sending in the paratroopers but by African nationalists fighting for their own freedom.

As for the social snobbery of myself at nineteen, you learn better as you get older: because the nastiest, most aggressive people make the most noise in some political group you detest on principle, that's no reason to lump together an entire category of opponents as loathsome. No, not even all Tories are 'lower than vermin', the Nye Bevan remark flaunted on some Labour T-shirts. In my mother's dying last days, she was so kindly and affectionately cared for by Collette, a white Rhodesian woman, earning money for a few months at a time as a carer in England to take back to her now poverty-stricken family in what she called 'Zim'. In her stories of life back home now, she sounded like the vanquished Southerners of *Gone with the Wind* after the American civil war. I just never discussed Ian Smith with her – and by then, so many decades later, there was no disagreement between us about Robert Mugabe and his vicious regime.

Beyond supporting prisoners' families, Amnesty's aim was to fund test cases to challenge the Smith regime's legitimacy. When I first arrived the Rhodesian courts had not yet opined on the legal status of government actions: there was a chance the judiciary, or some of them, would declare the unrecognized Smith regime and all its actions illegitimate. Some white liberal lawyers were imprisoned and there were virtually no black lawyers, but Walter Kamba was an exceptional man, one of the last of the black lawyers still free. When I approached him he was one of the very last willing to dare take a test case of a prisoner and challenge the courts to declare his arrest and detention illegal.

Peter Benenson turned up on a flying visit together with Commander Cunningham and his fat suitcase: he seemed to be spinning round the globe at speed, and he was keen to accelerate the case. Much later I came upon a secret letter of his that revealed the Wilson government was behind this push for legal action, using Amnesty as a cover and providing the money to finance this last chance to topple Smith peaceably using his own courts. Benenson had twice been a Labour candidate and had access to Harold Wilson: in the letters that emerged later he wrote to my predecessor running the Salisbury office using a pathetically transparent 'code' where he referred to Wilson as 'Harry'. 'Harry has developed a sudden enthusiasm for litigation. What with North Hull, Harry wants a fair buzz of legal activity. Harry's financial problems apparently have been solved and he's in a generous mood.' Kingston-on-Hull North was a crucial by-election that increased Labour's puny majority from three to four. The money flowed in to take test cases.

But just as Walter Kamba was about to take the case to court, there was a sudden screeching U-turn. The order came to me from Benenson to drop the case immediately, plainly due to some real or imagined British government change of heart. I was outraged since Kamba was taking such a huge personal risk, and he still thought there was just a faint chance the Smith regime could be challenged in law. I had to break the news to him, without having any explanation to give him for this betrayal, myself as angry as he. Shortly after the case was cancelled Walter and Angeline Kamba fled the country for Scotland where he took up a professorship in law at the University of Dundee.

Not long after, I had a phone call and then came a knock on the door. I was commanded to an interview with the Rhodesian secret service Central Intelligence Organisation. I imagined a cell in a police basement, interrogation lamps, threats, manacles or worse. But no, this police chief wanted to meet me in the bar of the Salisbury Hotel, the second best in the city. He had a rubbery red face, fat fingers and a purring smoothness that both intimidated and cajoled, faintly flirtatious, faintly contemptuous. His name was Gary and he said he might be able to help. Help? With what? You will be deported, expelled, extradited immediately. What for? Subversion of the state, encouraging subversives. Amnesty, he said preposterously, was an organization that helped prisoners escape over the wire. This was no surprise since previous Amnesty staff had been expelled, as had people regularly from many foreign charities. Do you want to leave, he asked? I said no, of course not. Ah, then I might be able to help you stay, if you are enjoying yourself here with your new African boyfriends. (Hear the sneer.) If I was willing to report to him on the activities of 'liberals', 'revolutionaries' and 'terrorists' who I had been consorting with, black and white, but especially on the doings of Eileen Haddon and Judy Todd, then I could stay indefinitely. Perhaps he thought the delight I took in camping trips up in the green and yellow hills was enough to turn me into a spy against my friends. Indeed, the landscape was spectacularly beautiful, though I looked out on it with a pleasure mixed with sadness at this lovely but cursed country which war was already tearing apart.

It was, I thought, a sign of their stupidity, their utter incomprehension to expect anyone in my position to turn spy: the Stasi and the KGB could only turn people into their agents because they had a brutal life and death stranglehold over their family. Gary had nothing on me, except extradition.

I was escorted onto the first flight to South Africa the next morning: sanctions prevented direct flights from Rhodesia to London or anywhere else. The last manic message I received from Benenson was a mysterious telegram: 'Proceed at once to the Kalahari.' I looked it up on an airport map but it looked like a big desert, and he didn't say where exactly. Besides, I was under arrest, with no choice where I was going as they firmly escorted me onto the plane. When I reached Johannesburg, I was taken down the aircraft steps by South African police and locked into a police cell for a day and a night – concrete bed, one dirty blanket, no window, bang on the door to be taken to the lavatory. There was some desultory questioning about why I had been helping prisoners and criminals escape, but it felt pro forma. It was a little, but frankly not very frightening. The man from the British consulate, who suddenly appeared at my cell looking bored and irritated at being called out, had no idea when I might be let out or where I would be sent. However, I was taken to the airport and escorted onto a plane back to London the next day, with no undue roughness, rudeness or violence, as I was safely white and safely English.

Arriving home I was surprised to find my father had come up to London to meet me. He was already a bit drunk by then. I remember sitting at the top of the stairs while he was talking loudly to a friend on the only house phone in the hallway, boasting proudly, 'Extradited! Isn't she a chip off the old block!' and feeling inexplicably furious. Following in footsteps, chips off blocks, acorns falling not far from the tree, none of these are what anyone wants to be.

Back home I joined campaigns for a free Rhodesia. There was a fair amount of press coverage of my deportation, and I was invited to speak for the cause of British intervention: tremulously, I made my first ever public speech standing on the stage beside old campaigner Fenner Brockway in

Conway Hall, home of free-thinkers and radicals down
the ages: though I didn't know it back then, it turned out
my great-grandfather, grandfather and father had all given
speeches from that same platform on liberation causes of
one kind or another. That's where my father had spoken
often, including his disgrace on returning from the Spanish
civil war to report back from his student delegation, when
he was too drunk, lost his notes and was booed off the
stage. They didn't boo me, but I am sure those forebears
would have spoken with more panache, experience and
knowledge. I was shaking like a jelly and politically naïve.

On the evening I was leaving Rhodesia I was handed
secretly a parcel of letters that had been left in a hotel safe
by Robert Swann, my predecessor, with instructions that
under no circumstances were they to fall into the hands of
Rhodesian officials. These were the 'Harry' letters, which
I didn't read until I got home, but they revealed the extent
of Benenson's collusion with the British government, his
antagonism to the freedom fighters of Zapu and Zanu as
communist infiltrated, and his willingness to do whatever
Wilson wanted to ease the Rhodesia question out of the
news in the run-up to the 1966 election. I never thought
of exposing how this supposedly independent charity had
been willingly used as a pawn of the British government,
as I knew the harm it would do 'non-partisan', 'non-polit-
ical' Amnesty International around the world: like the Red
Cross, its reputation relied on defending all prisoners of
conscience, free of any government influence, regardless
of nationality, ideology or creed. Besides, by then I knew
the eccentricities of Benenson had separated him from the
organization he founded. His Rhodesia operation had

been closed down and he had disappeared for a while into a French Trappist monastery 'to think things over'.

I went up to Oxford and I must have talked about it, told the story, mulling over Rhodesia's fate among friends and fellow campaigners and it must have seeped out. But it wasn't until a year later that I was contacted by a *Sunday Telegraph* journalist and I was about to get a hard lesson in the non-ethics of my future rough trade. How green, how innocent I was when I should have seen the red flashing warning lights in any approach from an arch-Tory newspaper. The journalist told me he had discovered that money had been channelled from Harold Wilson to Amnesty for political purposes. How did he know, I asked? All had been revealed to him, he claimed, by an Amnesty insider and he was just asking for my anonymous confirmation, as he knew that I knew and so I would be in trouble if I lied. But the story appeared the next Sunday as an exposé by me, with all my quotes – and some that weren't – but there was no information from anyone else. My words, my story was used to damn both Amnesty and Harold Wilson's deviousness. It caused enough stir for Wilson to be questioned in parliament that week and he admitted he had suggested sources of money for Amnesty in Rhodesia. I was appalled that I'd been duped, but there was nothing I could do. At a conference in Elsinore in Denmark that year Amnesty's headquarters were removed from Britain. I was summoned to Amnesty's board who ripped into me mercilessly: 'Do you realize prisoners will die around the world because of what you have done by politically contaminating our work?'

Those deaths were probably fictitious. But those thousands of black Zimbabweans killed in the thirteen-year

Bush War were real enough. The US furtively backed Ian Smith's Rhodesia Front and his claim to be defending the global front line against the falling dominoes of communism. Robert Mugabe's Zanu was supported by Russia, while Joshua Nkomo's Zapu received arms and training from China and North Korea.

Could the bloodshed have been prevented if Harold Wilson had invaded? Impossible to know. But British voters would never have backed that war: Margaret Thatcher's popular Falklands War defended our white kith and kin against Argentinian 'dagos', but this would have been the wrong way round. Besides, as well as being a political impossibility for a government with a knife-edge majority, military tacticians claimed conquest was logistically impossible too. That was one lesson in political disillusion.

Later came another political lesson: revolutions are breath-stoppingly exciting, a cocaine snort of exhilarating hope. The Arab Spring, the overthrow of Egypt's Mubarak, Syria's awakening, or go back to the storming of the Winter Palace, the romance of the Long March or Wordsworth's French Revolution, 'Bliss was it in that dawn to be alive!' Closer to home and considerably quieter, Labour winning general elections in 1964 and in 1997 after years of Tory rule felt to me like explosions of hope. But like delirious love, these grand political emotions usually have other endings. In those 1960s and '70s years of warring Marxist, Leninist, Troskyite revolutionary splinter groups, I was with Labour, never a revolutionary. That's typical of the bourgeoisie, was the comeback from far leftists. Are they right, the Robespierres? Only those who have nothing can ever be trusted as true revolutionaries? Possibly.

Walter Kamba was a key legal adviser to Robert Mugabe at the Lancaster House conference which drew up the new Zimbabwe constitution. He came home from exile in Scotland to his new majority-ruled country in 1980 to become the first black Vice-Chancellor of the University of Zimbabwe, a supporter and admirer of Mugabe who started out as the most radical and inspiring leader. I was a Mugabe supporter too, as were most I knew, full of hope when he won the first election fair and square. Mugabe began impressively, admirable, clever, astute.

But by 1991 Kamba stood down as Vice-Chancellor in protest at Mugabe's dictatorial and tyrannical power over the university as over everything else. Like so many other former Mugabe supporters, Eileen and Michael Haddon were forced to leave their multiracial co-operative and escape to Zambia for fear of persecution. In 1984 Judy Todd was raped by a senior officer in Mugabe's military on his orders, after she criticized his genocide of Ndebele civilians, the traditional opponents of Mugabe's own tribe. She founded a newspaper but it was banned. Finally she was stripped of her Zimbabwean citizenship and fled.

One more political lesson: thirty years on, the National Archives in Kew released a letter from Peter Benenson to Harold Wilson's Lord Chancellor, Gerald Gardiner. Wilson had indeed supplied £10,000 for Amnesty's Rhodesia work, but he had solicited it secretly from Charles Forte, hotel chain owner. Bold as brass, Benenson had suggested to Forte in a letter that in return for the donation, 'it was not altogether unlikely that the name of such a well-known caterer would appear on a future honours list'. Forte paid up, though he and his family were always and unequivocally

Tory supporters, and later became close Thatcher confidantes. Honours dangled for cash, what's new?

Some months after I came back from Rhodesia a letter arrived at my family's Pelham Crescent address from the Department of Immigration Headquarters, Salisbury, signed by Chief Immigration Officer M. Bryer: 'I am directed to advise you that you are persona non grata in regard to Rhodesia and that in terms of the Immigration Act 1954, your entry thereto will not be permitted. Should you at any time in the future, endeavour to gain entry into Rhodesia, your entry will be refused.' I was proud of that letter and I had it framed.

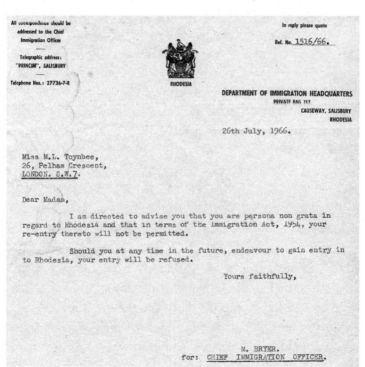

All correspondence should be
addressed to the Chief
Immigration Officer

Telegraphic address:
"PRINCIM", SALISBURY

Telephone Nos.: 27736-7-8

RHODESIA

In reply please quote

Ref. No. 1516/66.

DEPARTMENT OF IMMIGRATION HEADQUARTERS
PRIVATE BAG 717
CAUSEWAY, SALISBURY
RHODESIA

26th July, 1966.

Miss M.L. Toynbee,
26, Pelham Crescent,
LONDON. S.W.7.

Dear Madam,

I am directed to advise you that you are persona non grata in regard to Rhodesia and that in terms of the Immigration Act, 1954, your re-entry thereto will not be permitted.

Should you at any time in the future, endeavour to gain entry in to Rhodesia, your entry will be refused.

Yours faithfully,

M. BRYER.
for: CHIEF IMMIGRATION OFFICER.

But here's yet another political lesson: as it happened, years later I did try to gain re-entry for an article suggested by the *Guardian* to compare life in the Smith Rhodesia Front era, as I had seen it, with what had now become the harsh, violent and starving Mugabe days. But the *Guardian* stopped me going at the last minute following Mugabe's edict that any foreign journalist entering the country would be jailed for two years instantly and without trial.

Josephine at Pelham Crescent

11

Josephine

CHILDREN OF DIVORCE, our lives parcelled out between parents, spend more time together than others, travelling to and fro with our matching attaché cases, as we shunted between South Kensington and Suffolk, two households poles apart. I tagged along behind my sister, protected by her presence. She found me an irritant, especially when our mother dressed us in matching clothes – a sailor hat and coat, the same party dresses – but even so my existence protected her from being the only one shuttling between these starkly contrasting family lives. She had my admiration for her daring, as I followed along after her.

Josephine inherited our father's strong compulsion to do good. She strove for it all her life, admirable but sometimes with disastrous consequences. Like him, she was an impulsive plunger, diving for answers, leaping for better ways to live, seeking escape from the drag anchor of our class. She always seemed to me remarkable – with her great shock of bushy carrot-red hair, as fiery in appearance as in nature. No beauty, she was striking. And she struck me quite a lot as a child: I annoyed her, she blamed me – and as a result I always thought her superior in brain, in imagination, in bravery and above all in a selfless desire to make the world a better place. She was unworldly, I was not. She was reckless and dangerous, I was circumspect and cautious. Observing her rashness, I learned from her some important self-preserving life lessons in what not to do.

Our parents' divorce hit her hard, a damage she felt all her life. She admired and loved our father, disliked our stepfather who was unkind to her, and she held onto an illusory vision of some Garden of Eden that was our Isle of Wight early childhood before the split. Maybe my father breathed those thoughts into her ear: he wrote a well-reviewed modernist prose-poem novel, *The Garden to the Sea*, about a paradise lost where a serpent (my step-father) steals away his Eve. His publisher had to ask my mother's permission to print it, since it was so transparently about her. She agreed, so long as it was kept away from us: he retaliated by sending us home with our muddy wellingtons wrapped in proof copies, after our alternate weekends with him.

Whatever the reason, Josephine was often unhappy, sent to an analyst as a difficult teenager, always vehement in her views, brave and awkward, complicated and unpredictable – but never dull. I felt pallid beside her, but secretly I knew that I could navigate the world while she zigzagged across turbulent seas. She simply refused to follow the map, as she struggled, sometimes comically, to free herself of the guilt of our English privilege.

She would sneak out late at night without my mother knowing, once coming back with whispered tales of a

Josephine

Caribbean club she had found. She would slip out to visit the Partisan, a left-wing Soho coffee bar, where she pretended to be older than her fifteen years. I watched her set off one night wearing a dress she'd made from a hessian sack, returning with gripping tales of vigorous debate and heated argument in the anti-espresso bar founded by the likes of Eric Hobsbawm, Stuart Hall, Kenneth Tynan and Naomi Mitchison. Named the Partisan after Tito's fighters against the Nazis, it served notoriously disgusting Partisan filter coffee, or milky Fabian coffee. Regulars included Quentin Crisp and Doris Lessing. Here CND's radical breakaway Committee of 100 for mass civil disobedience was founded by Bertrand Russell. Here the first Aldermaston marches were planned. Aged about eleven, by then in boarding school in term time, I had almost no idea what Josephine was talking about, but I caught her excitement – and the danger, as she told me she was grabbed by a much older man and dragged into a dark passageway: I only dimly guessed what this meant, or chose not to know or ask.

Though like me, she was an 11-plus failure, St Paul's Girls' School gave her a place, hoping she would flower into following their esteemed alumna, our great-aunt Jocelyn, the Cambridge archaeology professor. Indeed, she did flourish and her cleverness earned her a Cambridge place a year young, and a good English degree. Afterwards she signed up with Voluntary Service Overseas (VSO), and she was sent to teach in a distant village north of Bamenda in Cameroon. All I knew of the country was from *The Bafut Beagles*, by Gerald Durrell, a childhood favourite of mine about collecting animals for a zoo, but that was well beneath her intellectual horizons. I saw her as a Mary Kingsley intrepid pioneering explorer, and as she left, she suggested she might never come back. She wrote me lyrical letters of the bountiful land where palm oil and palm wine flowed from trees freely, yams, fufu and cassava burst from the fertile soil, people and nature in perfect harmony.

As it happened, on my accidental Amnesty International journey from Nigeria to Rhodesia, due to multiple mistakes, lack of visas and money, I found myself hopping from one country to another and I landed in Yaoundé, French Cameroon's capital, late one night. I was shut into a caged area of the airport without a proper permit, where I was allowed to make one call: I rang Josephine. If I imagined she would be pleased to see me, that was an error. Hardly surprising, since it was a very long drive to collect me, down a perilous highway from British Cameroon, along a notorious road that was one way half the week, and one way back the other half of the week. The first thing she said, as she looked at me through my cage, both of us red-faced and dishevelled in that hot deserted airport, was 'I came all this way to get away from you all. How dare you follow me here!' That reminded me of those walks we didn't share as children, where she asked which way I was going and then set off herself in the opposite direction. But she had a point: I was invading her private world and collecting me was a long and arduous journey. But she was stuck with me until both my entry and exit visa arrived, following a message from Amnesty to proceed to Salisbury.

I had imagined her living in a mud hut with a thatched roof of the kind picturesquely painted in childhood geography books, those old books we learned from where the sun never set on the great pink blocks on the imperial map, of which British Cameroon was a part. But when we arrived at her house, many irritable hours later, I was disappointed to find no mud hut in a village with a chief, but a comfortable house with a patio on the edge of a college campus, and, astonishingly, a cook and a house-boy in attendance, who bowed to us. She was sheepish about them, but said they came with the VSO house, and there was no sending them away or they'd be fired. So, there she was, a colonial memsahib, I teased: she wished I hadn't seen it.

A monkey on a string was perched in the porch, and a baby owl. In the wake of the famous Gerald Durrell animal collections, it had become a local habit to bring stray baby animals to any British people in the district, whether they were zoo collectors or not. There is no escaping the empire, she said, with a sigh, but she was fond of them. Other colonial habits died hard. She complained the books she was given and the curriculum set for English literature

Josephine in Cameroon

were well-nigh impossible to teach: how to explain Jane Austen, let alone Thomas Love Peacock, though Dickens proved a little easier.

But the reason for recounting this episode in Josephine's life is the story of Jimmy. He was tall, lithe, graceful with boldly upturned eyelashes, as if they had been curled in a salon. Beautiful, charming, funny, bright, it was easy to see why she had fallen in love with this student from her English class, only a year or two younger. Jimmy was one of eight children, the son of a farmer with some land, ambitious and determined to get his children educated, and Josephine was keen to help the family. When her VSO time was over, his father was delighted and grateful when Josephine asked to take Jimmy home to London with her, promising to send him to a college in England to get qualifications.

Jimmy lived with us all in South Kensington for several years, but spent term time in a college in Chippenham where Josephine had found him a course in agriculture that she paid for: that was what Jimmy's father had ordered him to study, so he could bring home better modern methods for the family farm. But Jimmy never did go home. His student visa depended on him studying, which he did, a bit, but his heart wasn't in it, though he made friends wherever he went. In London he adopted an American accent, and often pretended to strangers to be American, with a cowboy hat, a fringed shirt and a book on American slang. We were all fond of him, enjoying his cheeriness, but things didn't go well. Year after year he failed all his exams: it was not the subject he should have been forced to study. As the two of them were separated

Jimmy and Josephine

during term time, they drifted apart, both had other affairs and we all felt the tensions between them as Josephine frequently lost her temper with him.

Finally, disaster struck. His student visa ran out when the college wouldn't take him back for yet another round of retakes, and Josephine's patience with paying the full cost of yet another failed course ran out too. But he refused to go home. He wept. He dared not face his father with the truth that he was returning with no qualifications. This suddenly became an emergency as immigration officers were about to expel him now he was no longer registered as a student, so what was to be done? Then she had a brainwave. She had once spent a summer working on a kibbutz in Israel, and surely that would be the perfect place to send him, even if agriculture and rural life were definitely not what he liked. So that's where she sent him and we all saw him off at the airport: I don't know if he had any idea where he was going.

Not long after he left England, he wrote enclosing a cutting from an Israeli newspaper with a glamorous picture of himself surrounded by people welcoming the first ever Cameroonian to join a kibbutz, but after that we never heard from him again. He vanished, leaving all of us feeling anxious and guilty. This was a colonial act, to pluck a boy out of Africa and transplant him randomly in Israel, abandoned to whatever his unknown fate might be.

Josephine taught for a while in a school in the East End, and was later a social worker in a West London housing association. But Africa had inspired her: she took an MA in anthropology, and after hearing him lecture, she fell under the intellectual spell of the charismatic rebel Catholic priest Ivan Illich. She went to join his Intercultural Centre for Documentation in Cuernavaca, Mexico, where he preached against the values of modern civilization, its education and its medicine, entirely in keeping with the spirit of those times. He fought against the missionaries Rome was sending into South America, he fought against the US Peace Corps and the other troops of do-gooders sent, as he saw it, as neo-colonialists to impose the wrong culture on the wrong places. Those same people were being sent to his institute by their institutions to learn before setting off on their development programmes, but he urged them to go back and work among the deprived in their own culture, one which they understood. His book *Deschooling Society* called for pulling down all formal education in favour of peer-teaching networks, perfectly suited to the drop-out, anti-establishment mood of the moment. He accused modern medicine of medicalizing death, pain and sickness: his best argument was that health in developing countries should be low-tech, brought to villages by barefoot doctors instead of wasting funds on unsustainable gigantic high-tech hospitals in a few cities for the urban privileged. I met him once when I reported for the *Observer* on the Zeno conference of philosophers in Cyprus. He was indeed mesmerizing and a brittle contrast with the huddle of English philosophers, of whom my stepfather Richard Wollheim was one, as they clung to obscurantist linguistics and regarded this real-world stuff as threateningly outside the realm of true philosophy.

A couple of years later Josephine arrived back from Mexico with a husband, and pregnant with his child. Juan (not his real name) represented everything she aspired to, a simple rural barefoot primary school teacher, semi-literate, but, she thought, a man of the people. We found him bafflingly silent, even when we had Spanish-speaking friends to help translate. She hoped to return to Mexico after her son was born, to live the simple life with Juan in his village, putting into practice all she had learned from Ivan Illich. But things didn't work out that way: that was

Juan and Josephine

absolutely not Juan's intention. He had escaped that simple life and he knew it far too well to find it romantic. They rowed, a lot. He wanted to be a footballer, she wanted them to farm. In the end he went back to Mexico, leaving her to bring up their child alone. His mother wrote letters from time to time, but once she died not long afterwards, Juan vanished.

Later Josephine married a twice-divorced former Anglican priest and they moved to Shropshire to take up ecological subsistence farming. They had a beautiful flock of long-eared goats, kept chickens and grew vegetables. The plan was to make goats' cheese in the big stone pantry, but they never found a reliable enough market to earn a living. He was a powerful and alarmingly controlling figure, frightening us with the way he seemed to have transformed my strong and fiery sister into a nervous and obedient wife. They became much involved with the local church, although he was barred from officiating. When farming didn't provide even a bare subsistence, he took up teaching work in Birmingham to pay the bills – and then suddenly and heartlessly he abandoned her, disappearing. I haven't been able to find any trace of him: I'm not sure how hard I want to look.

She sold the goats, left the farm and took her son to live in Birmingham where she worked for the council. She was put in charge of one of the local neighbourhood housing and social assistance hubs the council was opening then in the name of devolving power from City Hall. Her hub was in Nechells, a deeply deprived district, where she found herself at war with the council, because although they built the hubs they never let go, never devolving power let alone funds to neighbourhood control. That left her facing the daily demands of council tenants in real need, without the resources to do anything but pass their requests on upwards. Here is the fate of so many on the front line of social destitution, faced with obvious need and equally obvious simple solutions to problems, but frustrated without the means to do what needs to be done: the worst kind of working hell is responsibility without power. (I belonged to that opposite profession, the one Stanley Baldwin famously damned as 'power without responsibility – the prerogative of the harlot throughout the ages'.) She used to shake with indignation sometimes when she described her helplessness in trying to support those Nechells residents.

Active in the Labour Party, she met Bill Challis, an older former metal worker, autodidact of considerable knowledge and a left-wing trade unionist. In this third marriage to Bill, here at last was a thoroughly decent and good man, matching her in his constant state of outrage at the inadequacies of Labour politics.

Josephine died in 1998 at just fifty-five, of breast cancer. In the last decades of her life she and I had made our peace and enjoyed each other's company: I stayed with her in Birmingham and she with me in London. She never blamed me for choosing an easeful life of well-paid London journalism, instead of doing good. As the BBC's social affairs editor, I was merely reporting on the issues she was grappling with daily, gritty and all too real, but sisterly resentments had burned themselves out. I am sorry we didn't spend more time together once we had finally made friends. I miss her all the time, for her fire and for her memories, for there's no one left now who remembers the years of our early childhood.

What became of Jimmy and Juan? Years later an American woman called Maude contacted me after reading an article of mine and asked if I was related to Josephine. She told me that soon after Juan returned to Mexico, she met him there while on holiday and had spirited him off to the Midwest, where they married and had two children. But that too had failed soon after. He was last heard of living in a mobile home somewhere on the west coast of America, but no one knew where.

In 2011, out of the blue, I had an entirely unexpected email from Jimmy who had seen me on *Dateline*, a BBC World Service TV programme. He was not on his kibbutz living an agrarian life, but, amazingly, in Stockholm, working as an electrician. Full of curiosity, I hurried over to meet him there to hear what had become of him. We sat for several hours in a hotel bar talking about Josephine, both of us in our sixties, he no longer that beautiful lithe boy, but a rather solid man, nattily, if surprisingly, dressed in a dapper three-piece tweed suit and a tweed deerstalker, as English as he could be. His surname had been Enoh, but had now become Bridgewater, devised I imagine by himself.

Here's the story he told me. When he arrived in Israel he was warmly welcomed on the kibbutz and enjoyed life there – though not the farming. Eventually he was allowed to take an electrician's apprenticeship instead. While he was there a film crew arrived to make a new version of *Jesus Christ Superstar* and he was thrilled to be cast as Judas – what else? He showed me the photographs. He hoped it was the start of a movie career, but though he went to Tel Aviv in pursuit of acting opportunities, that never worked out and he returned to the kibbutz. There he met a Swedish girl, Birgitta, who had come to work for a summer just as Josephine once had. She took him back to Stockholm with her, where they married and had three children. He told me they had since separated and he was now on his own.

He talked of Josephine with great fondness. I asked if he felt he had been plucked from his roots. But no, he was full of gratitude, saying he felt in the end they had both behaved badly to one another. I had brought with me a photograph I had found that I thought he would like to have. Josephine took it of Jimmy with his Cameroon family on the day he left home, all of them standing in the bright sun with his parents and his brothers and sisters.

Did he ever get in touch with them, ever think of visiting or taking his children to see them? Tears fell down his cheeks and he said he just couldn't and didn't: he had left it too late and the longer he left writing that letter the harder it got. They never got to hear what became of him, their lost son.

Jimmy with his family in Cameroon

I tried to keep in touch with Jimmy, but I stopped receiving any replies to my emails. I wondered if he had been upset by our meeting, by my questioning him too personally about his life. Two years later an email arrived from Birgitta, his ex-wife, informing me of his death. She asked for details about Josephine and Jimmy's life in England to tell her daughters, so this is my reply. But she says she is saddened to read it and prefers not to show it to her daughters.

Reporting on industry for the Observer

12

Escaping Oxford, Starting Work

I THREW MY education away, and I regret it. Think what millions of others would have done with all those learning riches. Though I was miserable at an expensive school, it was good enough with a few excellent teachers, but I ignored whatever didn't offer instant gratification – Shakespeare, history and art yes, Latin grammar, maths and physics shamefully neglected. Though Holland Park comprehensive temporarily rescued me, I threw away my unexpected Oxford scholarship, abandoning university midway through second year. Why?

It's far too long ago to summon up an honest answer: I could say my time in Rhodesia made me impatient with mediaeval Latin and French, reading Bede or even grappling with Gibbon, Macaulay and Hobbes. I could say arriving mid-disastrous affair with a married roué TV presenter the same age as my mother, a famously seductive character, notorious (I didn't know) for a succession of young girls discarded in turn, until a few years later he killed himself. I could say that having my first novel published in first term was an act of such presumption that it set me up for a crash landing at Oxford. I could say it was that Gamble scholarship's unbearable pressure to get a first, with my two great-aunts walking their dog down to visit my tutors regularly to enquire after my latest essays. Maybe it was taking up with Jeremy Sandford, screenwriter of Ken Loach's *Cathy Come Home*, and living part time on his ramshackle Brecon Beacons farm looking after ragged sheep and ponies. In truth, I can't recapture the blend of woe and impatience that propelled me out. My shocked tutor, Jenifer Hart, said, 'You will regret this for the rest of your days. Everyone who leaves here tries to come back and we never, ever take them.'

It must have taken the cocky self-assurance of a secure middle class background that I never doubted I would earn my living. It was 1968, drop-out era, jobs were plentiful and no one worried. It was another universe for my luckiest of generations, compared with my pressured grandchildren who will emerge into a land of ferocious competition for fewer chances. But I did feel a fundamental distaste for Oxford and all its ways, its conceits and arrogances, its denizens' obnoxious certainty of their superior merit. The very beauty of its colleges seemed an opulent affront. Whatever the reason, I threw it all away recklessly. Because everything is preserved forever by the recording angels of the internet, those on the right who detest what I write in my *Guardian* columns sometimes dredge up my lack of a degree as ammunition to prove my stupidity and evidence that I don't know what I'm talking about.

Tate & Lyle

Insofar as there was a plan, this was it: I had to pay back my scholarship money, and I would earn my living by working all day with my hands, leaving my mind free to roam over the next section of the second novel that I would sit down and write in the evenings. I was not intending to write about work or factories, just to earn enough to get by for now while I wrote my modern *Middlemarch*. I took a job on the production line of the Tate & Lyle sugar-packing factory, beside a trickling remnant of the River Wandle in South London, where it was easy to walk up and straight into work.

Inside the great vaulted works, issued with overalls, hairnet and cap, the shattering, clattering and clanking battered the ears, while deep vibrations sent clouds of sugar dust up into the air. At first sight, these mighty machines gave me the same initial thrill I felt riding the combine harvester. I'd been working as a waitress in a Wimpy and then in a Golden Egg, but I preferred the drama of a factory, the sheer ingenuity of what these machines could do. Besides, factory work paid more into the weekly brown paper pay packets of notes and coins, because it was well unionized with everyone a member of the Transport and General Workers' Union.

'Sitting next to Nelly' was the only induction, training or safety instruction in manual jobs back then (so is it still in many jobs, I later found). How you got on depended on what kind of Nelly you were lucky or unlucky enough to be put beside. The sugar came cascading in a torrent down chutes into the waiting blue and white Tate & Lyle paper bags that whirled round the conveyor belt at high speed as metal levers shot out and folded down one paper flap after another, adding a dollop of glue before scooting the bags down the line. There were two basic jobs: one was standing under the chute by the metal levers to pull out bags fast if any misfired, split or failed to seal. The other, less skilled, was heaving in turn first six then eight bags off the line to stack into boxes on a slower conveyor line behind. Rhythm was vital: too slow and the bags risked falling off the end, so new girls were not welcome until they fell into the quick-heaving routine. At two pounds a bag it was back-breaking, until you learned – or Nelly showed you – how not to put your back into it. There was music, not quite *Workers' Playtime* as broadcast from a factory every day until a couple of years earlier, but the big bands and early 'light' music of Radio 2.

Camaraderie was warm, but it was the enforced cheeriness of soldiers at the front: you kept going because you had to. But of course I didn't have to at all. Given the choice, none of these women would have been standing there on aching feet all shift long, day after day, hoisting, heaving, singing and bellowing to one another now and then, to keep at bay the sheer boredom and the mind-dizzying speed of the revolving sugar bags. They struggled to keep some sign of human wit alive above the noise, humans used as engines of the humblest sort: it was the machines that did the clever work.

I would get home exhausted and aching, but beyond that, deadened in the brain by the noise and the transfixing monotony of the same action repeated ten thousand times over. So how was that second novel coming along? How was all that working with my hands to keep my brain free for higher things? It was a sharp lesson in why factories, construction sites, laundries, cleaning agencies, warehouses and catering kitchens don't seem to produce their fair quota of literary output. I stuck it out for a couple of months, as a matter of pride, to prove to myself I wasn't a middle class weakling, too soft and spoilt to do an ordinary job. But I lasted no longer. Not a word emerged on paper of an evening onto my old black Remington typewriter. What finally propelled me out of the factory was a growing bloom of a rash, all up my arms and then legs and face, itching like fury, unhelped by Pond's or Nivea. The other women laughed: they all got it, they said, the sugar rash, but it usually wore off after six months as your body got used to it. I didn't wait to see.

An accidental journalist

Why would you, if you had a choice? And I was born with choices. At university after my novel was published I was commissioned to write sometimes for the *New Statesman*, including an ill-advised attack on Oxford that caused a measure of outrage. I had never intended to be a journalist: George Eliot was the aim. But asking around for any writing work, by luck I discovered the *Observer* needed a temp for a week or two to cover for someone away ill on the Pendennis column, a miscellany of short pieces. When Anne Chisholm, the page editor, came back, she said she'd been wanting an assistant so she kept me on, no one apparently noticing an extra job added to the payroll. When I talk to young aspiring journalists now, all with not only a degree but an MA from a good post-graduate journalism course, they are amazed it was so easy to slide into newspapers, but 1968 was a lotus time of plenty. Not just newspapers with their burgeoning magazines and arts sections but a mass of good and interesting jobs were expanding to embrace my lucky generation. That's not just what I observed, but it's backed by statistical evidence on the growth of good jobs absorbing all the graduates from new universities and mushrooming white collar jobs taking in the children of blue collar families. If I were starting out now, without qualifications I would never get near a newspaper job.

I never meant to be a journalist. But once I was there, sent out with notebook and biro, I was gripped by reporting. Writing the real world was more exciting, more intellectually perilous, more unexpected and alarming than anything I was capable of inventing for myself. Things are never as you anticipate, never as you plan, people don't say or do what you expect. I think I might have taught myself to become an adequate work-a-day novelist, but never good enough, whereas curiosity takes you a long way as a reporter, just needing to know, looking and asking, prying into people's way of life and their thoughts, with an urge to capture and pin down on the page what you have seen and heard, quick, before it slips away.

Cyril Connolly, in *Enemies of Promise*, warns the would-be great writer against journalism for its devouring deadlines, its corrupting instant satisfactions, fast into print and rapidly rewarded with a fee. But I found plenty of promise in reporting. His other enemy was 'the pram in the hall', and that from a man. I was fortunate, of course. Though my career slowed right down for a while with four children, with my class, money and two-earner household, childcare was not the impossibly expensive nightmare it has become for my children's generation. Neither journalism nor children were my enemies because the truth was plain to me: I had never had George Eliot or Virginia Woolf promise, the kind that does require a sound-proofed writing room of one's own, without deadlines or prams in the hall.

I gravitated to the news desk where, whenever possible, I pushed to report on work and labour. Industrial stories, strikes, strife and unions were staple news and I was drawn to reporting on the nature of work and its conditions, eager to puncture the myths of all that 'dignity of work' extolled by those not doing it. The right-wing press fulminated at *I'm All Right Jack* strikes about tea breaks but if, from a newspaper office chair with the laxest of working hours, you never saw conveyor belt work, you wouldn't know the value of every precious tea break minute – for a smoke, a tea, a pee or just to sit down briefly and rest your legs. If you didn't understand the monotony and ache of each extra five minutes watching the clock, then the indignation at being cheated of extra pay for extra time would look trivial.

But what did I know? Feeling ignorant of the world beyond my upbringing, I took time off to set out around the country, taking jobs in different towns and industries to try to understand work and a working class world a planet away from my South Kensington background. I meant

At the Observer office, 1969

to see life from the ground floor, not the upper landings. I wasn't setting out to explore grinding poverty, but ordinary unskilled manual work in jobs I could walk into without question. Often the middle class writer's eye is instinctively drawn to extremes, to the romance of the gutter, to the homeless on the streets, to the near-starving and desperate cases. Traditionally that attraction to the lowest depths came with a Victorian disapproval of the undeserving or else with a philanthropist's pity or just sometimes grim fascination with how far humans can fall. Instead, I wanted to report on the ordinary, the everyday work it took to keep a family's head above water. That's where the great class divide yawns, right there, the grand canyon in education, life chances, surroundings, sense of security, expectations, presumptions – there in the nature of work itself. Setting out as a journalist, I needed the knowledge for my own inner exploration to acquire some sense of the world beyond the thin air of my rarefied background.

'A Working Life' – Lyons cakes

That journey is now over fifty years ago: I was twenty-three in 1970. Living standards were lower, everyone had less of everything than now, telephones, central heating and cars all rare, but most people were acquiring more. Some working conditions were worse back then, but the gradual improvement in safety and pay seemed inevitable and irreversible.

But I was wrong. Back then, I would never have guessed so many legal working rights, hard-won by the unions, would be lost half a century later in the world of Amazon warehouse semi-slavery, delivery driver zero-hours hell and gig economy home carers.

I started out at a large Lyons cake factory in West London, working the machine that put cream on the long stream of pink and yellow angel cake before it was cut into smaller slabs and wrapped further down the line. Each factory had its own rhythm, its own habits and foibles, I learned. I could have sought out backstreet slum work-shops for more shocking stories, but I chose famous name companies, so no one could claim these were untypical.

Lyons, however, turned out to be dirty and nasty, the wages not good for London. The squalid environment made the staff spiteful and resentful with one another, the noise far too loud for conversation, not even shouted. All communication was non-verbal, but just as expressively abusive. Trying to capture the obsessive details of the daily work, here's what I wrote at the time.

I found myself being maddened with rage by the woman sitting opposite me, large, sour and middle-aged, who had worked there for years. She was controlling the flow of the cream machine and it was her job to put the top layer of the cake onto the second layer as it emerged. I had to lift both layers and put them onto the third. As we sat opposite one another the speed at which she worked determined the rate at which I had to work. As she did her bit first, it meant I had to do mine later and a little further down. If she was slow or held onto her cake for an extra moment, I had to lean further down the line, which was uncomfortable and she knew it. We never spoke a word but there was a great deal of aggression between us. She would hold onto the cakes longer and longer, and sometimes I would have to get up and walk down the line to catch up. We also had to clean up the spare cream that often came out onto the belt. She was quicker than me with the palette knife and would clean up my bit too. Then I would get better at it and poach onto her bit. The point was that sometimes no cream came out of the machine and we had to spread it ourselves from the cream in the bowl beside us. The cream in the bowl was the spare cream we had gleaned off the belt, so we had to collect as much of it as we could. That is what preoccupies everyone on an assembly line. Ask what we were thinking – we were thinking about how infuriating the person we worked with was, or we were waiting for the next bit of spare cream to spill onto the conveyor belt. A stupid boring job makes a stupid boring mind.

A theme of the book I wrote, *A Working Life*, was that no human is stupid enough for dehumanizing work such as this. I found some research that I can't now trace because it may be apocryphal, that said in America during the war some chimpanzees were set to work on a conveyor belt, and productivity rose.

Port Sunlight

I went to work next at Unilever in Port Sunlight outside Birkenhead on the Wirral. There is a romantic appeal in the great industrialists who strove to create whole communities of better living standards around their factories – Saltaire in Bradford, Bourneville in Birmingham or New Lanark, south of Glasgow. Port Sunlight is a quaint village of mock-Tudor cottages built as model worker housing in the 1890s by William Hesketh Lever, later Lord Leverhulme, 'to make cleanliness commonplace; to lessen work for women; to foster health and contribute to personal attractiveness, that life may be more enjoyable and rewarding for the people who use our products'. Getting off the bus at the entrance to Port Sunlight, I was delighted with the charm of the place, with its tree-lined grassy verges, a garden to every half-timbered house. Everything is in miniature, its gothic community halls, a Roman temple, an art gallery, a bowling green and open air swimming pool. Here was the embodiment of the philanthropist's fantasy, imposing cultural as well as physical improvement on the working classes. People come from miles around now to admire this strangely artificial little world.

The rich often fantasize about ways to straighten out working class lives: at least Lord Leverhulme put his money into it, even if his methods were dictatorial. On a Sunday he would order a parade through the village with the Sunday school and the band, marching at its head himself, obliging villagers to come out on their doorsteps to watch politely. In the early days Lever started out with a small token profit-sharing scheme, but it amounted to nothing much and was abandoned, nothing to resemble the genuine generosity of John Spedan Lewis who gifted his whole company to the workforce of John Lewis & Partners. Or indeed, C.P. Scott who bequeathed the *Guardian* to an independent non-profit trust in perpetuity.

The village was Lever's toy, his social experiment, and the rules were strict – no washing on lines in the front, gardens to be kept neat on threat of eviction, only the right sort of families to be offered housing here, where the rent was still cheap when I lodged there. This is the kind of power and influence wealthy donors often seek, as they lean heavily on those charities they sponsor with their own amateur ideas on how to do good to the less fortunate. I think of City lunches I have sat through among donors who pontificate at length about the lack of aspiration or moral fibre that are the root causes of poverty. Philanthropy is their justification for stupendous wealth, although the statistics show that the rich give less as a proportion of their income than the poor. Expect no introspection from the plutocrats as to whether, just possibly, they themselves and their overweening political influence might be major contributors to the politics that permit poverty.

Since I wrote about Port Sunlight, historians have uncovered shocking facts about Leverhulme's Belgian Congo operation where he had set up plantations producing palm oil for his soaps. The Congo was the most brutal of all European colonies, controlled personally by King Leopold II, whose regime murdered an estimated ten million enslaved Africans. Leverhulme arrived in 1911, just after Leopold's era, and though he attempted to build African village versions of Port Sunlight for his own employees, beatings and forced labour were an integral part of his Congolese operation. As a result, statues of him are named in Black Lives Matter's list of monuments that celebrate colonial atrocity, to be removed or at the very least to bear an accurate historic record of his use of slavery.

I lodged with the Parkins, in their fifties, who had lived there since they married. Mr Parkin was Port Sunlight born and bred, went to the village school and worked all his life in the soapery. They rented the house from the company and let out rooms now their children had grown up and fled village life. Their other lodger was a silent man hired by the dredging company working on Port Sunlight dock. Mr Parkin was terse and orderly, a strict non-conformist and a Conservative voter though only earning an average working man's wage. Mrs Parkin was more rebellious. 'Father,' she said, 'is a great believer in the village. I think you have to be born here to accept it. It isn't just that it's a dead place with nothing happening, it's because it belongs to the firm. Everything belongs to them, every bit of grass and breath of air. Other women here feel the same way.' No shops, no cinema, no bingo hall and the one melancholy pub, the Bridge Inn, was closed on Sundays. Most people went to the Brown Cow in Bebington outside the village, where I sometimes met women I worked with: I find it has closed down a few years ago. Most of the women I met didn't live in the village and shuddered at the thought of being trapped in a home owned by their employer. At that time the village had a sad, run-down air and the communal activities felt dusty and desultory, the boys' brigade, the girls' club, various sports clubs. These days, when I revisited, I found it brightened up, owned by a trust separate to the company and bidding to become a World Heritage Site, but its inhabitants and its visitors are ageing: only 10 per cent of homes have children.

Mr Parkin's one sin, his only indulgence, was a little mild gambling, doing the Littlewoods pools on a Thursday evening, when he would draw up a chair at the table and show me how it was done, with a booklet explaining full perms, and Lit-plans, filling in the forms with intricate precision: 'two entries of lit-plan 80 = 120 lines at 1P = 50P'. He was full of stories he'd heard of people doing the pools for twenty years, but when they thought they'd won, finding they'd filled the forms in wrong for all that time, wasting all that stake money. On a Friday night the Littlewoods man came round to collect the money and the coupons, always with a cheery 'Could be your lucky week!' But Mr Parkin was tight-lipped about what he'd do if he won. The pools, in pre-Lottery days, were a daily dream, a non-stop topic on the shop floor where I worked, the only distant possibility of escape. Everyone needs a window of a chance that life might change, even if it's only a pinprick of light.

The housing back then was in a bad condition, the Parkins' the dampest I ever came across, the curtains in my room wringing wet. The village was built on a marsh not quite reclaimed, Mrs Parkin said, as her washing wouldn't dry. But at the time it was built the housing was exemplary: 'Best in neighbourhood, bar none,' Mr Parkin would say. It had an inside bathroom but an outside toilet. He had remedied that by building one for the household in a slice of my room, separated by a thin hardboard partition through which, I wrote at the time, every sound was audible 'from the snap of elastic to the crinkle of lavatory paper'. (No knicker elastic these days, and lavatory paper doesn't crinkle like the Jeyes of those olden days.)

One deterrent to living in Port Sunlight was the over-powering smell. The soap was everywhere within a mile's radius, enough soap in the air to make your nose itch, sometimes the smell of Lifebuoy, sometimes Surf, sometimes just sulphurous and chemical, with a constant roar from the factory at one end, which glowed in the dark at night. Sometimes when there was rain after a dry spell, foam appeared on the roofs and in the village gutters.

My job was in Number 3 Block, the scourers' department, on the belt packing Dot, a lavatory cleaner, and Vim, a bath cleaning powder. The bright blue and green powder poured down a high chute into plastic canisters, creating a faint blue haze in the room, sneezing silicone dust in your hair, your eyes and clothes and under your fingernails, a cloying sickly-sweet industrial scent. My job was to watch the lids slammed down on the fancy pink bathroom packs and pull out the faulty cans fast when the machine glitched, before they were tipped on their sides and fell on the floor. Dot was caustic, so a small spill made holes in your tights.

As in every workplace, there were unofficial traditions and habits: here there was 'spelling', when one spare person would come up to you and say 'Shall I spell you?' and you could slip off to the toilet for a smoke and rest five minutes before the supervisor came after you. When you came back, you 'spelled' someone else in rotation. But it doesn't take much to upset such dull routines: the shock came when the old toilets, there since the place was built, were closed and Josie the attendant was forcibly retired. She used to make her favourites cups of tea, chatted and cheered people up: she cried on her last day, offering everyone cocktail biscuits and sherry in tiny painted glasses. In the new toilet block, at the far end, was a new and stern attendant, who to everyone's horror wouldn't allow smoking; 'Fire regulations,' she said. Spelling was tightened up after that. Trivia? That was the point of reporting from the factory floor, at a time when tea breaks and working patterns caused strikes and made news. Ridiculously petty unless you work a nine-hour shift, day after day and every break in routine is infinitely precious.

One evening I had a drink after work in the Brown Cow outside the village with Linda, the same age as me who stood by me on the same belt, and Freda, a serious drinker in her late forties. Yes, I'd been at university, I said, and yes I was only working here for a while. They tried to imagine university and other aspects of my life but the chasm was so wide there were too few points of common experience to explain what that social divide meant. I hadn't the words or the heart to try to describe what it meant to be me, and so we settled on talking about things we all knew, our culture in common, pop music, TV programmes, supervisors at work, pay. One woman on the line who was a Girl Guide leader had asked me if there much Guiding at university: I said I hadn't seen any. But they did know university was the golden key to another world, and as Freda said, 'Well, of course if I'd had the opportunity, things would have been different.'

Linda said what I heard people say over and over: 'I should've tried harder at school, but I messed about. I was bored. Stupid, isn't it, how you throw away your chances?' And I thought about how casually I'd thrown away mine, but those chances boomeranged back to me effortlessly in a way they rarely do for the Lindas if they miss that one-and-only step up on the schoolroom ladder. Because my class stuck out like a sore thumb, this was a conversation that came up again and again. I wrote at the time about how people blame themselves. They see in some mysterious way that school was a chance, but because they failed – or their schools failed them – it must be their own fault that they ended up paid a pittance in a drudgery job without prospects. Here's the distressing corollary: that must mean anyone who made it through exams and on upwards probably deserves it. Polling shows most people want to believe that they live in an essentially meritocratic society, because it may be unbearable to think the cards are stacked against them from birth. Each time I left a job, leaving behind people who had been friendly, warm and interesting, I stepped back across the rope bridge between the two worlds, indignant, ashamed, but of course overwhelmingly relieved to be back on my own home turf.

A strike

I wrote a chapter about each job, but I'll only sketch them out here. Finding lodgings in Birmingham, with the usual lino floor and single ceiling light-bulb, I got a job as a switch cable operator in one of the city's eleven Lucas car parts factories, stamping cables into bulb holders with a hot cutter and a press. While I was there a strike by foremen and charge-hands caused 19,000 car assembly line workers to be laid off for a short while. This was the first strike at Lucas for as long as anyone could remember: the high drama of it shattered the monotony, and it sharply divided workforce opinions. Now there are no Lucas plants left, with those just-in-time car parts delivered mainly from abroad instead. Were strong unions to blame? Checking the records, it's worth noting that in that year three million days were lost to strikes – but 146 million days were lost to industrial accidents and diseases. It's the winners who write the history, so the 1970s have gone down in mythology as a time of out-of-control industrial action and union power gone rogue, though the root cause of economic distress was the oil price crisis and soaring global inflation that forced workers to fight to prevent their pay falling behind rising prices.

Coal and steel

I lived for a while in Brinsworth in Rotherham, with a retired Steel, Peech and Tozer steel worker and his wife, where I spent time in the steel works and down Manvers colliery, one of eight in the district. I watched steelmen firing up the gigantic furnaces, faces pitted from spitting hot steel, and miners working all shift bent double in a seam only two and a half feet high. Coal and steel, jobs of high intensity, high danger and high pay, carried the old prestige they had in the war as the mighty backbone of the nation's industry. But they were already teetering on extinction, a tragedy in the making. I am glad I was there to observe the true nature of those 'heroic' industries that were so ruthlessly shut down by Margaret Thatcher. There was always that essential conflict: the work was back-breaking and ferociously dangerous, so these men's sons should have been better off for never following their fathers down the pits: sentimentality and nostalgia should have been misplaced when they closed down. But instead those jobs were replaced with nothing but unemployment or low-paid security guard work.

I'd had no idea how appalling the conditions would be. The journey to the coal face from the shaft was a long rail ride, followed by a half-mile walk stooping low, very low for men, in a tunnel that grew hotter the further you went, at risk of tripping in heavy boots over rocks hidden in the ankle-deep water. The helmet was essential, protecting against jagged outcrops overhead. To reach the seam itself we had to worm along the final 200 yards of tunnel, very low now, never higher than two and a half feet. At the face men spent their entire shift crouched over or on their bellies operating lethal coal cutters in a cramped space, weaving between hydraulic pit props only a foot or two apart. Even when they stopped for a rest, they couldn't sit upright, but rested their heads on their knees. In those days, unsurprisingly, some 700 miners a year were killed or permanently crippled.

This was a decade before Margaret Thatcher swung her great wrecking ball at heavy industry, but the writing was already on the coal face about the demise of mining: the steel workers I met already feared they would be next. In the book I report one Steelos' union shop steward's sad prescience. Listening to the men boasting to me about their pride in steel-making while underplaying the hardship and the danger of their work, he said to me out of their earshot, 'In the old days you'd have found some miners saying the same things about the glory of their work, when mining was an essential industry. Now, for them, it's nothing but a dreadful job.' Work propped up by government subsidy was, he said, just charity on borrowed time, and they knew it. Then he added, 'It'll be the same for us very soon. They make steel cheaper in other countries. We look at the mines and we feel in our bones that it won't take long.'

He was right, but both industries put up a fight. A decade later in 1980 the steel industry went on strike for the first time in fifty years, striking for pay to keep up with inflation, but above all to stop the closures they feared. After fourteen weeks out, with great hardship, they returned to work with only what they called a 'slimline' pay rise. A year later, steel works were brutally shut down in Corby, Shotton, Consett, Scunthorpe and many more. The miners' last stand was their strike in 1984, a fatal, tragic year-long struggle, badly led and nobly suffered, to no avail: in 1984 Britain had 174 deep mines, but only four were left by 2019. Nothing replaced the catastrophic loss of well-paid jobs in these old heavy industries.

Later came a good example of what might have been done: when the Berlin Wall fell and East Germany, an impoverished rust belt of bankrupt industries, joined prosperous West Germany, a colossal investment of $2 trillion was the price paid from the rich to the poor sector to level up this newly unified country. That took thirty years of a 5.5 per cent Solidarity Tax from Westerners to invest in the East. Despite giant strides, the East still lags a bit behind, but nothing like the chasm that divides our North and South, or our rich and poor. Now we have a government promising to level up all those places 'left behind', mostly northern ex-industrial towns still devastated forty years after Thatcher, but without a whisper of that rugged and generous-spirited West German determination to unify through sacrifice.

The political wickedness was that failure to provide other well-paid work, letting globalization rip with importing instead of manufacturing. 'On your bike,' Norman Tebbit famously said, and some did manage to move away from workless towns, but most hadn't a hope of finding expensive housing in the better-off places rich in jobs, so those communities remain as barren scars, the next generations bereft of status, money or purpose.

The Army

I joined the Women's Royal Army Corps (WRAC) for a while, at the barracks outside Guildford. Eager to recruit, they had a scheme where you could sign on for six weeks, and then leave if you changed your mind. Here I found class stratification fine-tuned into an art to keep officers and women in their ordained places, non-commissioned officers below the salt, warrant officers uncomfortably perched straddling the two. The officers were posh girls who went to schools like my boarding school: I was a very rare posh girl in the ranks largely peopled by vulnerable lost girls from the poorest places. The WRACs were trained to do nothing but service roles, which meant servicing the men: they were drivers, potato peelers, secretaries and dogs-body auxiliaries to relieve men from irksome drudgery for fighting at the front: back then women were banned from fighting, no guns allowed. The WRAC wasn't disbanded until 1992, when relegating women to subservient roles had finally become politically unacceptable.

I worked next as a ward orderly – now renamed health care assistant – in the maternity ward at the old St Stephen's Hospital, in London's Fulham Road. That's been pulled down, merged with the Westminster teaching hospital, rebuilt and renamed the Chelsea and Westminster, replacing the run-down former workhouse where I worked.

* * *

When I ended my explorations, well aware of the pitfalls and potent absurdities in this kind of class-crossing expedition, my book was published and serialized in the *Observer*. Here's a comically revealing episode: I was invited to talk about it on the Michael Parkinson TV chat show, stepping down his famous glittering staircase in a long dress, with the band striking up as if for a movie star's entrance. What was I doing, of course he asked, a posh girl like me, taking these menial jobs? What did working class women make of me, with my middle class accent? But mainly he wanted the grim details of life in the dark satanic mills of Britain's factories. That felt odd: he interviewed me as if I were an intrepid Victorian lady traveller returning from the jungles of the Dark Continent, bringing home reports from some uncharted wild place. Yet I had been nowhere except right here, in our own country, right next door, down every ordinary street. That, I felt, proved the purpose of reporting the world of low-paid work in this first person style. By doing the jobs myself, by taking readers on a kind of travelogue, I could bring the likes of us – Parkinson, myself or *Observer* readers – on the journey across the great them-and-us divide. I wondered uncomfortably if any of the people I had worked with might be watching me describe their ordinary working lives as if they were the freakish oddities, as if Parkinson and I were the norm, amid the artifice and razzle-dazzle of a television studio.

Philip with the Barn House commune's cow

13

Philip – Older But Not Wiser

ALL HIS LIFE my father struggled to do good, and mocked his own failed attempts. By nature he was a millenarian, living with apocalyptic fears that the end of the world was nigh. And so it may well be, the planet tipping perilously towards disaster. Astronomers know without doubt the world will end when the sun dies, however many millions of millennia beyond our imagining. The question is whether it ends sooner out of sheer human idiocy.

He was one of the early founders of CND: he launched a peace march across Europe to Hungary in the 1950s. I set out on my first Aldermaston march with him at thirteen, after listening to him speak in Trafalgar Square, his voice echoing oddly around the lions and fountains. Unfortunately, we never got to Aldermaston. As was his wont, he stopped off at the Bunch of Grapes in Knightsbridge before the march had left Belgravia, and we got no further, as I waited and waited on the step outside with orangeade and crisps.

I did go for the whole four-day CND Easter pilgrimage every year after that, without him. To be honest, the Aldermaston march was the great social event of the year for me and my friends, we who aged fourteen had proudly founded the Chelsea YCND group. Aldermaston was the Glastonbury of my generation. We were genuinely terrified of imminent global obliteration – but we had a very good time too, spending the night in community halls in sleeping bags, partly partying along the way.

My father's fears of nuclear annihilation were so serious that halfway to a holiday in Abersoch, the family car had to be turned around because he had forgotten the large jar of death pills he had accumulated to mercy-kill everyone in the event of nuclear war. We went a few times on holiday to Decca Mitford's island, Inch Kenneth, off Mull, though by now she was so thoroughly Californian she barely ventured outside into the brisk Scottish climate, certainly not for the one mile walk around the island nor for rockpooling or fishing on the breezy beaches. Once

Philip at Inch Kenneth

my father was so panicked at forgetting the killer pills he begged the island's bailiff to row him across to Tobermory to buy up the town's entire supply of aspirins. We had all read Nevil Shute's *On the Beach*. We knew what was coming. We knew exactly what Strontium-90 fallout does to you and how you die. We knew that RAF Fylingdales' early-warning system would give us just four minutes to say goodbye and I carried banners on CND marches listing what you can do in four minutes: boil an egg, run a mile...

The songs of those marches have stayed with all who were there:

> *Don't you hear the H-bombs thunder*
> *Echo like the crack of doom?*
> *While they rend the skies asunder*
> *Fallout makes the earth a tomb.*

There were many verses and we know them all.

> *Time is short; we must be speedy*
> *We can see the hungry filled*
> *House the homeless, help the needy*
> *Shall we blast or shall we build?*

The rousing refrain ends 'Ban the bomb, for evermore!' But it hasn't happened, not yet, so the bombs are still here, now bequeathed as precariously as before to our grandchildren. At the time of writing, the British government is planning to increase its supply of nuclear warheads, though the existing 160 are each capable of incinerating a large city and all its inhabitants, but yet we need more.

However, those first throat-gripping, middle-of-the-night terrors of nuclear holocaust did somehow fade into the background over the years. Listening to my father, I expected the world to end before I got old. But here I am and so still are the death-dealing H-bombs. If anything, those nuclear arsenals are more unstable than back in the heyday of our CND demonstrations, now in the hands of countries not sanctioned by the UN to possess them, while sooner or later some terrorist will build a lethal dirty bomb in a suitcase.

But that gut-churning panic moved on to embrace other alarms. My father's end-of-the-world anxiety turned to sustainability. The ecological collapse of the planet took over. He was right, and he was early onto the plain fact that meat-eaters were and are the cause of global hunger; if everyone ate plants there would be plentiful food for all. Rearing a kilo of chicken flesh takes the equivalent of two kilos of grain. Cows belching methane use twenty times more land than plants to produce a gram of protein... But he was a meat lover, so it was a sacrifice: he compromised with three days of meat and four vegetable days. He had never cooked before, but he made himself unspeakable vegetarian stews – chunks of carrot, parsnip and potato boiled up with dollops of Marmite – so inedible he would wait until a minute past midnight for the next meat day to cook himself a late-night steak. I try, I eat very little meat – but my children are genuine vegetarians as are many friends, and I am not as good as them. No, I have no worthwhile explanation for this dereliction, nor for my many other short-comings in ecological and social virtue.

Suffering increasingly from severe depression, my father set off in search of enlightenment to ease the pain. At first it was encounter groups, communal searchings for self-awareness in the alternative world of meditation, spiritual experience, something, anything to reach out for meaning and fulfilment. He tried hard, though he was supremely unsuited to these intense social gatherings. By now he had become quite solitary, seeking less and less company beyond his family. The struggle with drinking and smoking continued.

So it was an act of extreme self-denial, renunciation of his own nature and state of mind when he decided to set up an organic farming commune in his own home, Barn House in Brockweir. It would be self-sufficient, growing its own produce through the sweat of its brow, while raising its sights to higher things in a communal search for something spiritual. Sharing everything would finally solve his life-long problem with social inequality and his endless tussle between God and Mammon. Here was a way out of the inexcusable, unforgivable guilt of a middle class life of ease while others toil for a pittance. The commune would mean sharing everything. (Though, of course, not quite. Never quite letting go of the purse-strings.)

Self-denial it might be, but it was extraordinary dictatorship too, since poor Sally and Clara, his youngest child still at home, were dragged along in this endeavour. Sally joined him in all he did, as in his later religious seekings, but it was never her choice to cut their house up into cubicles, tear out central heating and modern labour-saving devices like the washing machine, and invite in a host of communards who arrived in answer to ads in the alternative press.

Tragically she joined him too in alcoholism – or not joined him but took to her own particular secretive drinking style. She would leave the room and reappear some time later flushed and talking with elaborate enunciation, so as not to slur, and quarrels would begin. It was a clever kind of revenge on him for all he had done to impose his own will forcefully on her life.

He writes in his diaries, *Part of a Journey*, 'Sally was very dubious about the capacity of either of us to endure a communal life. She knew that although I had ostensibly once lived a life of almost frenzied social activity, I had become no less frenziedly dependent on longer and longer intervals of total privacy. But at this point nothing and nobody could have stopped me and I joyfully took part in making the drastic structural changes to Barn House which would enable ten people to be accommodated.'

The perversity of this struck friends and family alike as a madness, a kind of martyrdom, choosing to do good in the way that would cause himself most pain. Of course Decca Mitford, the great mocker and unsentimental leftist hard-liner, made relentless fun of the commune's airy aspirations, as did many other friends, visiting gingerly and infrequently, staying in a local pub. She writes, 'The unanswered question in my mind was why this absurd, pre-doomed experiment? I feared to ask Philip, who was often in the throes of "clinical depression". A pit of despair unimaginable to one who had not suffered it.' Other oldest friends shuddered in horror. His great friend Paddy Leigh Fermor said that when Philip had revealed the commune idea on a picnic at Tintern Abbey, 'I had never heard a worse plan. He appeared to me at once a figure out of

Peacock, determined to put theory into immediate practice, like the Shelley or Byron figures of the novels.' And of
course my father was well aware of all those absurd possi-
bilities and their comedic potential. But he drove himself
on with extreme determination to force himself to try to
do what was right. Admirable and unbearable to watch.

Josephine did visit and try to participate in my father's
spiritual endeavours: she too had struggled often with
depression and was in permanent search of meaning. But
I stayed well away, barring short rare visits, appalled and
resistant. By then I had young children, as well as a job
and a husband who was entirely uncomprehending of this
self-induced suffering, so I mainly avoided the commune.
Philip was only half joking when he would wag a finger
at me and my metropolitan ways, warning that we would
come crawling to the commune door from a starving
London, begging for a cabbage when civilization collapsed
around us. He did send us all matching commune tunics
for Christmas, Tolstoyan apparel he adopted to suit his
new Tolstoyan beard.

The commune started out intent on farming. But by
1977, the Barn House communards collectively drew up
the wording for a new prospectus that showed the way
it had already drifted: the commune was 'united by their
wish to experience community living and by their common
interests in organic gardening and farming. But over the
years there has been a gradual and quite unplanned shift
of emphasis in the attitudes of most members towards the
deeper purposes.' Indeed, it was an 'unplanned shift' away
from farming, digging and self-sufficiency to meditation,
chanting and 'deeper purposes' that didn't include much

manual work. Two days' work a week was prescribed, but work might be following 'our individual paths, which currently include pottery, puppetry, music, drama, herbal medicine, yoga, tai-chi and private meditation'.

In writing her memoir of Philip after his death, Decca recalls her frequent visits, casting a mordant eye on the commune's progress.

> Sally's commodious kitchen had been converted into a sort of scullery for the preparation of natural food, vegetables and the like. The environmentally offensive central heating had been taken out. The elegant staircase had been demolished and the hall divided into ugly little cubicles to house the inflow of communards and their children... The cast of characters was constantly changing as the Alternative People came and, having scant experience of the rigours of farming life, soon departed. Disaffected urban school teachers, university students bent on Finding Themselves – flotsam and jetsam of English society.

This, Sally later said, was too harsh, and a tad snobbish of this old communist, but Decca wasn't far off the mark.

Decca noted that Philip 'never relinquished his comfortable quarters, while Sally was consigned to one of the cubicles'. On her last visit there, Decca writes, 'The Commune had turned, predictably, into a horror scene.' She tells of resting in a bedroom one afternoon. 'It was freezing cold. Soon Sally came back with an electric blanket saying as she plugged it in, "For God's sake don't tell Philip. It consumes electric energy, he doesn't know I've still got it."'

Decca, my mother, Philip and Sally at Barn House (the couple at the back right are Terence and Joanna Kilmartin)

The aim was total self-sufficiency. He cut down the apple trees to make a pasture for a cow and intended to do away with any electricity not generated by their own windmills; Sally said later the engineering had defeated him, 'so toasting forks and scrubbing boards became the order of the day'. Decca brought her no-nonsense daughter Dinky (Esmond's child, Constantia, always known as Dinky) to stay with her young children, and a row ensued: Dinky is as firm a socialist as Philip was but also a strong feminist, a concept he never grasped, as she championed the rights of downtrodden women communards hand-washing their nappies now the washing machine was dismantled.

My father couldn't survive here long: his depression and need for privacy made his ideal of shared living unbearable in practice. They escaped to Woodroyd, a small cottage nearby in St Briavels. 'We would remain associate members of the now flourishing Barn House community and I fully intended to work in the fields which I had worked so hard at clearing of their trees and shrubs only a year before,' he wrote in his diary. Indeed, he always had a Stakhanovite appetite for hard physical labour, and had made and remade many gardens and vegetable allotments all his life. Just before the commune he had spent two years creating a complex water garden, now all pulled out for farming.

But his failure to live the communal life and his shame at escaping from it cast him into his deepest depressions yet: 'my inability to tolerate community life had seemed to me like one of my life's major failures'. He spoke of coming to terms with not 'living above one's moral means', a good phrase: the commune had stretched his moral means to bankruptcy. He had also just come to the end of twenty-five years of his daily writing of *Pantaloon*, the poetic work he called his 'tragi-comic epic'. Searching for the reasons for his distress, he adds, 'I still had a full array of childhood mistreatments for the benefit of any psychiatrists who may lay hands on me. But I could not find that any of this was enough to explain the real horror and anguish which I was experiencing. Even my vague and undulating spiritual beliefs were being crushed and ground, so it seemed, in that terrible mill of pain.' Amid plentiful anti-depressants, he finally opts for ECT, electric shock treatment, which helps, but doesn't cure.

His diary entries on the ending of the commune after years of struggle are comic and sad and irritable. They appear as light relief in his book. For at this point, to my shock, contrary to his upbringing of all of us, strongly against the grain of his atheist father Arnold and atheist grandfather Gilbert, he plunged quite unexpectedly into deeply religious thought and belief. Even he, who had always shaken his fist at any God up there who could inflict such undeserved suffering on wretched earthlings below, even he, in extremis, turned to the supernatural. His mockery of religious absurdities was dinned into me with my first breath, so this intense God-bothering felt to me like a great intellectual betrayal, but then he was in far worse pain than I could ever imagine. Nonetheless, I couldn't bear his attempts to draw me into any conversations on the subject. His book chronicles his spiritual searchings, his experimentations, musings and meditations, his impressively omnivorous theological reading, his intellectual contortions over God and the curse of depression. His suffering demands pardon for anything that helped relieve it, but all the same, I find the God-seeking just as excruciating as I re-read it now.

He never joined a denomination, but towards the end of his life he discovered the nearby convent at Tymawr where he visited often. Those wise nuns took him under their wing, discussed and disputed with him, offering calm. They admitted him as an honorary oblate – one step before becoming a novice, a kind of associate membership. Years after Philip died the convent sent me a prayer card in memoriam for the death of their mother superior, Sister Paula, who had been his spiritual mentor.

Whenever I meet someone who asks if I am related to Philip and proceeds to praise this particular book of his, telling me how much it means to them, I wince. I know at once this reader is a Christian, among whom the book still has quite a wide circulation. They love its blend of searing honesty about himself, his inadequacies, his suffering, his humour, his erudition and his seriousness about theological thought and a God of love.

But I find it an unendurable read, both for the agony of his pain and for the false balm of his new-found religion. He brought me up to be not just an atheist, but rabidly anti-clerical, forever making rude jokes about what God was up to, pointing skywards and shaking a fist. In the war he and a friend would put on dog collars under their army uniform and go out drinking, behaving uproariously, telling filthy jokes until fellow soldiers would say, 'Steady on, Padre!' I have been President of Humanists UK and am life Vice President now, of which I'm proud and I've been delighted to find I am travelling in my great-grandfather Gilbert Murray's footsteps. I am not just not religious, I am an enemy of all religions that seek to impose their laws on others. We live only once and the only purpose is to try to improve life on earth (in which we mostly fail). No, that is not in itself a 'religious' idea, as some claim, but a naturally evolved impulse towards progress among humans as social animals who, unlike animals, know the certainty of their own death and that propels the need to feel something is achieved in their brief life.

I can relish the culture of the bible and Christian mythology because it is so deeply embedded in history, literature, ethics and art that it can't be shed from my cultural identity. The same is true for every religion: everyone is wrapped in the stories, values, imagery and culture of their mosques, temples or synagogues. But that cultural history doesn't require belief.

My father tangles with Voltaire's old conundrum: what monster of a God would kill the innocent indiscriminately? In an echo of Voltaire's assault on God over the 1755 Lisbon earthquake, Philip writes, 'Is there weeping in heaven for the poor victims of the Italian earthquake? Surely there must be: and yet Heaven is supposed to be a PLACE OF JOY! Really there are times when all this kind of thing seems so puzzling and contradictory that I wonder whether it mightn't be better to think no more about it, (As if I could!)'

That is the heart of the impossibilism of belief: my father's perverse solution was an all-loving God who unfortunately, despite being creator of all things, is for some obscure reason not all-powerful. I thought that a preposterous evasion. My atheist grandfather and great-grandfather might point to more convenient religions which solve that problem: the gods of Olympus or Valhalla or Hinduism are not good, but sympathetically human in their failings, jealousies and foibles. They are dangerous and capricious gods who need appeasing, but not necessarily forces for good. As Gloucester bewails in *King Lear*, 'As flies to wanton boys are we to th' gods; / They kill us for their sport.' If you must have gods, that at least makes sense.

Since both Philip and his mother, in their different ways, converted later in life, Christian admirers of my father's book look askance at me. Retired vicars sometimes write me letters on Basildon Bond notepaper: you'll be next to see the light, wait and see, and sometimes they send me old copies of books like C.S. Lewis's *The Screwtape Letters*. But I would regard a deathbed panicky plea to a newly summoned God as a shameful abnegation of a life intent on facing the finality of death.

However, avoiding the theological ramblings, the diary extracts from his everyday life are as acute, disarmingly honest and gratifyingly redolent of the best of himself as ever. So I shall use his words to describe the ending of the commune.

November 1977. Enthusiasm continues to wane. Lip service is paid to work as prayer, the holy soil etc., but meditation, yoga, zikr, even astrology, now take up much time and energy.

6 March 1978. This insistence on 'doing one's own thing' can simply be a form of selfishness... Mary, for example, is going off for her third meditation course next week just at the time when intensive work on the land must be underway.

14 March. Simon tells us that there is no longer any enthusiasm for getting the vegetables sown or planted – as indeed I'd guessed from the state of the fields.

Standing high on a scaffolding with Simon, painting the outside of the house, 'Suddenly we heard a frightful scream from down the hill.' They dashed down and into the wood to find communard Phil 'a little abashed. Once out of earshot I asked Simon what on earth was happening. "It's only Phil's primal scream therapy," he said and I broke into howls of primal laughter.'

That same Phil features shortly afterwards:

As I was starting the fearsome task of clearing the big front flower bed at Barn House, Phil came up and offered me a whetstone for my hook. Then he stood, watching me work, with the full intensity of his shaggy earnestness. I gestured, as if whimsically, at a particularly tall clump of dock and thistle: and Phil thought this over for some time before saying, 'If you mean you want me to do some work, Philip, I'm afraid I can't because I'm just going up to meditate with Rose.' Later, refreshed I suppose by his meditation, he appeared again and delivered a little homily to me as I sweated away with hook and stick... Hilarious looked at in one way... I realised Phil will never do any work here... I thanked him quietly for his advice.

Things went from bad to worse in May. One evening a fanatic called John 'made a dramatic entrance just as we were beginning Sunday's communion'.

We were aware only of a rather mysterious, bearded presence as we made a place for him in our circle and he sat impassively through all our goings-on. He revealed himself to be a fundamentalist and revivalist Christian, a quiet unquestioning fanatic of the most alarming kind. He likes to be an enigma, will tell us very little about his background, except that he was once an actor and a sinner, but suddenly saw the light in South Africa. Since then he has lived in total poverty, preaching the word, relying on God to look after his bare material needs.

We quickly discovered that any sort of religious discussion was quite impossible: his only method of argument is to quote from the New Testament; or to say he knows the truth because Christ is always with him.

An impressive, infuriating, deeply worrying young man.

The new arrival divided the community between the susceptibles who fell in at once to become John's obedient disciples: 'John has come and has brought me back to Christ,' one announces. And the others, eclectic in their patchwork of Sufi, Buddhist or pagan compendiums of practices, who kept their distance.

As it happened, John had walked in from no one knew where at the excruciatingly awkward moment when Philip and Sally had decided to announce that the commune would be closing, the house would be sold and they must all leave within a few months. John came as if he were 'a Bailiff of the Lord', my father notes to himself wryly, as his divisive arrival perversely helped to seal the commune's fate. It was a fate predicted absolutely by family and friends, which only made it the more excruciating.

'I felt basely materialistic when I reminded them of the present economic situation: no money in the kitty; the pick-up a wreck and quite incapable of passing its MOT; the fields still a mess; the house itself in desperate need of renovation...' Many of the original communards, the ones my father was fond of, had departed already. It would now need five more people willing to work 'to save Barn House from dissolving into an irredeemable mess'. He argued with them: 'Who will weed the fields? Rotovate them? Rake them? Sow them? And when? "Don't worry so much, Philip! It will all get done if it's meant to be done." Inside my head I tear my hair; outside I heave a heavy sigh.' Argument swelled up, with one of them accusing him of thinking the commune was indulging in 'too much spirituality. Too much spirituality', repeated with bitter emphasis. Discussion slid away into the abstract question of the nature of the spirit, 'where every practical issue is vaporised as soon as raised'.

They wouldn't commit to staying for any fixed time when he tried to find out 'how many were reasonably sure they would be there in twelve months' time... six months' time... three months' time. But the usual answer was that he/she could make no promises at all, for who could tell when they would be directed to do something else.'

He tries hard to feel this has not all been a failure. 'The bargain had been a fair one; we provided them with the physical means of living and growing together; but I doubt they learned half as much from us as we learned from them. In fact I doubt whether they learned anything at all from me, for what did I have to teach? Whereas they, for all the rich confusion of their ideas, taught me a great deal about openness of heart and mind. The more tragic if they should fall under the aridities of dogmatic fundamentalism.' Many of them did fall under the spell of John's absolute certainties, about which my father talked to wise Sister Paula of Tymawr; 'Ah,' she said, 'the hotline to God. A dreadful danger.'

Philip had always known, of course, that ownership is the root of capitalism, the fundamental truth that defines, undermines and belies all human relationships. It can never be airbrushed away. From now on, he writes,

I could not help but be aware (and nor I'm sure could anyone else) that I had bared my teeth at them for the first time: brought out into the open for the first time the hard fact of ownership; the hard fact of who pays the piper. We have been so scrupulous over these four years never to pull that on any of them; always to present ourselves as simple members of the community... This would be a community without a boss. We had said that after five years we would turn Barn House into a trust and completely resign all special property rights in it. But at that time we were envisaging a stability that has never in fact been realised.

The original members had scattered, the newcomers were not committed to farming, and the final thunderbolt from hell was John.

Philip confronts, honestly as ever, the difficulty of giving everything away. He sees himself as the man turned away by Jesus because he was rich and could not or would not part with his wealth, the man as unlikely to enter the kingdom of heaven as a camel to pass through the eye of a needle. Not that my father was rich, with only this broken-down house as capital and exceedingly low pay from his weekly *Observer* reviews. But all wealth is relative and in relation to these communards who had nothing, he was Croesus himself. In him, as in all middle class left-wingers, God and Mammon are always at war and Mammon tends to get the upper hand. But before anyone throws that old stone – the hypocrisy of left-wing would-be-goods – which of them ever contemplated giving their property away?

John was by now breaking everything apart, a terrifying man with ferociously manipulative skills.

I knew I was falling into the pit of hatred for this intruder. Mixed with indignation at his invasion of our Barn House, his taking of our good friends and comrades, his brutish disturbance of our community... this unholy anger got mixed up in my restless mind with an equally unholy anxiety about the sale of our thirteen acres. Will we get enough? Will we get it before it becomes too late to let the fields for this year's grazing? Anger, greed and fear – a hideous trio of tormenting demons.

Depression, new anti-depressants, deepening agony, God, guilt and days unable to get out of bed follow: 'I woke to that aching lassitude which is the physical aspect of depression. So I stayed in bed all day and without guilt...' These are interspersed with fretting about money. 'The looming sale of Barn House has stimulated my greedy anxiety to an almost unequalled pitch. Have we asked enough from that very pleasant potter from St Briavels? Could we get more if we restored the house to its pre-community state? How much shall we give the children?' Oh, that's another perennial cry of every parent who has any capital: is giving them money bad for them? But how can you have money and not share it with those you love more than life itself? That's why inheritance tax, the fairest distributor of wealth, is by far the most overwhelmingly unpopular in every poll. He ponders, 'How much should we give to a good cause? How much will be left to protect me from my fears of destitution – a life without beer?' He pauses to consider Arnold's money fixations. He worries his thoughts are 'alarmingly like my father's almost pathological obsession with money. But unlike him I am not only fearful of ruin but also giddily extravagant. New speakers – again! – for the music centre: an electric lawn mower; and now at last a colour television. This last was always a symbol for us of the grossly unnecessary possession; so it was with some relief when buying the set to learn that 70% of the population now own or rent them.' Here's his comical addendum to that purchase of a colour TV for Woodroyd cottage: 'A large part of my motive for this new acquisition was the naïve but persistent belief that gadgets can help me towards the Truly Good Life. As I watch Cousteau's frogmen glide between shoals of brilliant, variegated fish I shall suddenly fall on my knees and praise God for what I have apprehended by means of those paradisal shoals. At only £270!'

At Barn House things went from bad to worse. 'A very ugly scene. I'd gone over there to start the huge task of

Commune workers at Barn House

clearing up the garden, having begged them to do a little of this themselves. But not only had nothing been done, they were lying and lazing about in the ruined garden, soul music from the open window, one very pregnant girl sitting naked on the edge of the swimming pool in full view of the road. What's more, half the people were strangers. A crash pad...' Lest you imagine Barn House was ever a seat of luxury, the 'swimming pool' was a small plastic contraption propped up on the grass.

'I delivered a violent harangue to which nobody spoke a single word in answer.' As I read this I shudder a bit. Oh yes, we his children know well what it was like to be on the receiving end of one of those full-volume angry harangues, truly terrifying. He writes, 'It was Them and Us with a vengeance now; the sweet freaks and children of nature up against the angry proprietor whose only thought was to drive them all away and sell the empty house for a fat sum.'

5 August:

Our *Times* ad of Barn House appeared on Wednesday – 'ideal for any form of community or retreat project'. Only one bite, by telephone but when we met the couple – elderly and rich – we knew from their first dismayed glance at the house that they wouldn't dream of buying it. And as we looked at our old dishevelled home through their eyes we saw all too clearly what an unattractive proposition it had become. How different from the bright, neat and charming house we first set our eyes on in November 1959.

That reminds me how fond I was of that house in the early days. It was never smart or beautiful, but welcoming. I was twelve when they moved from Suffolk to the Gloucestershire/Monmouthshire border, glad they were now close to where I was miserable at boarding school in Bristol. Some weekends I was allowed out for the day to take a train from Temple Meads through the Severn tunnel to Newport, where my father collected me for a day of adventure with him, stupendous food and warmth from Sally and the pleasure of playing with my three half-siblings, safe from the many torments of a boarding school Sunday. I look back on that pre-commune house in my childhood as a haven of escape, a far cry from what it had now become. My father's drink problem was contained by his strict daily routine, only bursting out whenever a visitor came. It took a few years before I finally recognized Sally's growing alcoholism. I remember early Barn House days as a place of comfort and refuge from school.

Continued ill-feeling, alas, with the remnants of the commune. Surely, we say to each other, they could do something to improve the appearance of the place, seeing that the damage had all been done by their long negligence as non-paying guests... Dave R told us that two of the communards were just going off on yet another meditation course. 'No', I said, 'they can bloody well stay and do some work, or bugger off for good.' 'Ok, Landlord!' said Dave and stabbed me in the heart, as he intended. But I pulled the stiletto out pretty smartly as I walked back fuming through the woods...

My God, I thought last night in bed, what an endless strain it is to try to live rightly.

A year later, the last stragglers from the commune had eventually departed, the house had been put back into some semblance of an ordinary dwelling and had finally been sold.

The contract for the sale of Barn House has at last been safely signed and sealed. So now we have a great deal of money in the bank, of which some – but how much? – will be given to Oxfam as a conscience saver. The gift won't be very effective in that function, but at least it may keep a few children alive.

Meanwhile in our unregenerate state, the thought of that solid sum to be transferred to a building society does give a certain cowardly comfort. It is also, of course, a barrier between us and God. Considering the interest that will accrue to us, I am again scandalised by a system that so brazenly adds more to them that hath. (But not, apparently, too scandalised to take advantage of it.)

At another point he agonized: 'The best thing we can do is to give up four-fifths of our income to the starving; live with the utmost simplicity, combined with the most apparent love; not cut ourselves off from ordinary company but bear quiet witness to our faith by what we have become and therefore are.' But of course he didn't become that holy abdicator of all earthly and material things.

Thus ended my father's heroic endeavour, his attempt to invest every part of his life and soul in being good, in living the good life, generously and openly. But as he said himself, this was living well beyond his moral means. Although it crops up time and again, mentioned in passing, he seems not to have given himself enough credit for some of the best good he did, in setting up Depressives Anonymous. For over thirty years he kept up long correspondences with many profoundly despairing people around the country, most of whom he never met, though he did sometimes travel to meetings. Plainly his patient and thoughtful letter-writing was a lifeline for large numbers of desperately unhappy people, as he generously gave away hours a week of writing time to ease their pain, and perhaps to some extent his own. Some of them wrote to me after his death.

But on the demise of the commune, friends and family had to button their lip and never say those killer words, we told you so: no gloating. The imposition on his wife and children of his moon-shots at saintliness seems hardly to have crossed his consciousness. The damage done to his youngest, Clara, the only one still at home to be dragged without her consent into the hell of commune life, took her years to recover from, she says. I was horrified when recently she told me that her mother admitted to her in later life she had been worried Clara might be born with foetal alcohol syndrome, due to her heavy drinking binges during pregnancy. Clearly not, but all three of my half-siblings later tell me how much they had suffered from both their parents. How lucky again in my life that my mother whisked me away from my father young enough to escape the effects of his atrocious parenting.

He was rather less curious about his children's characters than the character of God. I can't help being outraged that the only mention I get in his diaries is a brief pro-forma saccharine description of a visit to my family that shows he plainly had not the remotest idea – nor much interest – in my state of being. 'A very cheerful visit to Peter and Polly's house near Rye. I wasn't quite a witness to the love of God, but a good time was had by all. Decca and I clowned away together as of yore. S and I felt a great admiration for Polly, who is the most radiantly easy of all my children... She is a wise and loving mother, an unobtrusively good housewife and entertainer of friends and relations. The best kind of Martha – the one who would be too good-natured to make any complaint against Mary.'

Martha! Good grief! I don't think he ever read what I wrote: he took *The Times*, not the *Guardian*, so didn't bother to see what I was about. He never read the many years' worth of columns I wrote for the pioneering feminist *Guardian* women's page. He was encouraging about the novel I published while I was at Oxford, but I don't think he commented on my other books. This 'good housewife' stuff was the highest praise he could think of, the best a woman could be: feminism passed him by.

If I was in any sense the 'easiest' of his children, that would only be because I was the one least brought up by him, my mother having fled from him when I was three, for which I am grateful. My older sister partly idolized him and often yearned for his elusive approval in her own attempts to lead the good life. My half-brother had the hardest time in terms of intellectual expectations, bullied and chastised over exams and homework because he was a boy: my father was never much concerned about his four daughters' education. One half-sister felt neglected, ignored and then put-upon at a young age, summoned back home whenever they were in trouble, while Clara had a miserable adolescence in the commune psychodrama.

After the commune my father was, on and off, in a bad way. The depth of his depression and its physical effects hid a stomach cancer his GP had overlooked as psychological pain. By the time they opened him up, they took one look and sewed him up again.

He was dying just as I left the Labour Party and joined the newly formed Social Democratic Party in 1981, so our last conversation face to face in the hospital was his finger-wagging at me. Not that he was a Labour Party member himself, but CND had revived, women had gathered at Greenham Common's peace camps, where my sister arrived only to be turned away as she had a male with her (her six-year-old son). Labour leader Michael Foot was a disarmer, which, along with a policy to pull out of Europe and NATO, was a precipitating reason for those twenty-eight Labour MPs to split away and form the SDP. Misguidedly, I tried to do the impossible – to somehow bring together my betrayal of Labour with my father's CND beliefs I'd inherited, so at the SDP's first party conference I arranged a fringe meeting for SDP-CND: I think it was the only occasion in that polite new party that a riot broke out, and the meeting was forcibly broken up: SDP-CND was never revived.

As he lay dying Philip was desperate about the fate of *Pantaloon*, his epic poem, two thirds still unpublished. We talked on the telephone as I scurried around publishers and anyone who might help assure him that the whole work would appear in print. He had once told the author Robert Nye he intended the work to be *A la Recherche du Temps*

Perdu, Don Quixote and *Paradise Lost* rolled into one, and he was not mocking: after his death Nye called it 'a remarkable achievement, perhaps a masterpiece that will no doubt be published and hailed as such'. Frank Kermode and Stephen Spender were among those who had written glowing reviews of the first volumes that were published, and they did their best to help find a publisher before Philip died. Michael Schmidt was keen for his Carcanet Press to publish but it would need an Arts Council grant for such a huge undertaking: the grant wasn't forthcoming. I failed, but Philip died when publication was still a possibility. The manuscript sits among his papers in the Bodleian Library waiting to be found. Thomas Chatterton, he said to me wanly, was only discovered and published posthumously, thinking of the Pre-Raphaelite painting of the young poet lying dead in a garret. Philip died in 1981 aged sixty-five.

Philip at Barn House

Incidentally, 'John' the destroyer emerged in the press a little while after the commune closed. A court case was reported of a young man, not named John, of aristocratic family of some unfamiliar title who, together with a disciple, carried out an act of exorcism that involved the brutal beating of a young woman they proclaimed to be possessed of the devil. She died, but 'John' only received a five-year sentence. My stepmother said my father read that story and was outraged by the shortness of the sentence, but no one realized until years after my father's death that this was indeed the same religious maniac whose fanaticism finished off the Barn House community.

* * *

A postscript on the Barn House commune. One of the early communards wrote to me gently to say how fond he was of Philip and Sally, how much they had helped and supported him. Indeed, he was the one they were always fondest of, the model of the early joiners they originally intended to hand over to. 'Yes, we were all naive about the realities of that kind of lifestyle and fairly ignorant of the practicalities when we joined. However, as you say, in hindsight Philip and the rest of us were going in the right direction. We were fumbling our way, trying to realise a new model of living that nowadays seems spot on – alternative energy, organic farming, vegetarianism, recycling, anti-consumerism and involvement in the local community. Some of our systems were quite radical – all income was pooled (in a pot by the front door) with outgoings recorded in a logbook, each putting in all they could and taking out according to mutually agreed needs within a transparent trust-based system. Similarly, people contributed what skills and labour they could.'

He himself toiled in a local quarry and harsh mid-winter potato fields to assist. He says, however, 'My parents saw it the other way round – why was I contributing my wages from working in a quarry and labouring on the property at weekends without getting paid? Was Philip putting in his wages and share dividends? Wasn't I being exploited? I didn't see it that way but it was an understandable viewpoint.' He sends photos of hard work in progress in the fields. Certainly we who only looked at it from the outside were emotionally, intellectually, and maybe morally incapable of understanding the noble motives of those who helped found the commune.

Working as a dinner lady

14

Work, Thirty Years Later

FOUR CHILDREN LATER and thirty-three years after writing *A Working Life*, my first exploration of manual jobs, I set out again to see how much had changed since then. The political universe had pivoted on its axis several times. Labour prime minister Harold Wilson's utterly unexpected loss to Tory Edward Heath in 1970 was the first general election I covered as a junior reporter on the *Observer* news desk, and it was a salutary lesson in the danger of falling into group think: polls said Labour had an unassailable 12 per cent lead. Watching Heath's morning press conferences where he was knocked about daily, mocked and ridiculed by the press, by Tory papers too, it seemed to me inconceivable, impossible, unthinkable that this charmless and humourless leaden lump could beat the agile, astute, witty and canny Harold Wilson. But I learned an early lesson: Tories usually win, as they have for over two thirds of my lifetime. Last minute bad balance of payment figures gave Heath a very late swing. Another lesson: economics is as much a victim of fashion as hemlines, for who worries about the (habitually very bad) balance of payments now? Or, for that matter, the 1980s obsession with the money supply.

Years later, I have learned another lesson from that election: politics changes in retrospect. Looking through the rear view mirror, Edward Heath has become more of a hero, the man who, against all odds, and by sheer determination, managed to push and pull this recalcitrant country into the European Union – then the Common Market – where we belong. Compared to who came next, his detested usurper, he was the last hurrah of respectable post-war conservatism, the last leader to have fought in the Second World War, with the social awareness that came with that experience.

The seismic culture shock of my generation was Margaret Thatcher's 1979 win, securing her party eighteen long years in power, turning post-war Britain upside down. Not at the time, but only in retrospect did there seem to have been any kind of broad post-war consensus between Labour and Tories, sometimes called Butskellism, after Rab Butler and Hugh Gaitskell, two thinkers from each party neither of whom made it to prime minister. At the time the parties had always seemed far apart. Not until after the great tsunami of Thatcherism was it apparent there had been at least a mutual acceptance of government responsibility for key industries, the basic elements such as energy, water and rail, whose privatizations have turned into a serious error. Harold Macmillan had been the great council house builder but Thatcher's right-to-buy lost two million council homes and broke up old communities, as new landlords bought up council properties. That cast the next generation into private renting, home ownership their only and yet increasingly too distant hope. For the left, it was an agony to live through those eighteen years that changed the nature of Britain, its assumptions, its sympathies, its old post-war welfare state instinct for collective solutions. A generation grew up with no experience of those impulses, few trade unions, forced to be more individualistic because there was less of a national safety net for them.

By now I was a columnist on the *Guardian*'s op-ed page, an opinion writer, but I was feeling the dangerous aridity of sitting at a desk opining and not enough reporting. There is a risk, perched in our safe crow's nests, that we issue haughty judgements and instructions to the politicians and the policy-makers, the managers and the organizers. From up aloft we lob down our views on the heads of the people who have to confront society's problems day to day. I try to leaven my columns regularly with reporting, that fresh blast of unexpected actuality.

Five years after that 1997 euphoric election night of Tony Blair's 'new dawn', it seemed a good time to look again in close-up at how much Labour had changed people's lives, especially in the nature of work. Tony Blair and Gordon Brown had introduced a minimum wage, along with tax credit top-ups to low pay that eventually lifted a million children out of poverty. Were working lives altered for the better?

I had changed: I was only in my early twenties when I wrote *A Working Life*, naïve and just finding my feet as a reporter. With uncertain steps, I had been exploring for myself a working class world I knew nothing of, feeling my way in the dark. I was, in a sense, training myself as a reporter. Until sitting down to write this memoir now, I hadn't re-read that early book for years. Looking back, the reportage does capture the texture of those times vividly enough, but it feels to me jejune.

This time, in setting out to research *Hard Work: Life in Low-pay Britain*, I was far more sociologically and politically aware after many years of social reporting for the *Guardian* and as the BBC's social affairs editor. I had absorbed shelves full of social studies, including voluminous social class research, so I could better place what I observed in the context of the economics and politics of the last decades. This time I knew exactly what I was looking for and why I was doing it.

The question was simple: what quality of life is the reward for a standard manual job? A minimum wage is a step forward, but how easily can you live on it, pay the rent and the bills? How are people treated in low-paid work? Last time the purpose was to educate myself. This time I intended to make a more forensic analysis of exactly what kind of life a minimum wage buys – and what it can't. It can't buy so many things someone on my earnings takes for granted, things that are out of the question for anyone on the minimum wage. Last time I didn't count every penny or calculate the precise value of my pay packets. This time I determined to live only on what I earned, keeping a close account each day of costs: despite years of social reporting, I was shocked to find how little I had known of the true price of everything. If I didn't know, nor would most of my readers.

I went to live on the Clapham Park estate, only ten minutes from my home, and yet a world away. That's how Britain is, London above all, with interleaved council estates up close to the prime real estate that gleams in estate agent windows. Yet the two apartheid worlds are barely aware of each other's existence. This accident of geography has not created mixed communities: people in private housing never venture through the gates of housing estates. The closest that estate dwellers are likely to get to the inside of a Clapham Common home like mine is as a cleaner.

White House was one of a row of crumbling 1930s blocks of flats on the Clapham Park estate's west side, its once white façade pockmarked with deep holes exposing wires and concrete, scaffolding holding up nets to catch chunks falling off the roof. It had been waiting a long time for a facelift and repairs, dustbins overflowing outside, lift shaky, staircase evil-smelling. That's why I could rent one of its unlet flats temporarily from the housing manager. He was a man I knew well, as I had been following the fortunes of this estate since it was chosen as one of the country's thirty-nine most deprived, for Labour's New Deal for Communities improvement projects.

My fourth-floor flat was desolate and unfurnished. Counting out exactly how much – or how little – I would get from a social fund loan for a rehoused destitute tenant, I bought myself a bed, bedding, a pair of armchairs, a TV and basic pots and pans from a second-hand furniture charity; the money didn't stretch to curtains or a curtain rail.

Without trying this for myself and counting every penny, I would never have known that over the months ahead on the minimum wage, it was never possible to save enough for a pair of second-hand curtains: that's why you see so many windows covered, like mine, with a nailed-up blanket. I thought I knew what things cost: asking the price of a standard loaf or a pint of milk is an old trick for catching out Tory politicians. But when I was weighing up every penny in terms of the hours it takes to earn them, the cost of everything takes on quite a different complexion. With

Outside White House on the Clapham Park estate

a bad headache, I went out one lunch break to buy some Nurofen – but found that cost about an hour's work, and three times more than own-brand aspirin, which would do.

You don't starve, but living day after day on nutritious lentils, rice and porridge with an orange as a treat is atrociously dull. Spices are expensive when the hungry electric meter is ticking in the corner and alcohol to cheer a tired evening would tip you straight into debt. I was on my own: I thought how much harder it must be to budget with children clamouring for pizzas. With children, the emptiness of life would hurt: never taking them to a movie, nor shopping for anything but cheapest basics, no swimming sessions nor train rides, no holidays, refusing birthday party invitations because bringing a present is unaffordable, all that denial is everyday life for minimum wage families I had interviewed. Children often go hungry in families living with their noses pressed up against the windows of a consumer society they never join. How often, reporting on poverty over the years, I received infuriating letters, emails and comments on the online threads underneath my *Guardian* column from pious people smugly describing how well they brought up their children on simple food, homemade clothes, no trashy toys but good books from the library. I never believe these virtuous middle class puritans lived on this little.

But a critical mass of voters don't believe poverty exists or that it's caused by low incomes. Look, they say, these people have TVs and mobile phones! Those are the voters who ensure this country stays a largely Tory fiefdom. Some poverty-deniers have been forced reluctantly to accept footballer Marcus Rashford's personal evidence that children do go hungry, but then they blame it on feckless parents.

You can hear those opinions echoing down the centuries ever since the Poor Laws came in, the very same arguments that Beatrice Webb thrashed out in the Royal Commission on the Poor Laws, that helped drive my wretched great-grandfather Harry into the lunatic asylum. But I relish one particularly obnoxious recent example. Baroness Anne Jenkin, wife of right-wing Tory MP Sir Bernard Jenkin, chaired a press conference in 2014 to launch the House of Lords report of the All-Party Parliamentary Inquiry into

Hunger in the United Kingdom. People are going hungry, said the Baroness, not because they have no money but 'because poor people don't know how to cook'. She said, 'I had a large bowl of porridge today. It cost 4p. A large bowl of sugary cereal will cost 25p.'

The *Daily Telegraph* reported her findings that 'families are being driven to food banks because they lack the skills to shop on a shoestring. Lord Nash, an education minister, said the poor required more education in managing their money. Iain Duncan Smith, Work and Pensions Secretary, said people are going to food banks because they get divorced, ill or addicted to drugs, adding it's "ridiculous to blame the government". The reason children go to school hungry was "because their parents could not, or would not, wake up to make them breakfast".' As it happens, that year Chancellor George Osborne had announced another £12 billion to be cut from benefits: the biggest of all his cuts would be taken from families with children. Most households taking this cut were in work, but with their incomes topped up with tax credits as the minimum wage paid them too little to cover the rent and survive.

The reason I wanted to write in detail about living on low pay, accounting for every penny, was to rebut all those who choose to believe, like the authors of Baroness Jenkin's report, that poverty is people's fault, caused by their bad housekeeping and fecklessness. People on benefits, said the report, 'may have difficulties budgeting', because their money is too often 'devoted to non-essential items of expenditure'. Instead of cooking 'decent meals from scratch, they are more likely to rely on ready meals or takeaways'. Yes, Baroness Jenkin, a bowl of porridge for 4p is a bargain, but you try living on oats and lentils permanently and you too would yearn for takeaways.

Porridge has been rich folks' answer to poverty for centuries. I wrote the introduction to a reprinting of *Round About a Pound a Week*, a ground-breaking 1913 report by Maud Pember Reeves and a group of Fabian women who had for a year detailed the precise household accounts of mothers in Lambeth Walk trying to keep their families on the standard man's manual wage of £1 a week. These reporters chose only the most prudent working class women, with non-drinking, non-gambling husbands, mothers who scrimped every farthing to maximize calories with bread and dripping as their family's staple diet. Sure enough, at the time this meticulous Fabian report was greeted with exactly the same upper class response: if only these women weren't such 'bad managers'. Pember Reeves, so clinically analytical, lashes out contemptuously at the well-off who reply to her study by 'preaching the doctrine of porridge'. Anne Jenkin comes from a fine old tradition of porridge-preachers. Indeed, she warmed to her theme by inviting the *Daily Mail* round to lunch to show how she could cook up a meal for 57p: she served the reporter soup, rice and lentils, followed by banana and powder custard. The *Mail*'s verdict? 'Simple, filling and very tasty.' So here we are, back with the argument that never changes: poverty is caused by fecklessness and dependency, not by sub-survivable incomes.

* * *

Settling into White House, I got to know my neighbours: eccentric Mick next door became a friend as did the Somali family below. I might have been just out of prison, psychiatric hospital or escaping a violent partner, but no one asked personal questions because in London people don't. There was no lock on the block's front door, so at night sometimes there were people gathering, taking drugs, drinking or sleeping on the concrete landings, often alarming. Surveys on the estate found few residents felt safe.

At the local job centre, I found no shortage of work back then. The limit was on which jobs I could reach for an affordable bus fare, the tube far beyond the purse of a minimum wage worker. Mostly, I walked to save fares: the first essential of jobs involving standing up all day was comfortable shoes, but cheap shoes hurt.

The world of work had changed beyond recognition in the three decades since I wrote that first book. Factories were few and far between now. I looked for the Lyons cake factory, but it had closed down, as had all eleven of the Lucas factories in Birmingham. The mines and steel works had long gone. Jobs on offer were virtually all service work now, cleaning, catering, portering, caring, warehouse packing: broom, mop and cloth had replaced workbench, lathe and cutter.

By sheer good luck, the job centre computer came up with a job as a porter at the Chelsea and Westminster Hospital, which I knew well. Here I was, back at the same place I had worked decades earlier, but now unrecognizable from the old St Stephen's, its walls decorated with works of art, its central atrium hung with a great mobile sculpture, beneath which lunchtime quartets sometimes played.

But other changes were not for the better. I found I was no longer working for the NHS. All ancillary work was contracted out to Carillion – the huge company that later went bankrupt in ignominy, still paying its executives monster bonuses even as its finances were collapsing. But here's how outsourcing works: I was not working for Carillion either. As so often, that company had outsourced much of the work to agencies who in their turn often re-outsourced jobs. Where before I had a secure NHS job on NHS terms, now I was only agency, not covered by holiday, sick pay or working time laws. Where previously my supervisor had hired me and was responsible for me, now when I arrived I belonged to no one, the other porters from different agencies, our names unknown to anyone.

The old hierarchy hadn't changed, where the strict medical pecking order has the consultants kicking down to the junior doctors who took it out on the nurses who passed it on down to porters and cleaners. Trundling wheelchairs and beds around from ward to clinic to radiography or operating theatre, porters learned which wards had ferocious sisters who barked at us, and which had cheerful ones who sometimes offered biscuits. As it happened, this time I knew a number of the consultants here quite well. I had interviewed them often during my time as BBC social affairs editor. I knew one who had treated both my daughter and myself. But porters with their wheelchairs and walkie-talkies are invisible, not people but mere functions. Even if I smiled at them no one I knew ever recognized me, because I had become a non-person. That was something I experienced over and over in these jobs. Once you cross the threshold from middle class work to manual drudge, you pass through a green baize door of the mind into a nether world of unimportant, uninteresting non-personhood. Do you smile and say hello to your street sweeper? I do now. He may think I'm a patronizing Lady Bountiful but it makes me feel better not to walk past without acknowledging his work.

But here was the greatest shock, the most important revelation on my return to the world of manual work. In 1970, my wages here as a ward orderly had been £12.70 a week. Returning as a porter, a job on the same pay grade as a ward orderly, I now earned £174 a week. How did these pay slips compare? I asked the Institute for Fiscal Studies to calculate the difference in real terms, after inflation, some thirty-three years later and this is what they found. In real terms, my wages were now worth significantly less. To level-peg with 1970, I should be paid a third more, but I had fallen back while national income, GDP, had doubled in that time.

I hadn't expected anything so stark, but here was a graphic example of what the big graphs said: since the 1980s inequality had soared, the lid had flown off top earnings as pay at the bottom fell back and the pay gap yawned far wider. Here was progress spun into sharp reverse. This job was part of the explanation; the whole point of outsourcing state jobs such as mine was not for 'efficiency' or 'competition' but to shed old pay structures, to avoid trade unions and to cut pay. Old NHS jobs at NHS pay rates were cast out to the untender mercies of distant temp agencies who could get away with paying the barest minimum with no job security: I could be sacked any day. I kept applying for jobs that looked as if it would mean working directly for the state, but every time they turned out to be outsourced, working for agencies. Local councils, the NHS, schools, virtually every function and arm of the state had disposed of its manual workforce. That is the portrait of Britain going backwards.

In the minds of economists there is a perfect employment market, where underpaid labour will seek out higher-paid jobs, forcing employers to compete with better pay and conditions. But that's not how it works at the bottom end of the scale. Once you are low-paid, you have no freedom to set off in search of a better job elsewhere. Time and again I talked to women in lousy jobs who could certainly have found better, but how? Leaving early for work, home to children at night, fraught and frenzied lives had no time for job hunting. Take the cost of finding a new post: to get this hospital job I'd had to queue at an agency, return next day with forms and photos, and then pay for my own black and white work clothes, as agencies supply no uniforms. In charity shops and Bargainwear beside the estate I found cheap white tops and black trousers, but the flat black shoes were killers: in all, with Photo-Me photos for the agency, with travelling to the agency for two interviews where I had to sign away my working rights 'voluntarily', I spent £54.23. That was the price of starting a new job. Pay wouldn't come until the end of the month and I already owed back rent: offers of loans at outrageous APR interest rates came fluttering through the door. Changing jobs is precarious and expensive.

What you find when you apply for jobs is that you and your time are worthless. How often I walked far away to appointments that didn't happen, travelling expensively, wasting time, waiting in queues, told to come back the next day, bring forms back another time. Cheap labour is treated cheaply, though every hour wasted is a precious hour of pay foregone as bills mount. I needed to experience this contempt for myself to understand why people don't change jobs, don't 'aspire' as the politicians would have it.

Forget breaking away to retrain while the rent, electricity and dinner money wait to be paid, even if you had the energy, flat-out shattered at the end of every day. And for me, I was living an easier life without my children.

* * *

The world of work had changed, old jobs vanished, replaced by new service industries. I took a call centre job in Southwark, cold-calling on commission, selling cleaning services to any company you could get through to. By 2020 1.3 million people were doing this soul-destroying work. These days I am exceedingly polite, if firm and brief, with the aggravation of cold-callers reading off their scripts, because I know how dire that life is, hour after hour on the phone to angry people who shout and swear.

I worked as a dinner lady in a primary school for a while where the company employing us pinned up everywhere our brisk instruction, 'Always happy, never sad!' Though Maggie the head cook was weighed down with sorrowful stress, cooking and dishwashing not just for this school but for many others, as dishes went out and washing-up came back from schools whose kitchens had been closed by the company to save money.

I worked as a night cleaner in a distant wing of Guy's Hospital, travelling the night buses among that prostrate company of sleeping night workers slouched in their seats. I packed cakes in a scruffy back alley bakery, where I had to fight hard with the ferocious termagant of an owner to get my pay packet. Workers are often cheated.

By far the hardest job was working as a health care

assistant in a care home. I chose an upmarket, well-heeled one owned by a large company, the residents mostly private payers: it would be easy to find a run-down institution struggling to stay afloat on the under-funding for state-financed residents. The pay, of course, was the same rotten minimum rate wherever you work.

The other care assistants were kind, the nursing supervisors scrupulous, food decent – and it didn't smell of urine, the first nose test on stepping inside any care home.

Working at a care home

But even so, this was the most distressing of all the jobs I did. To be responsible, alone, for six fragile and doubly incontinent elderly people, all in varying states of dementia, is heart-rendingly difficult. Six residents per carer is standard, but it's too many and you can never do enough, never care enough. There's never time to talk and listen to those with no one else to talk to all day. It takes so long to get one difficult and resistant person up, bottom cleaned and creamed, hoisted into a bath, dressed and breakfasted, while the others are calling out for help. The last is still in bed at 11 a.m. when it's time to prepare the first for lunch. There is a not a moment when you aren't stricken by failure to do more, to be better and kinder.

It doesn't help that here, as in every other job, the equipment is skimped: we fought over surgical gloves, wipes, clean towels, all in short supply. It was the same in the hospital, as we all competed for too few wheelchairs, the canny porters hiding them away. Nappies were rationed in the nursery, with too few cleaning fluids, cloths and mops as a hospital cleaner. Here in the care home, as everywhere I worked, I found what these low-paid staff minded most was the obstacles to doing their job well, despite bad pay and often contemptuous treatment by managers. Yet the low-paid are treated as if they would skive and shirk without a whip at their back. The work ethic is astonishingly powerful, and it keeps people working for not much more than benefit rates. These carers gave of themselves emotionally, with little praise or reward.

By good luck one day on the Brixton job centre computer I found a job at the other end of life, with the young not the old. It was the best job by far, in fine surroundings among a babble of babies as a nursery assistant to work inside the Foreign Office crèche, 'no qualifications needed, life skills more valued'. Good!

But pause here and consider that: even in this grandest of nurseries, looking after the children of Foreign Office high-flyers, the nursery assistants on rock-bottom pay need no qualifications. It may matter less here, where these children will get all the stimulus, conversation, songs, books and play that middle class parents devote to their babies. But staffing nurseries with well-trained people to give those same things to children who don't have them at home matters crucially. Typically, most nurseries barely afforded by parents in poor places are staffed by under-paid scarcely trained young women who themselves failed at school. Fates are sealed in these early years, when a good nursery can see a disadvantaged child catch up with the rest before primary school. But it doesn't happen. Even in this grandest of nurseries, it was 'no qualifications needed'.

Signing in for my interview at the Foreign Office front desk, I sat in that familiar grandiose portico, head in my newspaper for fear of being recognized by anyone I knew, a fellow journalist, politician or civil servant. Reaching the nursery, I found it beautiful, airy, lavish in all its fittings, gleaming with new toys and books, climbing frames and easels primed with pristine finger paints. This well-staffed little paradise, this five-star childcare was a far remove from some of the struggling nurseries I have visited on estates around the country.

Starting work, I was given a bright Kinderquest polo shirt and a company-branded tabard. Each day we took the children out to walk and play in St James's Park. Here's what I wrote about finding myself in such familiar and yet unfamiliar surroundings:

> We set out in a long crocodile, a flotilla of triple buggies, with the good walkers holding on at either side, firmly attached to us by reins. We made slow progress out of the Foreign Office side entrance, past the security checkpoint, down King Charles Street, turning into Whitehall towards Downing Street. This was the time I really dreaded. In my usual life I walk down here many times a week. I visit departments, see special advisers and ministers, go to press conferences, hopping in and out of government buildings for one journalistic purpose or another. I rarely walk along Whitehall without bumping into another journalist, an MP or someone I know. I visit Downing Street quite often, usually for early morning seminars at Number 11 given by the Smith Institute, sometimes to Number 10, too, to see advisers or policy people.

(Remember I was writing this in Labour years: social policy detail never had the same priority in Tory times and nor was I much invited.)

> The police at the gates of Downing Street are well-trained to recognise thousands of faces and they might know me from when they tick my name off at the door. So the process of passing those gates at snail's pace was excruciating. We were quite a spectacle and people stopped to stare and smile as our outing made its stately progress towards St James's Park, not unlike

dog-walkers with our cluster of little children on leads. There I was in my purple Kinderquest uniform, pushing a big triple buggy with another child attached to my wrist, part of an eye-catching procession and my heart pounding with anxiety. What would I say to some fellow political journalist, some MP? I need not have worried. Women pushing buggies are unnoticed in Whitehall, part of the women's world that doesn't count. A middle-aged nursery assistant pram-pushing along with a row of others was an absolutely invisible non-person out there.

Except once. As we were turning into Whitehall a posse of neat-suited men stepped out of a doorway and bustled down the street in fast and purposeful group formation towards us. Of all the people in the world I would least like to encounter, this was he – Peter Mandelson, whom I have known for many years. There he was, the ever-elegant, sharp-suited paragon of style who carries with him the aura of a man who is where it's at, whatever the indefinable 'it' or 'at' may be. He misses little, his sharp eyes sweeping up and down whatever street or room he enters, taking everything in. So it was that he glanced at me, glanced again, gave half a nod, even a trace of a smile then looked away. His expression said he thought he knew me, might know me, but how or why he could not place. I prayed he would not suddenly remember. Behind him in his fast moving retinue was Philip Gould, the prime minister's pollster and general doom-watcher, who despite his morbid pessimism about all human nature, is good company and I have had several breakfasts with him at his favourite table at the Savoy. He looked straight at me and at our procession but didn't recognise me at all. We push on, my heart pounding for fear of further encounters. If challenged what would I say? And what could I say to my fellow nursery staff? How would I explain myself to both at once? But it didn't happen. We turned into Horse Guards, the children pleased at the sight of the Household Cavalry, their shining breastplates, red cloaks, tufted helmets and, best of all, their glossy horses. We crossed the great parade ground and entered St James's Park, filled with early spring crocuses.

* * *

I left my flat on the Clapham Park estate with no regrets, glad to be going home as I handed back the keys to the kindly housing manager. I went back to the estate often, still following the progress of the New Deal for Communities board of residents, watching the decisions they made with the grant they had been given and the inevitable strife and arguments. In a final audit, the estate project had worked very well, drawing in enough of its 7,300 residents to run the board that chooses what to do with the money awarded by the government. They hired wardens patrolling day and night who made people feel safer. They liaised with police to shut down crack houses and set up neighbourhood policing. They created a community hub, they held an annual festival, they arranged coach trips for families who had never had a day's holiday. The two children's centres at each end of the estate flourished. They invested in the local schools to help raise standards, they brought in a Job Shop with advisers for the unemployed. Things did get better, crime fell, school results improved, people felt better about the place where they lived. All this we recorded as part of *The Verdict*, the book David Walker and I wrote in 2010 to keep a record of all that Labour did well, and the things not done so well, so no one should later say 'nothing works' or claim the effort and money on social programmes was wasted.

I still drop back to Clapham Park once in a while to visit the tiny remains of that programme, struggling to keep going against the maelstrom of cuts that swept through after Labour lost the 2010 election. Only one old block has been rebuilt: White House, alas, still stands. These days I keep coming across traces of vanished Labour social programmes, where some academics have kept measuring the results, holding onto proof of what succeeds in improving lives for the future day, if it ever comes, when another government as keen on social programmes revives these attempts. For instance, as I write, research from the LSE has just landed in my inbox, showing that Labour's Health in Pregnancy Grant, designed to provide better food for pregnant women, did make a measurable difference to birth weights of babies of the poorest and youngest mothers. But that grant was abolished in 2011 by the coalition government, which dismissed it as 'a gimmick'. In one programme after another, there is ample evidence of 'what works': all it needs is a government of good will – and the good will of voters to elect one.

As I completed *Hard Work*, I was well aware of the rich potential for scorn at a middle class woman trying to 'live like common people' and 'do whatever common people do', as in the Pulp song. But I never had any delusions that I came away with an authentic notion of real life on the minimum wage. I could imitate it, I could earn the wages and pay the bills, calculating exactly what little I could buy. But that's just reporting. I could never experience a genuine sense of low-wage insecurity because I have never had a day in my life when I haven't felt cocooned in safety, not just financial but emotionally protected by a network of family and friends, themselves rock-solid secure.

It takes an unthinkable leap of the imagination to guess what I would have to do to lose all that protection: maybe commit a heinous crime, do something wildly shameful, turn to heroin, self-destruct in a religious cult or embrace the far right? In those great class-clash classics, Tom Wolfe's *Bonfire of the Vanities* or the film *Trading Places*, their writers needed to invent extreme scenarios to deprive their privileged anti-hero protagonists of everything that cradles them in the certainties of their birthright. So no, I don't know what it would be like to live a couple of pay packets from penury, as did most of the people I worked with and lived next door to: just before the Covid pandemic, one in ten people had no savings and a third of adults had less than £600. Nothing would save them if they lost their jobs, with barely a safety net, when the dole in Britain is the lowest among comparable European countries. To bring up children in that precarious state is beyond what families like mine can visualize, a class-dividing chasm too deep and wide to cross, except as a tourist.

Not long after my book was published I was invited to talk about it on the Radio 4 sociology programme *Thinking Allowed*, by its sociologist presenter, Laurie Taylor. But on the day, I found I was appearing with another author, Ellen Ross, an American professor of history who had just edited *Slum Travelers: Ladies and London Poverty, 1860–1920*. The blurb said, 'In the late nineteenth and early twentieth centuries, Britain saw many women in the privileged classes forsake dinner parties and society balls to turn their considerable energies and resources instead to investigating and relieving poverty. By the 1890s, at least half a million women were involved in philanthropy, particularly in London.'

Ha, a trap! That's me, I thought, a modern day version of all those Lady Bountifuls who fare exceedingly badly in literature – as in Dickens's *Bleak House*, where Mrs Jellyby, the 'telescopic philanthropist', is in ruthless pursuit of settling 'two hundred healthy families cultivating coffee and educating the natives of Borrioboola-Gha, on the left bank of the Niger'. Or her friend, Mrs Pardiggle, the bible-bashing missionary to bricklayers, whose 'one and only infallible course' was 'pouncing upon the poor and apply-ing benevolence to them like a strait-waistcoat'. I feared I was about to be done over.

But no, Professor Ross had selected the writings of impressive women whose reporting is often grittier and more realistic than Jack London or Dickens. By winning the trust of women, they had analysed with precision the wages and expenditure of households and they listened to the details of how their husbands' behaviour determined the family's collapse or survival. Male reformers, including William

Beveridge, never saw incomes as anything but wages paid into a man's pocket, a blunder in his later social insurance scheme, which left out women and single mothers.

Ellen Ross's *Slum Travelers* avoids the moralizers and the lecturers, the missionaries and the preachers, in favour of the reporters. One chapter reprints Beatrice Webb's experience of working undercover as a seamstress in a Mile End sweated-labour workshop. Margaret Harkness in 1889 gives a stark account of the lives of London barmaids working in the 'subterranean hotels' that were London Underground bars, harassed by men in their eighty-six-hour working week. Here was Annie Besant, too, writing in fine detail about the appalling conditions of match girls at the Bryant & May factory that led to their famous strike. Many of the writings here made a strong impact, Ross says, and many of their causes were eventually won.

Ah, but what's this? My heart sinks to find a relative of mine: I might have guessed. But I had never heard of Maude Alethea Stanley, sister to Kate who was Bertrand Russell's mother, so she is my great-great-aunt, sister to my great-great-grandmother Rosalind, Countess of Carlisle. Russell describes her as his 'stern and gloomy Aunt Maude'. She was the 'designated spinster' in a clutch of siblings in that large Liberal family, the one left unmarried to look after their widowed mother. But she broke out to devote her considerable energies to the slums of Five Dials, a now vanished part of Soho in St Anne's parish, where she set up night schools and clubs for girls, based in 59 Greek Street, as it happens, just a few doors down from where I rented a room for a while. She made friends with local young men and women in the squalid

Maude Alethea Stanley

Five Dials courtyards by playing cards and gambling with them. She created and then co-ordinated a host of London youth groups into a Girls' Club Union in 1880. She became a Poor Law Guardian, and manager of the Metropolitan Asylums Board. Ross chose a piece of her reporting that describes, quite graphically, the problems of drunkenness and its ruination of families. But admirable though her works were, I can't say I warm to Aunt Maude from the tone of her writing. I didn't let on to Professor Ross and Laurie Taylor that she was a relative. As things turned out, I needn't have been so defensive about my 'slum travels' as they treated my book well.

A few years after leaving Clapham Park, I unexpectedly met my neighbour, Mick, from the next-door flat in White House. Though I suppose it wasn't altogether surprising, given the circumstances. As austerity bit deeper into people's pockets, personal bankruptcies were soaring and I spent a day in the insolvency court, high up at the back of the law courts building in the Strand. There he was, in the crowded waiting room, jumping up to hug me, as cheery as ever despite falling on hard times. I knew from our many previous chats that he was an ex-social worker who had succumbed to serious and chronic mental health problems. Exactly what had precipitated him into this crisis wasn't quite clear, but the departure of a partner had something to do with it. He had fallen into the pit of trying to make ends meet on a sub-survivable single person's benefit. Rent arrears put his flat in peril, but declaring himself insolvent might save him. (I later found out that it did.) How was the estate, I asked? Going backwards, he said.

15

An Ending

THESE ARE SOME stories of my family trying, and often failing, to be and do the right thing in the battle against the forces of conservatism. It's about real people, with all our foibles, failings and perversities. By nature or nurture, I inherit much from them, though some seem distant to me, except my mother and those still alive too close to write about. I could have written a whole book about my philosopher stepfather Richard Wollheim, though true to form in my family, of course, he wrote a good one himself called *Germs*, elegantly reissued after his death by the publishing imprint of the *New York Review of Books*. Or I might have included the travails of my stepmother Sally transplanted from Ohio to my father's louche and drunken post-war Fitzrovia world. I might have name-dropped more of my parents' writer, artist, poet, academic or political friends – that family holiday in Yugoslavia where aged thirteen I stood on the quay and yelled for help and saved the lives of A.J. Ayer and Hugh Gaitskell who very nearly drowned – that kind of thing. But I've tried not to stray from my theme.

I could tell of two beloved Irish women who, one after the other, looked after my children while I worked, Tara and Sheila, both with family histories from a darker, distant, and mercifully almost unrecognizable Ireland of the 1960s. I haven't written enough here about the importance of having other women, yes, lower paid than me, to look after my children to give me the freedom to write about low pay. Never mind a room of one's own, a kind child-carer of one's own is what made my life easy. I would write so much more about Tara and Sheila, but picking my way through the contrary tanglewood of human lives, a writer has to choose some paths, some themes, not others.

I have seen forward leaps in my lifetime on liberal issues – but on the question of class and inequality, I find no progress: the dial has stuck. No doubt we ourselves are part of that stickiness, holding on, passing on to our children and grandchildren those same advantages. How could we not? When the right throws gleeful insults at us – 'Champagne socialists!' or just plain 'Hypocrites!' – we tend to cringe. But why? What should we do? Give up, shut up? One useful answer is to turn the searchlight back on them and take a good look at who they think they are. When I listen to rich right-wingers, I hear the self-same attitudes among these possessors of power and wealth ringing down the centuries with that age-old self-justifying complacency I might have recorded a hundred years ago.

Pause here and compare their way of being with our left-wing/liberal habits of mind. Look at their unshakeable belief in their own merit and their contempt for life's losers: the mild hypocrisies and moral contradictions of the bourgeois left pale into insignificance once you take a good look at how the unquestioning possessors think and behave.

In our book *Unjust Rewards*, on the rise of extreme inequality, David Walker and I took a close-up snapshot of them to explore how those cadres of super-winners justify their extraordinary income and wealth. With great difficulty we corralled some into focus groups, one with the highest earners among top City lawyers in Canary Wharf, and another with super-bankers in the City itself: their salaries ranged from around £1.5 million up to £10 million a year. (These would be far higher now.) This was in the wake of the great 2008 bankers' crash, when their culture of selling on the sub-prime mortgages of the poor brought havoc to the world economy, leading to severe austerity ever since. If ever there was a moment for intro-spection and reflection, surely, we thought, we would catch them at just the right time.

We brought Ipsos MORI pollsters to the focus groups to question them and collate their replies, with Professor John Hills, the great LSE expert on wage distribution, to dissect their answers. Trying to gauge their knowledge of where they stood on the earnings ladder, we asked them first to fill out questionnaires about their own standing and what they thought others earned, from street sweeper and factory worker, to nurse, engineer or average chief executive.

They revealed themselves to be utterly clueless about what anyone else earned. The general public are far more accurate than they about earnings scales, while these profes-sionals dealing daily with the flow of money through the nation's finances knew next to nothing of other people's incomes. They set themselves far nearer the middle, when in fact they were well beyond the 0.1 per cent, into the upper realms of the 0.01 per cent of earners. They judged the median income as four times higher than it was: the median is not the average, but the midway point (currently £31,400) where half the population has more and half has less than that. They thought most people were in the higher tax bracket and they found it impossible to believe that only 10 per cent of the population reached what they saw as this very modest level (now the higher rate starts at £50,270, which is reached by under 9 per cent of people). 'But everyone I know...' they said. No, they were emphatically told, 90 per cent were earning less than that, paying only the basic rate of tax. We had Professor Hills there so they couldn't dispute the facts of which they were so ignorant. He put his LSE charts up so they could understand what had happened to the explosion of unequal rewards in the last thirty years. In the ranks of high-earners, FTSE 100 top CEOs' pay compared with that of their median employees has sky-rocketed in the last three decades: top now is Ocado, where the CEO earns 2,605 times more than his median worker.

The discussion that followed, every word carefully recorded by Ipsos MORI, was deeply depressing: their resistance took familiar well-travelled paths. 'We are the geese that lay the golden eggs', was one escape route, ignoring how wealth has trickled up and not down on those charts. 'We work harder and aspire most,' said another. 'Quite a lot of people have done well because they want to achieve and quite a lot of people haven't done well because they don't want to achieve,' said another, to much agreement. They spoke of hard working all-nighters striking mega-deals across time zones: 'You won't find a teacher that works as hard as we do.' But did they work a hundred times harder? They regarded honourable vocations as a deliberate choice to be paid little: 'Some of these are vocational, things like nurses. It's accepted they go into it knowing that's part of the deal.' They were certain it was all a matter of choice. 'As long as you are aiming for it, the top jobs in the City are something that anyone can achieve.' A cursory glance at the shining path from public school to the City soon makes that look not impossible, but unlikely.

They didn't reach, as some of the wealthy do, for philanthropy as a justification: these were not natural philanthropists. But they did boast of how their earnings were all for the benefit of their children: 'I work hard, I've got two boys, I want to provide for them.' But where they saw inheritance as a moral virtue, my own family knew it to be the same old vice echoing down the generations: if not always in money, then in education, ensuring your own offspring get a leg-up ahead of others is nothing to boast about. While we thought inheritance the root of all injustice, they burst out in passionate hatred of the main mechanisms for redistributing wealth – inheritance tax and capital gains tax. They flicked away Professor Hills's chart showing the rich pay a lower proportion of their income in overall tax than those in the bottom 10 per cent, who pay out more of their earnings in regressive VAT and council tax: those paying PAYE have no clever means of avoiding income tax, such as partners in law firms.

As the discussions wore on, they became more animated and more dismissive of all evidence, perhaps aided by a glass or two of wine. 'Politics of envy!' one lawyer exploded furiously. 'I really object!' Redistribution, he claimed, 'won't help a poor person at all'. It was, said another, 'all kinds of bullshit crap which doesn't help people!'

Echoes of Ebenezer Scrooge's 'Are there no workhouses?' followed in one banker's protest that poverty is a thing of the past, or it only exists in Africa. 'People don't starve in this country. Compared to other countries, here you don't go hungry because you can just go and get money for free, right.' Ah, once they got onto the benefit system, they hit a rich seam of social ignorance. One banker thought a family of four would get benefits of £3,000 a month. 'They're not going to earn that sort of money, so where's the incentive for them to go out to work?' Professor Hills quietly told them benefits were a fraction of that sum. But the floodgates were open now: 'Single people get pregnant, then get a flat and more income. You just see everyone pushing prams so they'll get more income and a little flat they can stay in for life.'

They may have been ignorant of lives beyond their experience, but they did have strong views as to why paying out for the less fortunate was pointless. 'We don't think just chucking money at the welfare state is the answer,' said one, opening another flood of good reasons not to pay higher taxes. Government is always inefficient and should not be trusted with our money: 'Lack of ability is the main basis on which you get a job working for the state.' Others piled in with their view that public servants are feather-bedded and public money is all misspent. The entire public realm was dismissed in one sweep: 'I have absolutely no idea how my taxes are spent. It goes into a black hole.' One banker pointed out of the Canary Wharf window at the Millennium Dome across the river: 'Doesn't that say

all we need to say about waste?' As ever, one handy anecdote can beat a shed-load of facts.

Now these people may be excellent deal-makers in the
field of mergers and acquisitions, but it would be hard to
find a less intellectually inquisitive, less knowledgeable
and, despite having been to good schools, a less broadly
educated set than most of them. They did, however, like
everyone else, have a finely tuned sensibility about gradations of class nuance within their own cadre, naturally
more keenly aware of those above them than those below:
this was the world divided between the have-yachts and
have-nots, which moved into a finer distinction of those
who have yachts – with crews. They didn't feel wealthy
because others above them had more.

With minds this closed, taking their world-view from
the *Daily Mail*, whatever their low opinion of the public
realm they fell far short of the qualities required to reach
the upper ranks of the civil service, to be a chief executive
of a large city council, a manager of a complex NHS trust
or a head teacher of a large comprehensive school.

Most dismaying was their profound lack of empathy.
They were unwilling or unable to imagine other lives and
I don't know how hearts and minds so hardened by self-
interest can ever be changed. But that is what we are up
against and they are usually the political winners, we the
perennial losers. Right-wingers may loathe us as morally
smug, but so be it: we stand instinctively with the under-
dog, while they defend the selfishness of the possessors. So
no more cringing.

* * *

It takes no leap of imagination to guess how *Spectator*, *Telegraph*, *Mail* or *Sunday Times* writers may seize with glee on stories I tell here, using our own raw awareness of our contradictions as extra ammunition for their assaults on the middle class left. There is plenty of comic potential here. I could write it for them now and save them the bother: maybe I have. But nothing I or my family have ever written seems to make their tribe turn a mirror back to examine themselves or their motives. They don't question why their defence of inequality should dominate almost all the media and all the citadels of wealth and power, cemented in place by corrupting political donations and a dishonest electoral system. Introspection is inconvenient and it's not in their nature.

* * *

In the decades between my two explorations into the world of work, I married, I had four children, I worked at the *Observer*, in America for the *Washington Monthly*, back in London for the *Guardian*, the BBC, the *Independent* and back to the *Guardian* again, reporting on society and later on politics as well. My eleven years on the *Guardian* women's page changed my perspective on life, my eyes opened wide by viewing the world through a feminist lens. In 1983 I stood for parliament in the brief life of the SDP. Seven years in the BBC newsroom forced me onto a sharp learning curve, teaching me how to speak fire-proof BBC, how to make editorial judgements but without political bias – there's an important difference. This was in the later Thatcher years, when her people were watching out

suspiciously for any sniff of Guardianism in my reporting as social affairs editor. But as long as I stood on solid
paving stones of fact, they never laid a glove on me. Tories
always hated the BBC, but even under Thatcher, there was
nothing like the unreasoning virulence of their 'culture
war' crazed determination to destroy it now.

I was widowed very suddenly in 1992, my husband
dying of a galloping lung disease when my youngest
child was seven. Later I found a new partner. My life has
been filled with enchantments, a few disenchantments
and some shocks, such as everyone encounters. Nothing
clutches the heart as profoundly as children, and now my
six grandchildren. Nothing aches so much as memories of
time passing.

But in this book, I am confining the story of my family
and my life to chart the experience of middle class social
immobility and the embarrassments of the left living
comfortably on the moral high ground with uncomfortable consciences for as many generations back as I know.
In its way, this is intended to be as authentic an account
of the experience of class as those who write their stories
of rising up from tough working class roots. My story is
the opposite, a tale of generations staying almost exactly
where we are born. And, frankly, it has been a good
place to be.

It matters, who you marry. Every biography, every good
novel will tell you so: any romance needs to be candid about
an economic, intellectual and social marriage market too.
In the clunky language of sociology, 'assortative mating'
has been on the rise for the last few decades: couples are
even more likely than before to marry someone of the

same earnings and same background, as we described in *Unjust Rewards*. This marriage bonus is one more ingredient in the soaring inequality that took off in the 1980s. Sociologists are not good at translating this into human terms. Do fewer boardroom directors marry their secretaries, fewer dentists marry their hygienists, fewer princes marry showgirls? More of those girls now go to university, get degrees, aim for high careers and marry their equals in high earning potential. (Or at least near-equals, as women's incomes still fall well behind.) That helps the top echelons become more elite, more secure, more impenetrable to outsiders. Credentialism – the imperative to certify your worth with paper qualifications – helps cement class barriers, as the old tea-boy-to-boardroom stories are only found now among an older generation: the young need degrees that act as a hard barricade keeping out today's tea-boys. When people complain of the lack of working class MPs now almost all are graduates, they forget how many of the old working class MPs would these days have gone to university – a sign of progress. Of course all my four graduate children have married graduate partners.

But class is more than that. Subtle, sinuous and socially subversive in its ineffably fine distinctions, its miniature details crackling beneath the crude sociologists' radar. Every family can describe with fine precision its ups and downs, its rises and falls in fortunes and the gradations of nuance in the social status of the matches made, of cousins inching up and down the social scale. Sometimes it leads to feuds.

Britain is not alone in class rigidity, but we do make class distinction a curious emblem of nationhood. Look at all those absurd fossils of privilege – an unelected ermine-clad House of Lords, a knee-breeches-wearing Black Rod, a monarch in a golden coach opening our parliament and knighting with a sword anyone who can pay a political party enough to buy a mediaeval honour. Of course people laugh at a country where twenty of our prime ministers were nurtured at Eton.

But look abroad, and below democratic surfaces you can still see top echelons in Germany awash with Vons. It still surprises most people to learn that the myth of American classlessness was long ago dispelled by copious evidence of extreme social immobility: the route upwards from log cabin – or mobile home park – to boardroom or White House has been all but barred. And yet a narrative of the easy path of rags-to-riches is hard-wired into the American psyche and its nationhood story. The latest voluminous research that exposes this brutal truth is there in Michael Sandel's *The Tyranny of Merit*. Faith in the existence of a great American meritocracy hides the extent to which to be born in the USA is to stay fixed in your native social class more surely than elsewhere in the Western world, more even than in Britain. As Sandel writes, too few Americans understand what has happened to them in the decades since the 1960s. But national legend runs deeper than mere statistics, while meritocracy is a comforting national belief: everyone can make it if they try, and if they fail, then that's their own fault.

What about my own two partners? On the surface both would register as belonging to the same class as me, as successful well-paid journalists, both are ABs on a sociologist's or pollster's graph. But I add their stories here to show how these broad categories mask so many awkward gradations. Like everyone else, they have their own stories of their class origins, very different to mine and just as divergent from one another. So here are their experiences, to prove the wicked subtleties of class.

My husband, father of my children, political journalist Peter Jenkins, came from a small town England finely attuned to the arpeggios of class difference. Firmly separated rungs on the social ladder placed everyone in their correct milieu in the Bury St Edmunds of the 1940s and '50s. He would describe with fascinated horror and great ribaldry the rules, the snobberies, the barriers. He left the outline for a play about it at the time of his shockingly early death in 1992.

His mother Joan came from a successful family of fishmongers, whose entrepreneurial mother kicked off the dust of the East End and moved up-market to open branches in Bury St Edmunds and Newmarket, as fishmongers, poulterers and game dealers to the gentry. Joan was the first of her family to get a degree, reading biology at London University where she met her husband Kenneth who was studying pharmacy, also first in his family. He came from a lower middle class Welsh family from Swansea: one line in *Under Milk Wood* portrays his uncle sitting in a deck chair. Incidentally, Peter spent every summer holiday with his Welsh relations on the Mumbles beach, where he used to envy from a distance Michael Heseltine, son of a well-off local Swansea factory owner, his blond hair flowing, wearing tight bright blue swimming trunks surrounded by glamorous friends, with a canoe of his own. 'Ah, but,' Heseltine told us, when Peter told him this memory, 'I built my own canoe!' A good boast from he of the paddle-your-own-canoe party.

Peter's father, on marrying Joan, established himself in a chemist shop in Bury St Edmunds with giant bright coloured carboys in the window signifying a solid old-fashioned professional pharmacy.

But no, for all his qualifications, he wasn't called a professional. A doctor and a lawyer are professionals but running a chemist's was trade – that lower social degree trumping a university degree. Peter was sent to a Suffolk private boarding school to get a leg up the social ladder, but despite a private education, owning a pony and winning junior tennis championships, as the son of the town's chemist shop owner he was not quite the right class for Bury St Edmunds' pony club or tennis club circles. When he had to earn money in the holidays working for the hunt, being a hunt servant put him on the wrong side of the green baize stable door and ruled him out of hunting social circles and hunt balls.

When he did his national service in a naval aircraft carrier, he was swabbing the deck with other ratings when an officer asked, 'What are you going to do when you leave the Andrew, Jenkins?' 'Going to Cambridge to read law, Sir.' 'Good God, you'll soon be earning more than me! Better put you in for officer training.' And off he was sent on a WOSBy course, War Office Selection Board, picking out officer class material.

Peter's father had expected him to return from Cambridge to Bury St Edmunds to be a local solicitor, which would pull them all up the social scale. But he broke loose, appalled by suffocating small town social niceties, escaping to London and journalism: he never looked back, except with a shudder. Backgrounds are emotionally indelible. All his life Peter remained fascinated by the subtle delineations and injuries of class, and I am sorry he never finished his play, *Mr Attlee's Merrie England*, about the social absurdities and insults of Bury St Edmunds life.

Because of its then raffish air, journalism felt classless to him, escaping Bury's social claustrophobia. But the statistics say otherwise, showing the upper reaches of newspapers and broadcasting are dominated by the privately and Oxbridge educated. Peter and I met at a Transport and General Workers' Union conference in Southampton, myself dishevelled, returning from seeing Bob Dylan perform at the Isle of Wight Festival and writing about it for the *Observer*. He was there writing his political column in the *Guardian*, a sign of those times when every union conference was political news. I was there meeting trade unionists, to do some research before setting off on travels around the country to write my first book on work.

My partner of the last twenty-nine years, David Walker, also co-author of our many books, has his own strong feelings about his very different class origins. He was born in Aberdeen where his father was a plasterer, but the work was intermittent in winter. He seized the chance when the great Aberdeen migration came. The creators of Corby new town came up to Scotland to recruit workers willing to move south to work in Corby's new steel mills and to people the brand new post-war town still under construction. So many Scots moved in that great exodus that Corby still has a Scottish identity, Scottish products in the shops, Scottish accents still among the elderly.

They went south when David was six, but he still talks with a Scottish lilt – which has always been a useful classless accent to hold onto in the world of London journalism where most people talk middle class RP like me. At Peter's private school, their Suffolk accents were dinned out of them with elocution lessons. He said they were made to enunciate correctly, expunging the broad Suffolk 'Oi roide moi boik on a broight moonloight noight'. But I suspect he never talked like that: his mother and sister certainly didn't. Accents are still as strong a class indicator as they were in his late 1940s elocution days, though now in sophisticated circles, a regional accent can be a cool asset.

Corby may have been a brand new town, mostly inhabited by single-class steel workers' families, but one great class sorter remained, the 11-plus exam, dividing children between about a quarter raised up into grammar schools, the rest consigned to secondary moderns. That social guillotine was universal back then but is now confined to just a few backward Tory counties. It cut off most children's chances but elevated a few to higher expectations. No one who took the exam forgets the day the results envelope dropped onto the doormat. My sister and I failed, despite a private school cramming us non-stop with the infernal boredom of the stultifying 11-plus syllabus with its moribund similes: as white as... as black as... and there was only one correct answer, snow and coal. We both hated our Girls' Public Day School Trust school with its exam force-feeding, punishments and detentions and we both rebelled by refusing to learn. But it hardly mattered to us middle class children, unlike the great majority. Failing to get a grammar school place, we were whisked away to private schools instead, me to boarding school which felt like punishment, while Josephine was let into St Paul's Girls' School, on the coat tails of Great-Aunt Jocelyn's academic reputation.

The 11-plus raised David up into Corby's new co-ed grammar school, but his older brother was cast into the secondary modern, for no good reason: he went on to have a highly successful career as a chief executive of a local council despite that blow. The overwhelming evidence is that the 11-plus and grammar schools held most people back, while comprehensives saw a great leap forward in more pupils staying on for A levels and progressing to further and higher education. But the grammar school myth dyes deep in Conservative thinking, Tory MPs constantly calling for their return, and for expanding them in those few Tory counties that retain them, despite those counties having worse overall academic results.

Why this Tory myth? Because their grammar school ideal captures one of conservatism's deepest core beliefs. I heard a Tory minister at a Conservative Party conference express it perfectly when he spoke of the need to 'pick diamonds from the rough', revealing the assumption that most people are dross, but an elite must always be created. Even on its own terms, as an engine of meritocracy, the grammar school system failed: very few poor children, measured by those on free school meals, make it to grammar schools, knocked back at the 11-plus and marked down. Grammars get better results by picking children already destined for success, mainly by social background and extra tutoring. They add very little value to those who would anyway be heading for top streams in comprehensives, while damaging the rest as outcasts. There were more boys' grammar school places than girls', though girls out-scored boys in the 11-plus, so girls used to be systematically marked down as deceptive 'early developers'.

For those who took the exam, it still matters, it still hurts late in life: ever since I wrote about failing the 11-plus, I still get venomous Twitter posts claiming it proves I'm stupid, so my writing can be discounted. Those of us prone to impostor syndrome still secretly fear the damned 11-plus was a deep truth-teller, a divining rod that knew a sheep from a goat. But in fact some 30 per cent of grammar school children failed O levels at sixteen, while many who were cast into secondary moderns succeeded later. The myth that grammars were the secret of the sudden surge in post-war upward mobility has been exploded over and over: the secret was a great opening up of white collar, better jobs so two generations of children of blue collar families moved up to new better-paid office jobs, a movement that has now stopped.

David was one of the grammar school chosen few, but don't imagine jumping social class barriers is easy or painless. He won a Cambridge scholarship a year young and, like many, found arriving in those palatial halls from Corby into the throngs of entitled inheritors difficult. His fine-tuned antennae still note the differences between those like him who came from working class roots, and those like me who glide on a smooth path through life.

We met at an education conference in Zurich, both of us there for the BBC, where he was presenter of Radio 4's *Analysis* programme, and I was the BBC social affairs editor. Since then we have written eight books together, including *The Verdict*, chronicling the successes and failures of the Blair–Brown Labour era, and most recently *The Lost Decade*, on the social destructions of the great post-2010 austerity. We have tried to write a record of the social effects of the sharp swing between those governments, between those intent on making life fairer contrasted with those who deliberately made things less fair.

* * *

No family story makes sense without revealing its financial circumstances. In my generation, those who had struggled to buy relatively humble houses suddenly found their property sky-rocketing in value as boom followed boom. Before I knew him, Peter had been terrified at taking out a mortgage four times his salary in the 1960s, on a house costing £4,500 that he could only afford by letting out the top floors. But afterwards in decade after decade that house catapulted in value turning us into millionaires. London homes still often earn more in a year than their occupants. My mostly professional ancestors, the academics and writers, had not been property owners or their property was insignificant: now everyone of our age with equivalent occupations has acquired this unimaginable unearned wealth. Like many beneficiaries of that still continuing property bonanza, I now own a holiday home in Sussex.

At least we of the left argue honestly for wealth taxes to redress this unjust shift, against the right who somehow persuade themselves this windfall is justified, and so, they say, is passing it all on virtually inheritance tax free.

I often write about the explosion in unmerited board-room earnings. Median annual pay for FTSE 100 CEOs is now £3.41 million, 109 times the salary of a median full-time employee, with the top earner on £16.85 million. Look how steeply that has risen since the 1970s, the most equal era, when unions were strong and there was some sense of shame in the boardroom. Back then, those top 100 CEOs earned around ten times the pay of their average staff, according to the High Pay Centre.

I have argued for total transparency in earnings, with open book public tax returns, as in Finland. That would break a great taboo. It would let people know if they were fairly paid at work once everyone could see what every-one else earned and owned, exposing Britain's extremes of inequality. That caused right-wing commentators to challenge me to reveal my own various earnings, which I did – and they duly attacked me, of course, as a champagne socialist for my fortunate then £106,000 a year (though my highly paid attackers never revealed their own earn-ings). Like confessing my 11-plus failure, openness always gives added ammunition to your enemies.

My earnings put me in the top 1 per cent, according to the Institute for Fiscal Studies: I need to know that, just as everyone needs to know where they stand. In this controversy about unjust rewards discussed in our book, I was glad to be summoned to give evidence to the Public Administration Select Committee investigating excessive executive pay. I was touched when a group of forty-six MPs (Labour, Lib Dem and even one maverick Tory) unexpectedly backed me by putting down an Early Day Motion in the Commons, Motion number 38577:

That this House applauds Polly Toynbee, the *Guardian* journalist and co-author of the book *Unjust Rewards*, for volunteering details of her salary to the Public Administration Select Committee in its first evidence session on Executive Pay in the Public Sector; notes that she receives £106,000 per annum; and urges journalists, broadcasters, commentators, politicians and others to follow her example before pronouncing on pay levels in the public sector by first disclosing their own income, earned and unearned.

* * *

In the late Queen's long reign, her people voted more than twice as often for Conservative governments, so the entitlements of the masters of the universe, the inheritors and wielders of power, money and influence, have barely been disturbed. Even if they have few points of contact with ordinary British lives, they own and control the media that deceives and sways the votes they rely on. That is the nature of the enemy my antecedents have done battle with for many generations back and it has often left them in despair. At each defeat, the left picks itself up, dusts itself off and starts all over again (mostly fighting with itself).

This has been a book about self-conscious awareness of privilege, embarrassment at undeserved good fortune and uncertainty about how to live with uneasy consciences. Sometimes it leads to unresolved contortions and comic absurdities because, in the surge of inequality with its great property boom ignited by the Tories in the 1980s, we found ourselves its beneficiaries too.

Writing from the depths of yet another long era of Conservative hegemony, in depressed moments I might look back on all my family's endeavours as lifetimes wasted in the struggle for lost causes. Yet, if I could raise them up now to look at the far horizons, here is what I would tell them. Often in the end after their deaths their causes did win the day. In each wave of liberal consciousness and protest they won, whether for women, from suffragettes to #metoo, or on race, from the anti-colonial and anti-apartheid movements to Black Lives Matter. Or for LGBT rights, from Oscar Wilde in prison to equal marriage. At least there is widespread awareness of environmental peril, though the future of the world hangs in the balance. When I trace those causes back through several generations, each iteration of indignation does push the dial forwards. The young always do it better in each era.

But there are always those backward plunges too. I am glad these ancestors were spared witnessing the heartbreak of the 2016 Brexit vote. How appalled these ardent internationalists would be at this solipsistic isolationism, they who had worked unceasingly for the League of Nations, and when that failed for the United Nations and for European harmony. Yet I remain certain that this disastrous rift with our neighbours will be repaired and good sense will be restored. Life on the left demands perpetual optimism.

In the name of that unending hope, I would urge my ancestors to take the long view. Almost all the great leaps forward in social progress happened under Liberal then Labour governments. Even when out of power, change was breathed into the political air under the pervasive influence of liberal thinkers. It was Liberal governments of the nineteenth century that responded to the Great Stink of 1858 with what was until then an unthinkably gigantic public investment in Joseph Bazalgette's London sewers that ended cholera. Seeds of a universal education system were sown then, with working rights and safety standards. Later came Lloyd George's People's Budget of 1910 that brought wealth taxes, the start of state pensions and welfare. The dial moved permanently when things previously thought to be no business of the state were proven to be essentials only the state could provide. Under Attlee that lesson bloomed into the birth of the NHS and the social security welfare state, followed by Macmillanite Tory and Labour governments' monumental slum clearances and the building of social housing. The dial keeps pushing forward again and again in public attitudes to race, women, climate or LGBT rights. The Tories opposed all these basic human decencies, now attacking what they sneer at as 'woke' in their contrived 'culture wars'. Yet they lose every time and each progressive step forward is never reversed.

The left lives in hope of the next tectonic shift and another jump ahead. As I write, public opinion on inequality is confused: people are shocked by both food bank poverty and obscene mega-wealth. How do you persuade people that by living more equally, everyone gains? Scandinavian countries come top of happiness charts, paying higher taxes to enjoy a richer public realm. Margaret Thatcher used to say, 'You will always spend the pound in your pocket better than the state will.' But ask people what they value most in life and the answers are always the same: their family's health and education, their safety and security.

What gives most delight? Beautiful surroundings, fine public spaces, parks, schools, colleges, stadiums, sports centres, galleries, museums and well-preserved heritage to be proud of. A seedy, run-down public sphere depresses the spirit and diminishes us all. These collective assets bought through taxes are infinitely more valuable than anything Thatcher's pound in her pocket can ever buy in a shop.

That's what progress looks like. Looking back over the generations of my family as they struggled against the grip of a conservative establishment, the glacial pace of change may often have felt hopeless. But I would tell them to lift their eyes to see the broader sweep of social history and despite their lose, lose and lose again elections there is another story of the slow triumph of their social justice ideas. To shift public attitudes always takes the resolve of a few people over many bleak years, braving mockery and defying convention as a despised minority standing up for unpopular causes.

* * *

I have become keenly aware of the weight of ghosts that lie heavily upon us all as we grow older, trailing dead people in our wake, remembering with avid determination because our memories are all that is left of them. Those vanished lives will die again even more absolutely when no one is left who knew them. We all die twice. And memories are short: people famous a hundred years ago – such as my grandfather Arnold and great-grandfather Gilbert – are fading names. Journalists vanish even faster: my father's name is barely known now, cropping up here and there in footnotes and anecdotes in other people's biographies. My husband Peter was a well-known political writer, but within twenty years he was forgotten. I put 'Carpe Diem' on his gravestone, a note to myself of the transience of all but very few. Anguish at so many lost people risks turning us all melancholy in old age. Maybe it's that burden of duty to remember that makes some elderly people talk to themselves in the street, keeping alive old conversations, arguments, jokes, griefs and joys no one else knows that will soon be gone forever. The urge to make sense of memories and to clutch onto the meaning of lives has driven many in my family to write it all down. Now here is my contribution.

Acknowledgments

To my dear friend Anne Chisholm, my thanks for her patient reading of various drafts over the ten years it has taken me to assemble this book, with her sharp editorial eye for blunders and infelicities. Many thanks to Clare Drysdale, my editor at Atlantic Books, for her care and her enthusiasm. Many thanks to my astute agent Clare Alexander for nurturing this book and for her wise and thoughtful suggestions. Deep gratitude too to my agent of many years, Gill Coleridge, now retired, for her readings and advice.

To Christopher Ridgway, the learned Head Curator at Castle Howard, my thanks for his trawl through those archives on my behalf, and for the pictures he found. For valuable picture research, thanks to Jo Evans; for excellent copy-editing, thanks to Tamsin Shelton. My thanks too to the Guardian Foundation's archivist Clare Stephens, who sought out photographs dating back to my arrival at the *Observer* in 1968. Thanks to my aunt Jean Toynbee and my half-sister Clara Hayes and other family members for their memories and the photographs they found. My thanks to Professor Sir Simon Wessely for giving his medical opinion on notes from the St Andrew's Hospital archive on my great-grandfather

Harry Toynbee. My particular gratitude to the late much missed Professor Sir John Hills of the LSE for many years of patient education and information on all questions of poverty and inequality.

Notes

p. 9 **LSE research:** 'Deflecting Privilege: Class Identity and the Intergenerational Self', Dr Sam Friedman, LSE, 2021, p. 12 **Social Mobility Commission:** *State of the Nation 2016: Social Mobility in Great Britain*, Social Mobility Commission, 2016

p. 81 **Tony Blair:** Beveridge Lecture at Toynbee Hall, 18 March 1999

p. 86 **The Royal Commission:** *Report of the Royal Commission on the Poor Laws and Relief of Distress 1905–1909* (majority report), 1909

p. 89 **Webb minority report:** *The Minority Report to the Royal Commission on the Poor Laws and Relief of Distress 1905–1909*, Beatrice Webb et al., 1909

p. 90 **Beveridge's 1942 report:** *The Beveridge Report: Social Insurance and Allied Services*, William Beveridge, 1942

p. 92 **Archives at St Andrew's:** St Andrew's Hospital, Northampton

p. 378 **1.3 million people:** 'Britain's call centre boom', Grace Gausden, This Is Money, 2 July 2020: https://www.thisismoney. co.uk/money/news/article-8478819/Call-centres-report-huge-surge-interactions-creating-hundreds-jobs.html

p. 385 **Health in Pregnancy Grant:** 'The birthweight effects of universal child benefits in pregnancy: quasi-experimental evidence from England and Wales', Mary Read and Dr Kitty Stewart, LSE, 2022

p. 396 **Median income:** statistics from Office for National Statistics, 2021: https://www.ons.gov.uk/peoplepopulationandcommunity/ personalandhouseholdfinances/incomeandwealth/bulletins/ householddisposableincomeandinequality/ financialyearending2021

p. 397 **Rich pay a lower proportion:** *The UK Wealth Tax Commission: A wealth tax for the UK*, Dr Arun Advani et al.: https://www.ukwealth.tax/

p. 409 **Some 30 per cent:** The Crowther Report: *15 to 18: A Report of the Central Advisory Council for Education (England)*, HMSO, 1959

p. 411 **Median annual pay:** *Analysis of UK CEO Pay in 2021*, Andrew Speke et al., High Pay Centre and TUC, 2022: https:// highpaycentre.org/ceo-pay-survey-2022-ceo-pay-surges- 39/#:~:text=Median%20CEO%20pay%20is%20now,and%20 107%20times%20in%202019

Bibliography

Cockburn, Claud, 'Spying in Spain and Elsewhere', *Grand Street* (Vol. 1, No. 2, Winter 1982)

Glenconner, Anne, *Lady in Waiting: My Extraordinary Life in the Shadow of the Crown* (London: Hodder & Stoughton, 2019)

McNeill, William H., *Arnold J. Toynbee – A Life* (New York: Oxford University Press, 1989)

Mitford, Jessica, *Hons and Rebels* (London: Gollancz, 1960)

Mitford, Jessica, *Faces of Philip: A Memoir of Philip Toynbee* (London: Heinemann, 1984)

Murray, Gilbert, *An Unfinished Autobiography* (London: Allen & Unwin, 1960)

Murray, Rosalind, *Moonseed* (London: Sidgwick & Jackson, 1911)

Murray, Rosalind, *The Good Pagan's Failure* (London: Longmans & Co., 1939)

Power, Jonathan, *Like Water on Stone: The Story of Amnesty International* (Boston, MA: Northeastern University Press, 2001)

Romilly, Esmond, *Boadilla* (London: Hamish Hamilton, 1937)

Ross, Ellen, *Slum Travelers: Ladies and London Poverty 1860–1920* (Berkeley, CA: University of California Press, 2007)

Russell, Bertrand, *Autobiography* (three volumes; London: George Allen & Unwin, 1967–1969)

Sandel, Michael J., *The Tyranny of Merit: What's Become of the Common Good?* (London: Penguin Books, 2021)

Sennett, Richard and Cobb, Jonathan, *The Hidden Injuries of Class* (New York: Norton, 1993)

Shaw, George Bernard, *Major Barbara* (London: Archibald Constable & Co., 1907)

Spender, Matthew, *A House in St John's Wood: In Search of My Parents* (London: William Collins, 2015)

Toynbee, Philip, *Friends Apart* (London: Macgibbon & Kee, 1954)

Toynbee, Philip, *Part of a Journey: An Autobiographical Journal, 1977–79* (London: Collins, 1981)

Toynbee, Philip, *End of a Journey: An Autobiographical Journal 1979–81* (London: Bloomsbury, 1988)

Toynbee, Polly, *A Working Life* (London: Hodder & Stoughton, 1971)

Toynbee, Polly, *Hard Work: Life in Low-Pay Britain* (London: Bloomsbury, 2003)

Toynbee, Polly and Walker, David, *Unjust Rewards: Exposing Greed and Inequality in Britain Today* (London: Granta, 2008)

Webb, Beatrice and Webb, Sidney, *Soviet Communism: A New Civilisation?* (London: Longmans & Co., 1935)

West, Francis, *Gilbert Murray: A Life* (London: Croom Helm, 1984)

Wilson, Duncan, *Gilbert Murray OM: 1866–1957* (Oxford: Clarendon Press, 1988)

Wilson, Gwendoline, *Murray of Yarralumla* (Melbourne and London: Oxford University Press, 1968)

Books mentioned in passing

Austen, Jane, *Emma*
Connolly, Cyril, *Enemies of Promise*
Dickens, Charles, *Bleak House*
Dickens, Charles, *Great Expectations*
Garnett, Eve, *The Family from One End Street*
Mitford, Nancy, *Noblesse Oblige*
Orwell, George, *Homage to Catalonia*
Orwell, George, *The Lion and the Unicorn*
Orwell, George, *The Road to Wigan Pier*
Powell, Anthony, *A Dance to the Music of Time*
Thackeray, William, *Vanity Fair*
Toynbee, Philip, *Pantaloon*
Waugh, Evelyn, *Black Mischief*
Waugh, Evelyn, *Brideshead Revisited*
Waugh, Evelyn, *Put Out More Flags*
Wolfe, Tom, *The Bonfire of the Vanities*

Picture credits

All images are from the author's collection, with the following exceptions:

Pages 78 and 82: photographs reproduced with the kind permission of Toynbee Hall

Page 129: Photograph by Elliott & Fry © National Portrait Gallery, London

Page 268: © Topfoto

Page 310: © Hulton Archive/Evening Standard/Getty Images

Page 316: Photograph by Bryn Campbell © Guardian News & Media Limited

Page 327: Photograph by Jane Bown © Guardian News & Media Limited

Page 354: Photograph courtesy of Bim Mason and the Barn House archive

Page 361: Photograph by David Newell Smith © Guardian News & Media Limited

Index